Television Truths

To Tina Horton, who knows how hard it is
(to watch TV) . . .

Creu Gwir fel Gwydr o FFwrnais Awen*
In These Stones Horizons Sing
Gwyneth Lewis

*Creating Truth like Glass from a Furnace of Inspiration

Television Truths

John Hartley

Blackwell
Publishing

BLACKWELL PUBLISHING
350 Main Street, Malden, MA 02148-5020, USA
9600 Garsington Road, Oxford OX4 2DQ, UK
550 Swanston Street, Carlton, Victoria 3053, Australia

First published 2008 by Blackwell Publishing Ltd

1   2008

Library of Congress Cataloging-in-Publication Data

Hartley, John, 1948–
    Television truths / John Hartley.
        p. cm.
    Includes bibliographical references and index.
    ISBN 978-1-4051-6979-0 (pbk. : alk. paper) — ISBN 978-1-4051-6980-6
    (hardcover : alk. paper)   1. Television broadcasting—Social aspects.   I. Title.

PN1992.6.H366 2008
302.23'45—dc22

                                                              2007014548

A catalogue record for this title is available from the British Library.

Set in 10.5/13pt Galliard
by Graphicraft Limited, Hong Kong
Printed and bound in Singapore
by Markono Print Media Pte Ltd

For further information on
Blackwell Publishing, visit our website:
www.blackwellpublishing.com

Contents

Part IV What Can TV Be? (Metaphysics of TV)   221

Figures

Tables

Acknowledgments

Television studies, if history proves there to have been such a singular thing, has been a publishing preoccupation of mine since *Reading Television* came out while I was still in my twenties. Although life, job descriptions, and curiosity have tempted me into many another field in the interim, TV remains home territory. It has retained its fascination because "TV studies" is not really (or not yet) a discipline. The "field" in which it pitched its analytical tent is far from stable ground. Things have changed so much during the TV era that it may be argued – and this book does argue – that a paradigm shift can be observed. The way television itself is made, distributed, watched, used, and thought about has changed. Previously familiar intellectual and cultural horizons have shifted too. Returning to television studies throughout an academic career has proven far from samey; the "home" ground is always shifting under one's feet.

However, one thing has stayed the same, and that is the pleasure to be had from reading and working with colleagues, students, collaborators, and interlocutors from around the world and from some of the many different perspectives that have congregated on this interesting terrain. I thank them for their company, for their talent, and for what they continue to teach me:

- Colleagues and postgrads, present and former, at QUT; heartfelt thanks to all: John Banks, Bao Jiannu (Beijing Foreign Studies University), Jean Burgess, Axel Bruns, Christy Collis, Sandra Contreras, Steve Copplin, Stuart Cunningham, Joshua Green (MIT), Elaine Harding, Greg Hearn, Nicki Hunt, Michael Keane, Helen Klaebe, Li Hui, Alan McKee, Kelly McWilliam, Lucy

Montgomery (Westminster), Aneta Podkalicka, Geoff Portmann, Ellie Rennie (Swinburne), Angelina Russo, Christine Schmidt, Christina Spurgeon, Jo Tacchi, Jinna Tay (UQ), Jerry Watkins, Shannon Wylie.

- Television and other scholars, editors, and facilitators; thanks for your inspiration and collaboration: Sara Ahmed (Goldsmiths), Pertti Alasuutari (Tampere), David L. Andrews (Maryland), Lynden Barber (Sydney Film Festival), William Boddy (Baruch-CUNY), Mike Bromley (UQ), Roger Bromley (Nottingham Trent), Will Brooker (Kingston), the late Jim Carey (Columbia), Stephen Coleman (Leeds), Nick Couldry (Goldsmiths), Glen Creeber (Aberystwyth), Michael Curtin (Wisconsin-Madison), Terry Cutler (Cutler & Co.), Peter Dahlgren (Lund), Mark Gibson (Monash), Malcolm Gillies (ANU), Faye Ginsberg (NYU), Jonathan Gray (Fordham), Terry Hawkes (Cardiff), Joke Hermes (InHolland), Richard Hoggart, Amanda Hopkinson (East Anglia), John Howkins, Henry Jenkins (MIT), Jeffrey P. Jones (Old Dominion), Elihu Katz (Annenberg Penn), Charles Leadbeater, Richard E. Lee (Binghamton-SUNY), Lee Tain-Dow (Kun Shan), Martin Löffelholz (Ilmenau), Malcolm Long (AFTRS), Catharine Lumby (Sydney), Tara McPherson (USC), Toby Miller (UC Riverside), Susan Murray (NYU), Horace Newcomb (Georgia), Kate Oakley, Jan Olsson (Stockholm), Tom O'Regan (UQ), Laurie Ouellette (Queen's-CUNY), Mark Pesce, Monroe Price (Annenberg Penn), Kristina Riegert (Södertörn), Chris Rojek (Brunel), Andrew Ross (NYU), Avi Santo (Old Dominion), Jim Schwock (Northwestern), Jeffrey Sconce (Northwestern), the late Roger Silverstone (LSE), Lynn Spigel (Northwestern), Mike Stubbs (ACMI), Tony Sweeney (ACMI), David Thorburn (MIT), Olga Tobreluts (St Petersburg), Graeme Turner (UQ), William Uricchio (MIT/Utrecht), Jing Wang (MIT), Ken Wark (New School), Mimi White (Northwestern), Barbie Zelizer (Annenberg Penn), Zhang Haishang (CELAP), Zhang Xiaoming (CASS), Zhao Bin (Peking).
- A special thanks to co-authors Joshua Green and Jean Burgess; to Stuart Cunningham, Toby Miller, and Kelly McWilliam for reading the MS; and to Jean Burgess (again) for helping me with the illustration permissions as well as reading the MS.
- The peerless team at Blackwell: Jayne Fargnoli and Ken Provencher.
- As ever, the home team: Tina Horton and Karri, Rhiannon, and Sophie Hartley.

I acknowledge with gratitude the Australian Research Council's support via a Federation Fellowship which has sustained the research on which this book is based.

The publishers and I would like to acknowledge publishers Allen & Unwin Australia, British Film Institute Publishing, Duke University Press, Peter Lang, MIT Press, NYU Press, Sage Publications, and the University of Texas Press, and journals *South Atlantic Quarterly*, *TV & New Media*, *Cinema Journal*, *International Journal of Cultural Studies*, and *Australian Cultural History*, for the use of parts of articles or book chapters that were first published as follows:

- "The 'value chain of meaning' and the new economy." *International Journal of Cultural Studies*, 7:1, 2004, 129–41.
- "The frequencies of public writing: Tomb, tome and time as technologies of the public." In Henry Jenkins & David Thorburn (eds) *Democracy and New Media*. Cambridge, Mass.: MIT Press, 2003, 247–69.
- "Television and globalisation." In Glen Creeber (ed.) *Tele-Visions: Concepts and Methods in Television Studies*. London: BFI, 2005, 137–46.
- "Television, nation and Indigenous media." *Television & New Media*, 5:1, 2004, 7–25.
- " 'Republic of letters' to 'television republic'? Citizen-readers in the era of broadcast television." In Lynn Spigel & Jan Olsson (eds) *Television after TV: Essays on a Medium in Transition*. Durham NC & London: Duke University Press, 2004, 386–417.
- "Reality and the plebiscite." In Kristina Riegert (ed.) *Politicotainment: Television's take on the real*. New York: Peter Lang, 2007.
- "Live event television: From the 'wandering booby' to the 'death of history'." In Graeme Turner & Stuart Cunningham (eds) *The Australian Television Studies Book*. Sydney: Allen & Unwin, 2000, 155–70.
- "Kiss me Kat: Shakespeare, *Big Brother*, and the taming of the self." In Susan Murray & Laurie Ouellette (eds) *Reality TV: Re-making Television Culture*. New York: New York University Press, 2004, 303–22.
- "Sync or swim? Plebiscitary sport, synchronised voting and the shift from Mars to Venus." In David L. Andrews (ed.) *Sport: Playing With the Pleasure Principle*. *South Atlantic Quarterly*: Vol 105(2), 2006, 409–428.

- " 'Laughs and legends' or the furniture that glows? Television *as* history," with Joshua Green & Jean Burgess. *Australian Cultural History*. 26, 2007.
- "Is screen studies a load of old cobblers? And if so, is that good?" *Cinema Journal*, Vol 45 No 1, 2005, 101–6.

Television Truths
Argumentation of TV

Cornell Research: Children's TV Triggers Autism
A new study from Cornell University shows that television is re-sponsible for the developed world's rising rates of autism in children. If this is true, can parents and governments have any choice but to stop children watching it?
White Dot: The international campaign against television, *2006*[1]

Argumentation: TV Truths

What is it about television? Watching television is still the most popular pastime ever. Since Bhutan introduced it in 1999 there is no country in the world without a television system. The onset of new ways of interacting with TV, via the internet, mobile, and non-broadcast forms of production and distribution, have not supplanted but supplemented its role and reach. TV both shows and shapes contemporary life across the economic, political, social, and cultural spectrum. It plays a prominent role in producing and distributing what counts as true for many if not most people in commercial democracies. Once established, such truths play an active role in public and private life, from legitimating actions in war, business, and the "administration of life" to steering conduct at the personal level. More routinely they supply global audiences with evidence of the factual reality (or otherwise) of our mental and physical horizons. In short, TV truths are pervasive, persuasive, and powerful.

Television's aspiration to universal accessibility has been achieved in all developed and many developing countries. Almost everyone who can watch it does so at least sometimes. And yet TV is still among the most criticized phenomena of modern life. For an extreme but familiar example of this tendency, see the quotation at the head of the chapter (above), taken from the website of an "international campaign against television," whose activists are encouraged to go round with a device called the TV-B-Gone that remotely switches off TV sets in public places.[2] Getting rid of television altogether from people's lives is a persistent fantasy in poplar culture. It often involves the kind of scaremongering solution imagined in the quotation above: the call for state intervention to stop entire populations watching TV. Such a totalitarian intolerance to a communicative form is reminiscent of book-burning, although expressions of hatred for TV rarely attract the public opprobrium that results from attacks on the written word.

Despite such infantile fantasies, the experience of watching television is widespread, well-liked, and regulated into the ordinary routines and relationships of daily life. To that extent, everyone in the audience is also both an *expert* on TV and a *critic*, not only as fans or foes of specific shows, genres, stars, or serial forms, but also because audiences know quite a lot about TV's productive apparatus, cultural forms, and supposed effects. The main lines of critique are remarkably widespread as a part of informal common sense: TV's connections to corporate and state power structures; TV's supposed moral shortcomings and behavioral effects; TV's persistent failure to entertain, inform, or educate particular taste cultures or audience demographics. Such *informal* expertise is relatively autonomous from the *formal* apparatus of knowledge. Collective wisdom about television is absorbed from personal experience, general social and mediated intercourse, commonsense knowledge, and journalistic debate. Generally it does not trickle down from the professional expertise of a branch of scholarship called "television studies." Nor, however, does it trickle up from audience experience directly, because public discussion of television is one-sidedly negative, rarely dwelling on the *positive* "effects" of the tube (for a refreshing antidote see Lumby and Fine 2006). Experts who do get to comment on television in the media are likely to be drawn from disciplines like psychology, marketing, journalism, political economy, pediatrics, criminology, or, in the case of the "Cornell research" cited above, economics. In the main, such experts have not been sympathetic witnesses, unless they're discussing the TV industry as a business. In this particular case, the Cornell economists compared data on US children's TV watching with climatic data on rainfall: "This analysis showed that children from rainy counties watch more television. When autism rates were then compared between rainy and drier counties, the relationship between high precipitation and levels of autism was positive." The authors admitted that "there are no large data sets that track whether children who watch a lot of TV when they are young are more likely to develop autism" (Cornell University 2006). Despite this caveat the "White Dot" folks were keen to move straight to total prohibition. One definition of autism is "pathological 'self-absorption.'" Physician: heal thyself! Alternatively, try calling for a ban on rainfall.

Within the academy, the formal study of television has struggled to achieve high-prestige research status despite its popularity with students. Academics from other disciplines who harbor strong views against television are likely to have strong views against TV *studies* too, rather than collegiate respect for its exponents' expertise. Thus, the most *respectable* forms of expert knowledge about television tend to be the ones that evaluate it most *negatively*. Knowledge about television is at a low premium if it is gained via the experiential immersion of the domestic consumer, or even via research into that experience. Its prestige rises the further it is removed from the home. The economists who trawled the datasets did "urge further study by autism experts" (Cornell University 2006). They felt no need to consult TV scholars.

Is there something peculiar about *television*, or alternatively is there something odd about our ways of producing and distributing *knowledge*, that has produced this tension between a popular pastime and an expert system? *This book is a sustained reflection on the tensions produced by the problem of knowledge in and about television.*

Despite the low prestige of media studies compared with philosophy, and despite widespread skepticism about television itself as a dealer in truths, even though it is trusted by many, it is important to seek to understand, within the flux of symbols, meanings, statements, and stories circulating on TV, how TV truths are communicated, and how television achieves its much-vaunted power to command. It has fallen to media studies to undertake that task. Media studies is therefore at least part of *the philosophy of the media age*: it produces both rational and empirical knowledge about how truths are told today, from the detail of individual strategies and techniques right up to those truths that have power to command on a society-wide basis and to a global extent.

There's no doubt that important questions about the status of truth are considered in "disciplinary" philosophy but nevertheless, as a discipline, philosophy has gained a reputation (which may not be deserved) for cloistered abstraction and upscale taste, far removed from the cut, thrust, and mess of industrialized global sense-making in a world governed by media, PR, spin, entertainment, spectacle, celebrity, and power. Philosophy (with a capital P, as it were) is these days a minority pursuit in which technical expertise and mastery of a difficult field are both at a premium, setting practitioners apart from lay people, even though as with television itself the problems it seeks to address are embedded in everyday life and everyone is an expert in them. Meanwhile, media studies has gained a reputation (which may not be deserved either) for pursuing questions that are trivial rather than important, and even for dispensing with truth altogether while having fun on the postmodern helter-skelter: it is contaminated with the supposed attributes of its own object of study. So there's a double problem facing anyone interested in pursuing media truths: the object of study in itself, and the pursuit of knowledge about it, are *both* intellectually suspect, of low repute, easily dismissed. Like women's magazines, they are "easily put down," in Joke Hermes's grave joke. But this familiar default setting of our collective intellectual prejudice, which presumes that philosophy is high status and media studies is low (almost as an *a priori* "truth"), may be no more than the very kind of snobbery and class distinction in language that ought to be part of the object of study, not its framework of explanation. Certainly those who are interested in how truth is made to count, made "commanding" in popular culture and public life, ought to take account of the media and mechanisms through which everyone in a language-community can participate in its establishment. For everyone is an expert in truth, just as everyone is an expert in television.

Expert paradigm vs. viewing experience

A certain critical suspicion of media manipulation is always healthy, because the motives of those who exploit TV commercially and politically are not entirely pure. In fact, it sometimes seems miraculous that so much of interest, importance, and merit has resulted from a business plan that never liked viewers to come too close, and did its best to convince us all that we were exactly what it wanted us to be – passive consumers with a shameful habit.

The television business began as a standard modern industry, based on a "closed expert process." This system worked fine for engineering and manufacturing industries – cars and chemicals. In such a business model, profitability is ensured by keeping the creative talent as far away from consumers as possible. Experts are isolated in a lab where they can do what they like (the company owns everything they come up with). Their ideas are sifted and reduced to standardized products and processes, then sent down a supply chain, which is often also controlled by the company, to waiting consumers. On the well-established model of the Hollywood "star factory," this was the plan for monetizing television. Creative experts came up with innovative products in the form of each season's new TV shows. These were standardized into familiar TV formats and produced by industrialized technical crews. They were disseminated through a controlled pipeline (TV networks) to the grateful but passive audience. It was the same business plan that brought you DDT and the gas-guzzler. It was how TV was imagined in the 1950s – and for quite a while thereafter.

The downside of this extreme division of labor was that consumers were excluded from contributing to the creation of the experience, except as studio audiences and occasional "vox pops" or as victims in news stories. It was your job to be a wise consumer. That model of television reduced viewers to behavioral responses. Naturally that behavior had to be professionally manipulated by marketing and regulation, increasing the gulf between TV and its audience. We could love 'em or hate 'em; we just couldn't join 'em.

Is it the destiny of "the tube" to continue pumping out products and propaganda for Planet Landfill? Or are we now witnessing a change in the experience of TV for consumers and producers alike?

The *experience* of watching TV has always been very different from the point of view of audiences as opposed to experts. The television experience is not about the consumption of goods, but is part of culture; more simply, for each viewer, it's a "history of me." There's no such thing as a universal "me," of course. What TV means, how it feels, what it is "for," changes depending on your own character and taste, and also on socio-cultural determinants like gender, age-group, family, class, nation, and ethnicity. But everyone in modern society spends some of their time making themselves up as they go along, learning their own identity via stories, interactions, and relationships, often in those otherwise unproductive, ungoverned, and potentially risky moments when we're not doing much at all; just daydreaming on our own or getting up to mischief with peers. This is where TV reigns supreme. The miracle that broadcasting performed every day for over half a century was that the same restricted range of programming in each country enabled individuated viewing experiences among so diverse a range of audience demographics. And here's why audiences are far from passive. We are not consuming a product but using the imaginative resources of story, song, sight, and sound – some of the most powerful tools known to humanity – to think about identity, relationship, and community, in real time and space, often while our annoying family is making us dream of being somewhere else entirely. Television obliges that dream. Using its semiotic and social resources, we make ourselves up as we watch, which is why so many people have a store of shows, characters, even ads, that reminds them of how, when, and where they went about that task.

But things have already changed beyond recognition. TV is on the move. While you've been lounging on the couch, the broadcast era has passed, and a new epoch has begun. With the rise of the internet and the fall of transaction costs in electronic media, every home in affluent societies has become a potential multiplatform publisher and every consumer a potential producer. Home itself has become a place of productive capacity, not just a leisure-time refuge. The 1990s and 2000s were marked by the migration of high-tech computing power out of organizations and into the home, a process marked by the shift of corporate power from IBM (office-based mainframe) to Microsoft (personal PC). Already, technologies are migrating again; out of home, out of the office and into the car, onto the body – to mobile applications. Post-broadcast (i.e. customized) television will follow; not only migrating out of the lounge-room and into the kitchen, study, or bedroom, but out of the sphere of domestic identity altogether. The TV–computer interface also means that all sorts of online services can merge with TV content: travel, learning, government, health, science, etc. The propagation of innovation throughout society has begun. Consumption has become co-production. TV is about "creating my (or our) experience" not "consuming your products." For today's teenagers, of whom there are over a billion worldwide, each one wanting to make their mischief and fulfill their dreams, this will be the new "history of me."

The value of TV studies

When you get in close to the actual scholarship, intellectual hard work, audacious theorizing, painstaking investigation, attention to data and detail, the wry and knowing mastery of the material and sheer flair of delivery of some of the best work being done both on TV itself and in TV studies, the continuing low repute of both TV and TV studies seems wrongheaded, not to say mean-spirited. Unfortunately, both TV and media studies tend to be judged on their poorest performances, not their best. It takes more than mere evidence to change habits of thought about a medium or a method, because of course those habits are relational, not scientific. They're not really personal opinions based on observation and study, but places in a hierarchy of culture where high status can only be achieved in opposition to low status. Media and methods need to be placed at one end of a value hierarchy in order to sustain culturally preferred values at the other. Popular entertainment is easily consigned to the opposite pole from truth-seeking philosophy in a print-literate, science-based intellectual universe; one that has, however, forgotten that there was no higher form of truth-telling in ancient Greece than drama, or that the most popular entertainments like the plays of Shakespeare can also achieve the status of universal art. Currently, we're habituated to a hierarchy based on thought being separated from entertainment, mind from body, science from emotion and conflict, elite universities from mass-education colleges, high-prestige research disciplines, devoted to describing things, from low-prestige teaching subjects, devoted to inspiring people.

But what goes around comes around. Like magnetic poles, value hierarchies can invert over time. Is it happening again now? There is a good reason why it should, because the status of truth has power to command at the level of individual lives and societal decisions. "We" judge people and policies by their truthfulness. It must surely follow that the more widely understood such processes are, the more "expert" everyone can become in determining the status of truths that buttonhole us on a daily basis. That is why the very real immersion of media studies in the sensational, trivial, manipulative, irrational, emotional, duplicitous, dissembling, and tendentious world of human mutual influence is especially important – it is the very context in which entire populations have to decide for themselves what counts as true. There is no need to construe the world of popular culture as a "negative pole" to which critical expertise must be *opposed*; it would be much more productive – and more "critical" – to evaluate it more highly as the locus of cultural, political, and knowledge formation for whole populations, a prime site for further democratization of knowledge, and to esteem slightly less the self-righteousness of the alienated critic or isolated expert, both of whom may be suffering from "paradigm lost," as will become more evident below.

Television Truths – The Book

In order to understand television, these problems of knowledge, repute, and intellectual hierarchy, which beset both the medium itself and the study of it, need to be made explicit. Any new work must recognize that there are epistemological imperatives that condition and even determine what we know about television, how we know it, and how we suppose it produces and circulates its own truths. This book tackles the task of understanding television truths by setting TV, and the study thereof, within the context of changes in the history of knowledge. We have to look at what TV does when it establishes the truth, but we also have to analyze the apparatus we're using to look with.

The problem of TV truths is as much epistemological (how do we know, and what institutions have arisen to produce such knowledge?) as it is metaphysical (what is the nature of the object we're investigating?). Indeed, all the branches of philosophy – the study of truth – are needed to sort out what's going on in contemporary mediated sense-making. This book contributes to that endeavor by showing how knowledge has intersected with media, how "reading publics" are formed in both cases, and what needs to be done in both education and television to bring TV truths into better understanding. This is not a work of traditional philosophy (with a capital P); it is, however, interested in pursuing the classical branches of philosophy into the contemporary world of television, having something new to say about each of them in the context of contemporary realities.

A philosophy of the popular

Within that overall structure, the book seeks to show how media studies, as a *philosophy of the popular*, has something important to say not only about television but about education (what is it for and who will do it); politics (consumer-citizenship in the era of interactive multimedia); creativity (television's own evolving aesthetic); and the future (as one "regime of truth" or knowledge paradigm disperses and reforms into another).

In order to understand television in this way, the book pursues a distinctive and characteristic mode of inquiry that grounds forward thinking in a broad understanding of historical change, some of the latter very long-term, contextualizing discussion about contemporary phenomena and future change in a comprehensive argument about why and how the paradigm has shifted. While very much concerned with evolution and change, the book is nevertheless a corrective to those futurological scenarios that work from current business data and technological developments to predict the social outcomes of technical inventions. Instead it explains the dynamics of shifts that are already under way, and shows how apparently distinct areas, for instance the media and education, or entertainment and innovation, are in fact part of the same paradigmatic shift.

Structure of the book

This chapter introduces the topic by establishing its language and discussing the mode of argumentation; it is equivalent to the branch of philosophy labeled Logic. Thereafter the book is in four parts, each one presented as the equivalent of a branch of philosophy (see table 1.1):

Part I (Is TV true?) is more about the basis of knowledge within which we make sense of television than it is a direct description of things on TV. It shows how paradigm shifts associated with modernity have affected the status of knowledge, and how both TV and contemporary thought have been shaped as a result. This part goes on to consider aspects of television across time and space, showing how TV sits among other media and modes of communication and literacy both historically and globally.

Part II (Is TV a polity?) considers the relations between television and its audiences, in the context of current notions of media citizenship and the citizen-consumer. It analyzes the narration of

Table 1.1 TV truths – a philosophy of the popular

Branch of philosophy	Domain of truthfulness	Part of this book
Logic/language	Argument	Introduction: television truths
Epistemology	Knowledge	I: Is TV true?
Ethics/politics	Conduct/action	II: Is TV a polity?
Aesthetics	Beauty	III: Is TV beautiful?
Metaphysics	Existence	IV: What can TV be?

nationhood, the historical relations between the "republic of letters" and television's "reading public," and contemporary civic engagement, TV-style.

Part III (Is TV beautiful?) analyzes TV content, showing how television apprehends the world of the imagination via live events, reality TV – a dramatic format that has surprising antecedents – and sports programming as you've never imagined it.

Part IV (What can TV be?) looks at the past and the future of both television and television studies. Television's existence is determined contextually and historically, so there's nothing "metaphysical" about it, in the ordinary-language sense of that term – TV has no essence, no transcendent properties; there is no "it" that can be abstracted and universalized. The only way to identify what it can be is to investigate it in context, historically. Unfortunately, TV scholarship has neglected not only the history of television but also its historiography. This section shows how TV has been memorialized in both formal and informal knowledge in one particular national context, using that example to create a template for the future study of television history. The book concludes by showing how TV studies itself can provide a new template for university education as we head into the era of self-made media and distributed truth.

Each part is also prefaced with a short introduction to orient the various chapters toward the themes of the book as a whole.

Given that the broadcast era, dominated by commercial network free-to-air TV, is coming to an end, how does television make sense of its own history, its own future, and how do other cultural sites and institutions attempt to grasp the essence of television? As digital media platforms mature (spread further, more cheaply), what changes in television will be caused by self-made content, social networking, interactive TV, mobile and non-broadcast platforms, and new business plans based on the long tail rather than the mass market? Are there lessons from previous "new" media such as print? Does the rolling transformation of television suggest a new model for the propagation of innovation, change, and creative capabilities throughout society? I argue that television going forward needs to be understood via the creativity and imagination of its viewers as a complex adaptive system, rather than via a rigid institutional system controlled by industrial expertise. Upon this "truth" will depend TV's continued existence.

From popular culture to creative industries

The book as a whole tracks an overall logic or argument toward a new paradigm for understanding television, for television research and scholarship, and for the future of the medium itself. In this respect it mirrors a trajectory in my own thinking about television, which has evolved from a "popular culture" to a "creative industries" perspective, the latter being most evident in chapter 12 below, although it suffuses the book. That change has partly been provoked by technological and cultural changes in the way TV is produced, disseminated, and used. Lately the "active audience" tradition has been boosted in a quite spectacular way by the advent of interactive formats, consumer-generated content, and user-led innovation. For me, these developments are welcome because they allow for some long-standing problems of cultural communication to be addressed more directly, most importantly that of a continuing structural tension in the relations between "addresser" and "addressee" in popular culture, between professional/managerial expertise and control on the one side and consumer/network creativity and activism on the other.

The division of labor between producers and consumers that we've inherited from the modern industrial era had become so strong that it was hard to see "mass" media like TV as two-way communication at all, so much did the circulation of meaning belong to firms and the experts they employed, so little to people at large. So it is a definite step forward in the public understanding of media when non-professional audiences, consumers, citizens, members of the public (call them what you will) are at last recognized as being so active that they – or rather "you" – have been collectively honored as the *Time Magazine* "person of the year 2006." The *expert paradigm* has a competitor at last. *Time*'s managing editor, Richard Stengel, praised the idea "that individuals are changing the nature of the information age, that the creators and consumers of user-generated content are transforming art and politics, that they are the engaged citizens of a new digital democracy" (*Time*, December 25, 2006: 4).[3] However, old habits die hard. While declaring upfront that "the 'great man' theory of history . . . took a serious beating this year" from "community and collaboration on a scale never seen before" (p. 24), *Time* illustrated this thesis by featuring not the anonymous millions of "you" but a series of well-chosen "greats" who had achieved international prominence online, including a seven-page profile of Chad Hurley and Steve Chen, co-founders of YouTube (pp. 46–52).

The tension between the expert paradigm and consumer activism is evident in such coverage. It is a sign of longer-term changes, where the point of view of the consumer – the perspective of culture rather than industry – is no longer confined to "making sense" of ready-made entertainments prepared by experts. Audiences always have exceeded what commercial media required of them, but with the advent of user-generated content it is easier to discern how audience practices connect with creative, critical, or communicative efforts in a cultural context. It is only now that broadcasting is no longer the only available model of "mass" communication that we can begin to see more clearly some of the problems incurred when expertise takes over a communication system in which the whole population is in principle a participant. Expertise leads too easily to exclusion, control, manipulation, reduction of interactions to the profit motive or to ideological ends, and the production of disengaged passivity or resentment among those excluded, who are also the large majority of the population.

One practical consequence of this change is that television studies has to change too, from its original provenance as critique – an uneasy amalgam of political and literary criticism and behaviorism mixed with emancipation – toward something that is itself more active. Now, television takes its place as one of the creative industries and television studies needs to go there too. Expertise doesn't need to be overthrown, however; it needs to be widely distributed. Everyone in consumer societies is now complicit in what used to be arcane mysteries, from how to perform the self in public to telling stories, true or tall, using digital technologies. Conversely, where telling the truth used to be an individual speech act, now it's a media performance. Either way, more and more non-professionals know how to do it for themselves. Crucially, they also know how to communicate the results to the same "mass audience" (or reading public) that corporate media had originally manufactured for their own purposes. So TV studies needs to play an active part too, in uplifting the level of communicative ambition and entrepreneurial achievement among the general population, whether for commercial, community, or personal gain, using digital media and networks. Furthermore, the line between expertise and consumption is now so fuzzy that consumers play a strong role in innovation. TV scholarship needs to become more alert to the productive potential of the consumer paradigm, in which context it needs to encourage active creative production as well as reflective critique.

There are of course many books on TV. What makes this one unique is its attention to *longue-durée* historical processes, its broad focus on the context of knowledge within which television culture and scholarship both move, and its analysis of the imaginative content and cultural uses of television. It represents a new take on television from a writer who is steeped in that field. Given the evolutionary perspective, it would be surprising if the argument of the book neglected changes that press upon the medium, including further extrusions from the broadcast tube itself. But the real quarry of the investigation pursued in this book is not "the future of television" so much as "the future of knowledge" in a democratized, monetized, and globalized world where the "modern" paradigm of representation is giving way to a distributed and networked system in which some "eternal verities" have turned out to be far from robust.

Notes

1   See www.whitedot.org/issue/iss_front.asp.
2   See www.tv-b-gone.com.
3   See www.time.com/time/magazine/article/0,9171,1569514,00.html.

Part I

Is TV True?

Epistemology of TV

This part explores the ground of knowledge within which both television as a cultural form and TV studies as a critical discourse need to be understood. First off, chapter 2 sets the historical context by showing how meanings have been organized into significant paradigmatic clusters over successive epochs (pre-modern or medieval, modern, and contemporary or global). This chapter is the conceptual engine of the book as a whole. It has three main aims:

- first to identify how the causation or source of meaning has been located on a successive link of the "value chain" in each of these epochs:

  producer/author/originator → *commodity/text/document* → *consumer/reader/user*;

- second to show how each link generates characteristic meanings in different cultural contexts, producing a characteristic *knowledge paradigm* for each period; and
- third that these knowledge paradigms are *mutually incompatible*, analytically if not in practice. In other words, the meanings of one paradigm cannot be analyzed by means of the values of another.

It is in relation to the third point that trouble stirs in intellectual work. Modern scholarship has developed into a very strong knowledge paradigm, organized around the foundational scientific insight (dating from around the sixteenth century but not fully ascendant until the nineteenth) that the source of meaning is not divine but can be observed within the properties of things themselves. Most scholars now subscribe to this view, including me. The trouble is that you can't "read" contemporary *global* meanings directly via the *modern* paradigm without a sort of parallax error (meaning that your results are determined by the position from which you observe, not by the actual properties of the object of study) because, in contemporary consumer culture, the source of meaning can no longer be presumed to be located within objects, documents, or texts in themselves. In a market environment such things – from movies to clothing – don't have any meaning until they're used. The source of meaning is the consumer, user, or reader. The lesson here is that it is difficult to "read" such phenomena in their own terms if you approach them with a "modern" analytical toolkit. That is why scientists tend to be hostile to contemporary mediated culture: it locates the source of meaning in the "wrong" paradigm of knowledge from their point of view.

Here's where television comes in. Although as a technological medium it dates from the modern era and requires a good deal of science to produce and distribute, as a cultural form it is firmly within the contemporary paradigm, at the mercy of consumers and audiences for its meanings and values. It is important therefore to understand how it fits into knowledge paradigms and historic shifts. Equally important to recognize is how the *study* of television has been shaped by the same historical process, but that for the most part formal knowledge and scholarship still occupy a different position on the value chain from that of their object of study. There is a mismatch (a parallax view) between television, as a meaning-generating cultural system, and the means of studying it, modern empirical-observational science. Chapter 2 provides a template for the study of television as part of long-term shifts in the value chain of meaning.

One reason why there is a lag between entertainment culture and media scholarship is that the two operate at different *frequencies*. Like chapter 2, chapter 3 sets the study of television in a longer timeframe and larger context, this time related to the frequency of different forms of communication. Once again it transpires that popular culture and academic writing are related to each other rather than existing in chalk/cheese opposition. Where in chapter 2 the relationship was between paradigms, here it is a matter of where to tune in along a range of communicative frequencies. Popular culture and media tend to operate at higher frequency than does academic writing. Journalism for instance is "uttered" faster, with closer intervals between successive utterances, than is the case for scholarship. However, this difference is not an opposition but a gradient, as all "public writing" is uttered at high-, medium-, or low-frequency intervals.

This part of the book finally closes in on television just as it disperses spatially across the globe. Chapter 4 shows how television is both an agent and effect of globalization, but once again the chapter sets the consideration of TV's global reach into a larger context. Overall, this part seeks to address the *way we know about* television – its "epistemology" – within the same historico-conceptual analytical framework as the thing itself.

2

The Value Chain of Meaning

Television in the History of Thought

This chapter provides a template for the "value chain analysis" of media culture (see table 2.1 below). It shows *where* meaning is thought to originate – its presumed source or causal origin – and how that source has shifted along the "value chain of meaning" over successive historical periods. A "*longue-durée*" approach such as this takes a while to get to television as such, but the purpose is to show how television as a cultural form sits within such long-term trends in sense-making. It argues that where meaning is thought to originate is a structuring principle for successive historical epochs.

The Value Chain

In business rhetoric, a "value chain" is a banal concept. At one end of the process of shifting goods is origination and the producer; in the middle is found the commodity and its distribution; at the other end is the consumer or end-user, like this:

Value chain of merchandise (goods and services):

Origination	Commodity	Consumption
Production	Distribution	Use

"Value chain analysis" is a managerial process designed to pay proper attention to the possibilities of increasing revenue and cutting costs all along that chain, not just in the process of manufacturing or production (see Porter 1985: 45–52). Businesses like to add value at all points. Consumers have become the focus of intense value-adding initiatives. For instance, customers of furniture stores like Ikea supply their own labor to assemble the goods they buy. Users of interactive computer games like The Sims contribute to the development of the game itself. It's not just "user pays": it's also "user makes." Where Fordist manufacturers once relied on control of the production process to control the generation of value, now they need to pay attention to the *experience* of consumption.

Their interest in culture is hardly surprising. The source of value is no longer to be found only in the scale and organization of manufacturing industry alone; it is also to be found among the uses and creativity of consumers themselves. Garnering value is no longer merely a matter of the bottom line, which itself has tripled in order to accommodate social and environmental as well as economic values (see Leadbeater 1999: 10–12). It is now also a matter of partnership with customers.

If meaning has a value chain, then it links the author (producer), via the text (commodity, distribution), to the reader (consumer), like this:

Value chain of meaning:

| Author | Text | Reader |
| Producer | Performance | Audience |

Thinking about Euro-American Western culture (non-Western traditions may have different histories of meaning), value has been added to meaning over time by progressively extending its supposed source across the chain as a whole. The place where people have looked in order to determine what something means has drifted down the chain. In "epochal" terms, the extension of meaning to the next link in the value chain can be seen to correlate closely to successive historical periods, like this:

- In the pre-modern (medieval) period, the source of meaning was understood to be divine, fixed in texts such as the Bible by the Judeo-Christian God. Authorial intention was therefore unarguable: a text meant what its (divine) producer said it did. All that remained for readers to do was to work out what the Author "meant." Priests were on hand to provide that service; that is what priesthood is for.

- In modern times, taking modernity to coincide with the inauguration of popular sovereignty, industrialization, the Enlightenment, etc., meaning was sourced to the distributed commodity itself: the *object,* in this case the text. Locating the source of meaning in the "thing itself" was the basis of empiricism and realism, the scientific observation of actually existing objects, documents, or (precisely) "sources" to determine the truth. Texts were objects – and vice versa – and they meant exactly what they themselves said. In the realm of language this led to the heyday of modernist literary criticism and scientific semiotics. Literary readers must get at meaning themselves, without the help of authorities, by using techniques such as I. A. Richards's practical criticism – close critical reading of the text without reference to contextual features (I. A. Richards 1929). Meanwhile, linguists hoped to be able to reduce meaning to a "science of signs." For better or worse, contemporary academics, intellectuals, and critics are "modernist" – they are trained to source meaning to its commodity form.

- In contemporary times (since World War II), the source of meaning has drifted to the other end of the value chain. It is taken to reside in the consumer – the audience or reader. Given the anonymous popular sovereignty of mass democracy, this was an egalitarian approach to meaning. It required large-scale sampling and ethnographic methods to get at meaning, because a text meant only what several million people said it did. The way to find out what something meant, from an event in the news to the outcome of TV shows, was not to inquire into the intentions of the producer, or even to analyze the text, but to source meaning to the consumer by polling, ratings, survey, and sample – by plebiscite.

It ought to be said straight away that each succeeding era does not supplant but typically supplements what has gone before, just as new media do. So in the contemporary period there are plenty of examples of both modern and pre-modern relationships to meaning. Indeed, many skirmishes in the "culture wars" that characterize contemporary societies are fought over differences among pre-modern (religious), modern (scientific), and "postmodern" (relativist) "truths."

The Drift of Meanings

Extending further this periodization of value chains in meanings and merchandise, it is interesting to look at the institutions, relations, and personnel involved in situating the source of meaning at different points along the chain in different periods.

To begin with, it is clear that different populations have been invoked by different assumptions about the source of meaning.

- In the medieval period, with a divine author, the general population comprised the laity or "the faithful." They needed priests to mediate between themselves and meaning's supposed source. They looked to the church as a physical location for that encounter. The gothic cathedral is a material expression of the belief in a divine source of meaning.
- But in modern times, after Milton and Johnson, the laity was secularized and became the reading public and thence "the" public. The intermediary here was the publisher, of pamphlet, newspaper, scientific treatise, literature, fiction, useful knowledge, official information, intelligence, and the like. The location for these meanings was an already virtualized public sphere – the imagined co-readership of documentary sources on the "public record."
- In the contemporary period, the source of meaning has shifted to the "DIY citizen" (Hartley 1999); its location has shifted to private life and the consumer market. The intermediary now is marketing itself – PR, IMC (integrated marketing communication) or "marcom," spin, information and impression management, and the like:

In the wake of the 9/11 attacks in the USA and bombings in Nairobi, Bali, Madrid, London (7/7), and the so-called global "war on terrorism," it is salutary to reflect that meanings are a matter of life and death and of lethal force. The source of meaning, whether understood as having divine, national, or personal origins, could be disputed at the point of the sword. One's position as a "subject" of power (i.e. one's subjectivity) could determine one's fate. During the same historical periods noted above, the basis of power, force, and enmity also shifted along the chain, drifting from the sovereigns and feudal lords who wielded "pain of death" in the name of a deity (which they tended to confuse with themselves), to the modern institutions and abstract entities for and against which one was recruited to fight, and thence to the front line of contemporary warfare, which is less a conflict between sovereigns and nations, more a battle of identity, thus:

What theorist, subjectivity, power-base:

Bible	Marx	Foucault
Soul	Individual(ism)	Experience
Pain of death/hell	War	Administration of life ("market")

What sovereign power, arms-bearer, enemy:

Monarch/divinity	Nation-state	Self
Knight/crusader	Conscript/volunteer	Terrorist
Peer/heretic	Country	Civilian

British diplomat Robert Cooper has argued that contemporary states may be classified in the same way: as pre-modern or "Hobbesian" (Somalia, Taliban Afghanistan), modern or "Machiavellian" (China,

India, Pakistan), and postmodern (post-imperial countries like the UK, Germany, and France) (Cooper 2002). Robert Kagan (2003) has added to the debate, dubbing "postmodern" states "Kantian":

What type of state:

"Hobbesian"   "Machiavellian"   "Kantian"

Kagan argues that this typology explains why the US and "old" Europe are experiencing troublingly divergent strategic cultures: "Americans are from Mars and Europeans are from Venus" (Kagan 2003: 3). In other words, the drift of meaning has strategic effects, where modern states like the USA rely on power and hegemony, while postmodern polities like the EU (and the post-imperial nations within it) are force-averse and "security is based on transparency, mutual openness, interdependence and mutual vulnerability" (Cooper 2002; and see chapter 10 below).

In the realm of knowledge itself, the mode of inquiry appropriate to discovering and communicating meaning changed also, requiring quite different philosophical and epistemological approaches, and reach of education, to deal with the drift of meaning along the value chain.

- In medieval times, truth was revealed. To find its source required an understanding of "authorial intentions," which in this context meant theology. Not too many people were needed for that, so education was restricted to the caste of literate clerics.
- In modern times truth was regarded as a scarce good: an indivisible unity, and while people might contend over it they could not pluralize and therefore share bits and pieces of it (Milton agonizes over the metaphor of the post-lapsarian dismemberment of truth in *Areopagitica*, a founding document of modernity). Truth was like power: a zero-sum game. If I had it, you didn't; if I lacked it, I had to take it from someone in order to possess it. This notion governed the period when secular modernists hoped that knowledge was a coherent unity (albeit with many disciplinary "branches"), and they set about educating their own mass populations into sufficient literacy to be able to add value to it by scientific observation and empirical application.

- But in contemporary times truth has multiplied and fragmented, just as has power. In these days of difference, diversity, and diaspora, truth has become inclusive, plentiful (see Hartley 2003: ch. 1). It is revealed by plebiscite. Education is no longer purposed for the literate mass workforce only, but for universal learning services available on a commercial, customized, "borderless" basis to anyone, anywhere, of any age. Thus:

What philosophy, epistemology, educational reach:

Revelation	Scarcity	Plenty
Theology	Empiricism	Plebiscite
Elite	Mass	Universal

Interestingly, while schooling was "modernized" into the form of mass education a century or more ago, *tertiary* education outside of the USA has taken this path only since World War II (Robbins in the 1960s in the UK; Dawkins in the 1980s in Australia). But social democratic governments are already pushing on toward "universal" provision in the tertiary sector by combining further and higher education, augmented by voluntary and commercial learning services (e.g. the Thomson Corporation) and media-learning institutions like the Open University, University for Industry, and National Health Service University in the UK or Shanghai Television University in China.

What is the method required to identify meanings? In medieval times it was biblical exegesis and the "concordance" or commentary on sacred texts, both of which were secularized in the modern period in the form of literary criticism. But such criticism could no longer be anchored on the "intentions of the author." The preferred method was skeptical observation and attention to the empirical form and properties of the object of study – criticism became a form of "scientific" method designed to dissect and anatomize the textual specimen. But although the battle over the "intentionalist fallacy" is by no means won (it prevails in common usage), the modernist method no longer suffices either, because texts cannot by themselves mean what they say. Readers, audiences, and consumers, within a situated context of experience, decide what texts mean. Indeed, because there is just too much readily accessible and available meaning out there among the millions of people, media, sites, and sources, the method of determining meaning from among consumers is itself a creative process, but an editorial not an authorial one, using a textual practice that I've called redaction (Hartley 2000, 2003: 82–7).

Redaction is the creative editorial practice of bringing existing materials together to make new texts and meanings. It is both the art form of the age and a method for representing meanings sourced to consumers. Redaction has added value to the end of meaning's value chain. The new method is to "edit people's choices" (this phrase was used by a designer from Country Road at a recent conference to explain what fashion designers do).

Meanwhile, the characteristic creative form of each era changes: in medieval times it's the liturgy in the cathedral, that combination of space, paint, glass, smoke, song, sight, spectacle, and ritualized actions that cohere around the glorification of the superhuman source of meaning. In modern times it's realism: journalism in the realm of fact; the prose novel in that of fiction. Now it is "reality": factual and fictional performances that promise some element of transparency, universality, participation, and interactivity with the audience, like this:

What interpretive and creative form:		
Exegesis	Criticism	Redaction
Ritual/liturgy	Realism (journalism, novel)	Reality

Such developments were accompanied by, and required, changes in literacy, of which they were also a symptom.

- In the medieval era audiences were just that – they "audited" what authors had created. Literacy needed to be "hear only," whether in church or theater. Audiences only had to hear the divine word in the liturgy and sermon.
- Modern audiences were true readers, but their literacy was largely "read only." In order to take part in public life in democratic societies, for instance, the modern citizen had to be able to read the newspapers, but not write for them.
- The contemporary period is witnessing a further change in literacy – the popular audience is achieving a "read and write" capacity in publicly distributed media, via their participation in shows like *Big*

Brother, and in private communication, where digital equipment for making audio-visual texts and messages is close to achieving the banal and autonomous status of the pen. Thus:

What literacy:

Hear only   Read only   Read and write

How do you talk to such folk? The "mode of address" has changed from one that was designed to convert hearers to the faith, via one that wanted to convince readers to give their loyalty to a party or brand, a cause or campaign, to one seeking to converse with customers who might also be suppliers, competitors, or partners:

What mode of address:

Convert   Convince   Converse

Summary

If there is a "value chain of meaning," corresponding to value chains in business, then a correlation can be explored between author, text, reader (meaning) and production, commodity, consumption (merchandise) (see table 2.1, p. 28). I argue that meaning has been attributed to different sources in different historical epochs, and that these have been associated with successive stages of the value chain in pre-modern, modern, and contemporary (globalized) times. The analysis suggests that creative and cultural activities whose meanings are associated with one link in the chain (e.g. reader/audience/consumption) may be negatively valued or even unintelligible to those whose ideological or disciplinary training centers on a different link (e.g. text/performance/commodity, or author/producer/production). If observed from such a perspective, a critical "parallax error" may distort our view of creativity in the new consumer economy.

If the categories are read "vertically" as a "paradigmatic" list rather than horizontally as a "syntagmatic" sequence, it becomes clear that more

Table 2.1 The value chain of meanings

Era:	1 Pre-modern	2 Modern	3 Global
Value chain:			
of merchandise	Origination/	Commodity/	Consumption/
of meaning	production	distribution	use
	Author/producer	Text/performance	Reader/audience
When, where, who (time, place, population)			
When	Medieval	Modern	Postmodern
Where	Church	Public sphere	Private life
Who (population)	The faithful	The public	DIY citizen
Who (intermediary)	Priest	Publisher	Marcom/IMC
How (regime)			
Theorist	Bible	Marx	Foucault
Subjectivity	Soul	Individual(ism)	Experience
Power-base	Pain of death/hell	War	Administration of life ("market")
Sovereign	Monarch/divinity	Nation state	Self
Arms-bearer	Knight/crusader	Conscript/volunteer	Terrorist
Enemy	Peer/heretic	Country	Civilian
State	"Hobbesian"	"Machiavellian"	"Kantian"
Why (knowledge)			
Philosophy	Revelation	Scarcity	Plenty
Epistemology	Theology	Empiricism	Plebiscite
Educational reach	Elite	Mass	Universal
What (form)			
Interpretive form	Exegesis	Criticism	Redaction
Creative form	Ritual/liturgy	Realism (journalism, novel)	Reality
What for (communicative politics)			
Mode of literacy	Hear only	Read only	Read and write
Mode of address	Convert	Convince	Converse
Who says (choice control)			
Source of control	"Him" – divine control	"Them" – expert control	"Me" – self-control
Source of choices	No choices = **Fundamentalism**	Publisher/provider = **Modernism**	Navigator/aggregator = **Globalization**

than cultural history is at stake. Ideological commitments and imaginative vision are bound up with each list and its internal transformations (see table 2.2, pp. 30–2).

This exercise reveals that some terms are associated with categories that don't sit very easily with our habitual self-understandings. I would guess that most contemporary intellectuals, whether academics or activists, policy-wonks or journalists, are most comfortable with the terms in the middle column. For most practical purposes "we" readers are modernists. But the categories of "production" and "the author," to which many are still devoted, from political economists to film critics, appear here in the context of fundamentalism. Is it possible we are too wedded to ideas of primacy, causation, and prestige that are simply medieval? Should we be so certain that causation flows just one way? Do we love authors and production for merely metaphysical reasons? Is there a hint of Coleridgean "clerisy" (Coleridge 1972) in our desire to teach populations what "we know" rather than what "they want," and to regard the extension of meaning's source to consumers as "dumbing down," not "democratization"?

In political and cultural movements at large it is clear that column one has not lost its force except in the armed components of the "regime" category (at least in the West). Politicians still recruit votes by stirring up residual allegiances associated with pre-modern categories, while certain movements associated with religious fundamentalism actively pursue the society-wide reinstatement of column-one characteristics. So this periodization of the drift of meaning along the value chain does not imply "progress" from one column to the next. On the contrary it is a Ramist spatialization – a visualization of knowledge characteristic of early printing, when the linear sequence of speech was rendered into spatial layout on the page (Ong 1958: 314). It spatializes (and so renders "methodical" in Ramist terms) an insight that I sought to explain in *Uses of television* (1999), namely that contemporary sense-making is *trans-modern*, using pre-modern (oral, family-based), modern (rational, capitalist), and postmodern (textual, mediated) modes of *teaching* all at once.

The terms in column three include many of the most contested, derided, "unworthy" categories in current public discourse. That column also includes some terms that haven't been invented yet, being neologisms of my own coinage required to identify and to bring forward for analysis newly emerging phenomena to which modernist thinking is almost completely blind: in particular the concepts of plebiscite, redaction,

Table 2.2 Paradigmatic alphabets of meaning
(a) The fundamentalist alphabet – pre-modern values, centered on origin, author, and production

a	Pre-modern	**To convert – devotion, exegesis, revelation**
b	Origination	
c	Production	
d	Author	
e	Producer	
f	Medieval	
g	Church	
h	The faithful	
i	Priest	
j	Bible	
k	Soul	
l	Pain of death/hell	
m	Monarch/divinity	
n	Knight/crusader	
o	Peer/heretic	
p	"Hobbesian"	
q	Revelation	
r	Theology	
s	Elite	
t	Exegesis	
u	Ritual/liturgy	
v	Hear only	
w	Convert	
x	"Him" – divine control	
y	No choices	
z	Fundamentalism	

Figure 2.1 Ludovic Brea, *Scenes from the life of Saint Margaret* (1498) (detail). Collection musée des beaux-arts Jules Chéret, Nice. Used with permission

Table 2.2   (cont'd)

(b) The modernist alphabet – modern values, centered on the commodity, text, and distribution

a	Modern	**To convince – poster, politics, criticism**
b	Commodity	
c	Distribution	
d	Text	
e	Performance	
f	Modern	
g	Public sphere	
h	The public	
i	Publisher	
j	Marx	
k	Individual(ism)	
l	War	
m	Nation-state	
n	Conscript/volunteer	
o	Country	
p	"Machiavellian"	
q	Scarcity	
r	Empiricism	
s	Mass	
t	Criticism	
u	Realism (journalism, novel)	
v	Read only	
w	Convince	
x	"Them" – expert control	
y	Publisher/provider	
z	Modernism	

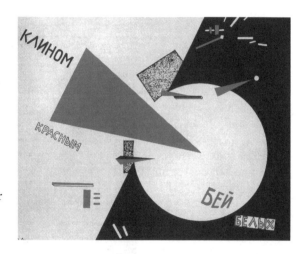

Figure 2.2   El Lissitzky, *Beat the Whites with the Red Wedge* (1919–20) ("klinom krasnym bei belykh"). See www.usc.edu/schools/ annenberg/ asc/projects/comm544/library/ images/706.html

Table 2.2 (*cont'd*)

(c) The postmodernist alphabet – global values, centered on the consumer, audience, and use

a	Postmodern	**To converse – computer, celebrity, redaction**
b	Consumption	
c	Use	
d	Reader	
e	Audience	
f	Postmodern	
g	Private life	
h	DIY citizen	
i	Marcom/IMC	
j	Foucault	
k	Experience	
l	Administration of life ("market")	
m	Self	
n	Terrorist	
o	Civilian	
p	"Kantian"	
q	Plenty	
r	Plebiscite	
s	Universal	
t	Redaction	
u	Reality	
v	Read and write	
w	Converse	
x	"Me" – self-control	
y	Navigator/aggregator	
z	Globalization	

Figure 2.3 Olga Tobreluts, *Sacred Figures I – Kate Moss* (1999), after Antonello da Messina, *The Virgin Annunciate* (1476). Courtesy of the artist

the DIY citizen, and "read and write" literacy for post-broadcast media content.

I'm suggesting that intellectual inquiry based on modern (and some pre-modern) categories – a devotion to *the public sphere, print literacy, the nation-state, government, empiricism, criticism, realism, the public* – is not necessarily best placed to understand culture and business organized around a newly emerging paradigm: *consumption, the reader or audience, postmodernism, private life, marcom, the self, the "plenitude of the possible"* (Foucault 1984: 267), *analysis by plebiscite, universal education, redaction, reality, the DIY citizen*. In the face of such contemporary phenomena, modernists are apt to revert to adversarial thinking. It's the Cold War all over again. But perhaps the *casus belli* isn't so much the culture as the categorization? And meanwhile, the object of study – culture "out there" – has moved to a different place, where modernist analysis may simply "misread" it.

The New Economy, Creativity, and Consumption in the Value Chain

This amounts to a kind of critical "parallax error," where the object of analysis is in a different position from the point of observation. My prescription for the analysis of television in the context of the new economy and consumer-led creativity is not to start from inherited presumptions (fundamentalist or modernist) about what "consumption" means, where it fits, and what it connects with. Instead, it is preferable to look directly at the way cultural practices themselves are organized and reproduced, to try to explain how the drift of the source of meaning to the "reader" end of the chain of communication is working itself through in various categories and media, including both broadcast and post-broadcast forms of television.

Paying more attention to consumers is anathema to critics who want to see control being exercised by powerful others, usually with malice aforethought, in the name of state, corporate, ideological, or divine power. Naturally, there's plenty of evidence that latter-day moguls do indeed seek control over assets and attitudes, so the case seems easily made. However, the preoccupation with ownership and control, and the presumption that it entails behavioral or ideological effects in consumers that can be known in advance and against which the individual is defenseless, both serve to deflect attention from other, equally interesting, "structural" features of the landscape of meaning that cast the consumer in a different light. Prominent among these is the drift of *control* and *choice* along the value chain along with the source of meaning, thus:

Source of control, choices:

"Him" – divine control	"Them" – expert (remote) control	"Me" – self-control
No choices	Publisher/provider	Navigator/aggregator

- In the pre-modern or fundamentalist paradigm, control over humanity was exercised by the divinity, to which "there is no alternative" (as Maggie Thatcher was later to proclaim about her own messianic program): choice was not an option.
- In the modern era, control was ceded to remote-control experts, administrators, and publishers (including media barons), who *provided* choices to grateful consumers.
- In the contemporary global era, however, consumers exercise their own choices (with the help of redactors like Google), carrying their own self-control mechanisms, and *navigating* the means and media of meaning that they want or can access, to deliver their own choices. The choices that people make are both guided and scaled, so that profitability comes from *attracting aggregated attention* (see Lanham 2006 for the "economics of attention") rather than "positioning" audiences or consumers by some kind of corporate head-lock.

This model does not apply to everyone, even in rich countries, but its generation and refinement in the intense competitive domain of digital content ("Web 2"), media entertainment, and consumer services (including television and its post-broadcast successors) is fascinating to observe. It is a distributed model of control and choice. Of course, as the man said (in *Casablanca*, 1942), "the problems of three little people don't amount to a hill of beans in this crazy world" (although *stories* about those "three little people" can indeed make a difference), so individual navigations, choices, and control strategies are aggregated and scaled up to form the "collective intelligence" of network culture. Television – tentatively – has entered this world, and the model of the malevolent mogul pulling the strings so that "we" all believe and do what "they" dictate is no longer appropriate: it's another parallax error. More interesting by far is to concentrate on how, for good or ill, the consumer paradigm will turn out, and whether its positive potential will counterbalance its well-documented (but less well-understood) down sides.

All this suggests that not just the media and informal sources of meaning, but also universities and other institutions of formal knowledge, need to think about their situation, even as they analyze the informal production and distribution of meaning by media such as television and its successors. Our own knowledge, values, and learning services are caught up in the extension of the value chains of goods and meaning toward the consumer-based "navigator/aggregator" model. We, modernist intellectuals working in barely post-medieval institutions, are no longer self-evidently the source, the "provider" of knowledge. One implication of the emergence of the new economy, creativity, and consumption is that now "we" have serious competition. We've dissolved into our other, but so has our value.

3

Public Address Systems
Time, Space, and Frequency

"My name is Ozymandias, king of kings:
Look on my works, ye mighty, and despair!"
Nothing beside remains: round the decay
Of that colossal wreck, boundless and bare,
The lone and level sands stretch far away.
Ozymandias, *Percy Bysshe Shelley, 1818*

This chapter approaches the epistemology of media by showing how the *frequency* of communication affects its status, use, and social impact. Like the previous chapter, this one is therefore not directly "about" television as a self-contained medium. Instead it sets TV into the context of a much wider frequency range of communicative forms, by means of which its cultural purposes may more easily be understood. It does deal directly with news, a form of truth-telling in which television is a major player. Again, however, journalism is barely explicable in terms of any one medium: news is a multiplatform phenomenon whose frequency has varied over historical time and in different media and geopolitical contexts. How then do we know what's news? The answer, to a surprising extent, is that we know what it is by its relative *frequency*.

News and Time

Time in communicative life can be understood not merely as sequence but also in terms of *frequency*. A "wavelength" of 1,000 years represents a very low time frequency, whereas the pip-pip-pip of the speaking clock or the up-to-the-second news bulletin represents high-frequency time. Time and news are obviously bound up in each other. The commercial value of news is its timeliness. Simultaneously, for the public, part of the quotidian sense of time in everyday life comes from keeping up with the news. For its devotees, news confirms a sense both of time passing, as stories unfold and new ones emerge, and of the concrete experience of the "nowness" of each day and time of day, as one pays attention to a particular news program or title.

Not surprisingly, therefore, the longest-lasting news outlets tend to be named after time itself, whether their frequency is the hour, day, or week; for instance the American weekly magazine *Time*, the British daily newspaper *The Times*, and the flagship Soviet/Russian TV nightly news *Vremya* (which means "time" in Russian). For more than 70 years BBC Radio has used the second-by-second time-pips to introduce its most portentous news bulletins. This convention is so naturalized that it has become unthinkable to begin broadcast news bulletins at any other time than "on the hour" (or half-hour) – the public simply can't be trained to tune into a news show at, say, seven minutes past the hour.

Clocks and datelines feature prominently in the design of TV news programs, such as the British ITN *News at Ten*. Indeed, over a 30-year period this show and its timeslot became tightly bound together with a widespread sense of British national togetherness. The commercial television network ITV was only allowed to time-shift *News at Ten* in 1999 (to make room for peak-time movies) after a failed attempt in 1993, a national inquiry by the broadcasting regulator (the ITC), and a hostile parliamentary debate. It seemed that messing with the news was tantamount to messing with time itself. The conjunction of *time* and *journalism* was thought to be significant to *national* identity. The "frequency" of news is thus a weighty matter.

"Public Writing" – from Slow-Mo to Po-Mo

Public writing is produced, circulated, and deciphered. Each of these moments in its career has its own frequency:

- the speed of *creation* – how long a given "text" of public writing takes to produce;
- frequency of *circulation* – intervals between publication;

- the wavelength of *consumption* – the period a given text spends in the public domain before being superseded by later "pulses" of text from the same source.

In news, the frequencies of production and consumption are designed to match that of publication. A premium is set on high-frequency news-*gathering*, on increasing the frequency (i.e. reducing the time lag) between the occurrence of an event and its public narration, although not all public writing shares this imperative. And all news relies on what they used to call built-in obsolescence: a high frequency of consumption. News that is golly-gosh today is chip-wrapper tomorrow. There are commercial and even ideological reasons for trying to keep the three wavelengths tightly bundled, although in principle they are not. For instance, news can sometimes take much longer to create than its daily rhythm would predict (investigative stories, news from remote locations, stories recovered from the past and re-run); and of course once published, news "texts" continue to exist long after their newsworthiness has expired. Given long enough, their value begins to appreciate once more; a copy of a seventeenth-century newspaper is much more valuable than this morning's.

In contrast to news, very low-frequency public writing, like an inscription on a public monument, which is designed to remain legible for a very long period, may take longer to create and to transmit than very high-frequency writing that is expected to be discarded after a day or two. In other words, carving is slower than speaking, and it also takes a given "interpretive community" longer to pass by a fixed building to read the inscription than it does to broadcast a news bulletin to the same proportion of that population. Low frequency should not be confused with inefficiency. The proportion of Americans who have personally scrutinized fixed inscriptions of the peak national monuments in Washington and New York is likely to be higher than the proportion watching any news show. "Bring me your huddled masses" is written on just one structure, located inconveniently in the middle of a very large harbor, but it is a better-known text than the lead item on the highest-rating news. People from all over the world queue to read it on the plinth of the Statue of Liberty.

Thus "public writing" displays high to low frequencies right through the value chain from creation ("writing"), via publication ("text"), to consumption ("reading"). For the purposes of this chapter, however, the primary "wavelength" will be that of circulation – the intervals between publication in any series, on the model of "journalism" itself (the word derives from "jour," French for "day").

As already hinted, "public writing" as a term refers not just to alphabetic print but to communication by any means that is designed to address its interlocutor as "the public." Such "writing" includes contemporary electronic forms of public address from broadcasting to the internet. Naturally it also includes print, from the tabloid press to book publishing. But "public writing" is much older than those forms that are currently recognized as "the media," and it extends to much lower frequencies. It certainly includes inscriptions carved into monuments, tombs, temples, and the like.

But in order to do full justice to the range of "public address" covered by the notion of frequency, it is in fact necessary to expand what is normally understood by the term "writing." Messages "written in stone" are clearly intended to be more permanent and portentous than those breathed into the air; "inscription" is a mode of public address somewhere along a continuum with speech. However, *stone itself* may be regarded as a form of writing. Sculpture and architecture are themselves among the earliest forms of "public address," the "mass media" of their day, certainly in Western (Egyptian-Hellenic) traditions. Tombs and temples, palaces and palisades, statues and sphinxes, were all, beyond their functional organization of *space*, also forms of public communication, using familiar codes, conventions, idioms, and styles. They were for their creators, and remain today, forms of "public writing," in fact. Furthermore they were designed to express long-term, stable meanings, and to communicate very serious messages. They spoke the language of death, eternity, empire, power, and beauty. They took communication from the personal to the collective plane, from individual to imperial. They remain to this day the lowest-frequency forms of public writing.

Indeed, the continued existence of ancient examples of "public writing," and the reworking of their "idiom" in contemporary buildings, demonstrates that "new media technologies," all the way from limestone and granite via print to electronic and digital media, do not supplant but supplement older ones. Writing itself has never been extinguished since the Egyptians and Sumerians first invented it some time before 3000 BCE, despite a number of "mass extinction" crises suffered by particular writing systems since then. Individual "texts," such as the pyramids at Saqqara and other antiquities dating back to the very earliest periods of public writing, are still belting out complex messages that "speak" to millions of contemporary readers (the Egyptian economy is dependent upon this fact). Such "messages" survive millennia, and communicate to cultures with meaning systems quite different from that of the original builders.

But more significantly, the "idiom" of ancient "public writing" in stone survives and is reworked to make new messages; it remains an active "medium" of communication among the many later media. Cities around the world are crammed full of postmodern, high-tech buildings that add their contemporary voice to the low-frequency mode of public writing in stone. Their facades are clad in granite (quoting Egyptian monuments for the eternal look), travertine marble (quoting the Roman Forum for the republican look), white marble (quoting the Roman emperors' palace for the imperial look), or Portland limestone (quoting St Paul's cathedral for a modern, rational look), even while their occupants are busy producing electronic, virtual, and digital public communication at ever-higher frequencies.

Some communicative syntax – for instance many architectural details understood as "classical," from the portico to the pediment, column to frieze – has been transferred from temples and triumphal arches to the facades of banks and media corporations. Presumably the urge here is to preserve rather than to change the temporal signification of stone. Such uses of architecture have become the very "language" of permanency and power, exploiting the ultra-low frequency of architecture and sculpture to "say something" *public* about *commercial* institutions, using the idiom of civic and religious communion. The classical temple, tomb, and palace, the imperial European city, the art deco American one, and the sprawling megalopolis of the developing world; all rework the low-frequency mode of "public writing" (see table 3.1 below).

Paradoxically, the most *enduring* human creation is the *ruin*. The ruin may indeed be defined as public writing that has outlived its author's intentions and even the language of public communication in which it was created. It sends what may be termed the "Ozymandias" message (see that name in Wikipedia). Ruins speak to the unfolding present from "time immemorial," but the "message" is unintended, a text without an author. The ruin, together with other "immemorial" texts, such as prehistoric cave-paintings and carvings, is the lowest-frequency of all forms of public address.

Some ruins remain semiotically active without a break for millennia – Stonehenge, the pyramids, the Great Wall, the tomb of Augustus or Hadrian in Rome. Although they are not "ruins" in the same way, even greater communicational longevity may apply to rock-carvings and cave-paintings. But it would not be safe to associate low-frequency public address with traditional and pre-industrial societies. Such societies also make widespread use of high-frequency forms, from the sand art of the Navajo and also of some Aboriginal peoples of Australia, to the painstaking making of the mandala by Buddhist monks who destroy their work on completion. But of course it is the low-frequency communication of traditional societies that tends to survive. While some "rock art" is perhaps tens of thousands of years old, it remains sacred and significant for the Aboriginal communities who live with it, and it is increasingly revered by official cultures as part of their unique "national" heritage.

Other ruins are intermittent signifiers, being lost or forgotten perhaps for centuries, later to be "reincarnated" as it were, to communicate new meanings with the help of archaeology. Such "texts" include "rediscovered" temples in Java or Cambodia; Maya, Aztec, and Inca ruins in the Americas; the tomb of Qin Shi Huang, first emperor of China; the moai of Rapa Nui.

If all media are forms of public writing, then the concept of "media" extends well beyond those forms that are currently recognized as belonging to the media sector of the contemporary economy. Between high-frequency marcom and low-frequency marble there are myriad media of public address, distributed across all frequencies from the moment to the millennium (see table 3.1).

Journalism Frequencies

Over its 200–400-year history, journalism has shown a consistent tendency to drift upward in frequency. New forms of news, especially those that attract the most intense capital investment and public disquiet, are ever faster. Journalism can range in frequency from the second and faster (e.g. Matt Drudge, spin doctors), down to the quarter (e.g. *Fashion Quarterly*), though the latter frequency (like the once-common bi-weekly newspaper) is now archaic for news; it has been occupied by academic and scientific journals.

At the very highest wavelengths, instantaneous reporting has appeared on the internet. This development has caused some commentators to predict the end of journalism (as we know it). The Monica Lewinsky affair in the USA during President Clinton's second term was the trigger for such concern, since court decisions and other news-sensitive information were released on the internet, bypassing the usual journalistic gatekeepers. On the publication of the Starr report, TV

Table 3.1 Frequencies of public writing

Frequency	Media
Before the event	Previews, leaks, briefings, PR, "spin," marcom
High frequency Instant/second	Internet, subscription news: e.g. Matt Drudge, Reuters Financial TV, Bloomberg.com
Minute	"Rolling update" news: e.g. CNN, BBC-24/Choice, Radio 5-Live
Hour	Broadcast news: e.g. CBS/ABC/NBC, ITN/BBC, Radio 4
Day	Daily press: e.g. *The Times, New York Times, Sun, New York Post*
Week	Weekly periodicals: e.g. *Time, New Statesman, Hello!, National Enquirer*
Mid frequency Month	Monthly magazines: e.g. *Vogue, Cosmopolitan, Numéro, FHM*
Quarter	Academic journals: e.g. *International Journal of Cultural Studies*
Year	Books, movies, TV series: e.g. *Harry Potter, Star Wars, 24, CSI*
Low frequency Decade	Scholarship, contemporary art: e.g. "definitive" works, textbooks, dictionaries, portraiture, fashionable artists
Century	Buildings, statues, canonical literature: e.g. Sydney Opera House, war memorials, Shakespeare
Millennium	Temple, tomb: e.g. Parthenon, pyramids
Eternity	Ruins: e.g. Stonehenge, "Ozymandias"

viewers around the world enjoyed the spectacle of CNN cameras pointing to a computer screen while the reporter scrolled down pages of internet text to find newsworthy references to non-standard uses for cigars (see the entry on Monica Lewinsky in the Wikipedia). It certainly *looked* as though the form of journalism that prided itself on its high frequency, i.e. the rolling update continuous "breaking news" format of cable TV, was reduced to the status of mere servant to the instantaneous internet. Furthermore, CNN got into trouble even for this second-hand timeliness, as commentators expressed discomfort at seeing the unexpurgated facts on a TV screen, although they seemed happy for the full text of the Starr report to appear on the internet itself.

Currently, then, there is a complicated readjustment in progress between the *previously* fastest and *next* fastest news media. Up-to-the-second forms of journalism are concentrated at the premium end of the market for news, targeted at the most highly capitalized sector of the economy with time-sensitive information needs – the financial markets. This is one place where news has attracted new investment and innovative format development. Reuters Financial Television and Bloomberg, for example, are locked in an international competitive struggle for this "narrowcast" but ultra-high-frequency form of journalism, which can be sold at a premium to corporate clients. Meanwhile, the *look* of the instantaneous format has been "borrowed" from the net to give the slightly slower TV screen the appearance of instantaneous news. For instance, CNN's on-screen design now resembles the aesthetic of the internet, with rolling stock-prices, text captions that may not relate to the pictures, and inset video frames with pictures that may not relate to each other.

It seems journalism can't get any faster than the instant. But with previews, leaks, spin doctoring, news management, and PR, a good deal of news crosses the time barrier into the strange world of "news *before* the event." Each morning's radio and TV news shows bristle with rebuttals and responses to government decisions or reports that haven't yet been released. The "get your retaliation in first" sector is in a phase of rapid commercial development and expansion. Of course its ascendancy gives the lie to the old-fashioned notion that news can only occur after some sort of event has occurred – a myth of news-making that has never been true. Just how badly news-before-the-event can tear the normal fabric of the political time-space continuum was demonstrated in 1999 in Britain, with the difficulties experienced by the government after the pre-release of part of the Macpherson Report into "institutional racism" in the Metropolitan Police (the Stephen Lawrence inquiry). The government tried to get an injunction on the publication in the daily press of sections of a report they themselves were due to release to Parliament two days later. By the time the full report was published the various players had already taken up their positions in the public domain. But within hours of the official publication the Home Office had to recall the entire print-run as the report contained the identity and addresses of witnesses. Thus, quite apart from its controversial conclusions and recommendations, the report became a political hot potato purely because of its *timing*. Released before their (albeit arbitrary) time of publication, the untimely facts caused unmanageable side-effects as they darted about in the public domain before their own release.

At the slower end of journalism's frequency range, the glossy fashion and style monthlies hold sway (see table 3.1 above). *Vogue* and *Elle* have been joined by the "lad-mags" for men, like *Loaded*. Some of these have proven so successful that they have become global brands, like *FHM*. Other booming sectors are lifestyle and "shelter" magazines like *Wallpaper*, and a proliferation of titles for teenagers and young women; the *More!* the merrier.

The *monthly* wavelength of the periodicals market is buoyant. However, the once-dominant higher-frequency *weekly* magazines for women, such as *Woman* and *Woman's Own*, are in decline. While their circulation tends to be higher per title than that of the glossies (reaching millions rather than tens or hundreds of thousands), this is no comfort to them. Their sales are steadily trending downward with declining profitability. The reaction to these tendencies by the top-selling Australian women's magazine, the *Australian Women's Weekly*, is interesting. For some years this magazine has been published as a monthly, despite retaining its title. Recently it has also begun to appear in international editions aimed at a general readership, so it's no longer Australian, women's, or weekly – its descriptive title ought to be the *International General Monthly*.

While news journalism tends to the highest frequencies, non-news journalism, from the political and gossip weeklies (*New Statesman*, *Hello!*), to the fashion and style monthlies (*Vogue*, *Numéro*), operates at lower frequencies. Weekend newspapers draw on aspects of both of these types. Non-news journalism on television also tends toward lower frequencies than "hard" news. While news is hourly, current affairs shows are week/daily, and lifestyle journalism (such as holiday, fashion, food, motoring, and consumer-watchdog shows) is weekly.

It is also apparent that increases in the speed of journalism are associated with new media. While (500-year-old) print dominates the wavelengths between the day and the week and below, (100-year-old) broadcasting predominates in the frequencies between the day and the hour. Non-broadcast forms of screen and electronic media, i.e. cable and internet forms (introduced only two or three decades ago), have taken over in the wavelengths between the hour and the instant.

Moving down to the mid-frequency range (see table 3.1 above), journalism is still present, but it is giving way to other forms. In the non-fiction area, its place is taken by book publishing, and by academic, scientific, and scholarly writing. Mid-frequency journalism includes books by journalists on current affairs. Sometimes these can be newsworthy in their own right (Andrew Morton's book on Diana, Princess of Wales), sometimes they can define an event for posterity (John Reed's *Ten Days that Shook the World*), and sometimes they might contribute to the practice of journalism itself (Philip Knightley's *The First Casualty*).

Academic writing is on the same continuum as journalism – generally speaking it is "public writing" that is produced and circulated at a lower frequency than the news. However, some of it, especially competitive science or medical papers published in journals such as *Nature, Science*, or the *Lancet*, operates at frequencies as high as news or even faster (i.e. by direct online dissemination), because this form of academic publication is connected to intellectual property rights that are established by being first to publish a discovery. Indeed the high investment associated with high-frequency science publication simply proves the point of this chapter; that different corporate and cultural purposes are served by publications at different frequencies. Academic writing is part of the continuum, and where it can be monetized its frequency can be as high as any other mode of public address.

Bearing in mind that different disciplines and countries will prove the exception to any rule, it can be observed that historically, and as a routine professional practice, academic publication has tended to occupy the mid-range frequencies. Its wavelength is counted in months and years (mid) rather than either days (high) or centuries (low). Scholarly writing, as opposed to scientific IP (intellectual property), is slower than both journalism and much commercial writing. The latter is geared to the financial year and is therefore rarely slower than annual. But it is not as slow as canonical big-L Literature, especially "classic" texts that are out of copyright (i.e. with a frequency lower than 50 or 70 years depending on the jurisdiction). Academic writing that attains classic status, such as Charles Darwin's *Origin of Species*, may be republished *as* literature, as it has been by the Folio Society for example, even though its value as a scientific text is far from spent.

The time lag between commencing a piece of writing and its publication in academic work is, in the main (with the exception of high-investment science, as noted above), much greater than that for journalism. Scholarly articles and books can take months or even years to write. This one certainly did. After that, the waiting lists for publication in some academic journals can be counted in years, even after a paper has been refereed over several months. In the case of books, an academic book takes from nine months to a year to publish after delivery by the author. It is therefore really difficult to achieve topicality in academic writing using print as the means of dissemination. E-journals have begun to change the situation, but as yet only at the margins of academic endeavor in the social sciences and humanities. Awareness of the slow frequency of academic writing has an influence on what is written; topical references and anecdotes have to be treated with care, and arguments or analyses have to anticipate unfamiliar reading contexts. Abstraction is consequently at a premium over immediate local, practical detail, especially in the humanities, where books are still more prestigious than papers and theory is more enduring than quotidian particularity. Once published, academic knowledge aspires toward stability. Academic books may stay in print for years or even decades. They are available indefinitely in libraries. Influential papers are cited in other people's works long after they are published.

As with other media (see below), there are internal frequency differences within the medium of academic writing. Topographical maps may be expected to be quite stable when published, lasting perhaps decades. Policy documents have a use-by date measured in months. Some academic knowledge is very high frequency at the point of discovery: witness, for instance, the regularly reported race to publish some new scientific or medical discovery first when the stakes – a Nobel prize or a lucrative patent – are high. But that same knowledge becomes very stable once published, especially in the "natural" sciences such as physics or astronomy. A double helix remains a double helix well after its first announcement, but the people who first announce it can set a premium on the timeliness of their work.

Meanwhile, textbooks tend to be lower in frequency than leading-edge research, more so at the most introductory levels. In the teaching context, knowledge can be really low frequency, maintaining theories, methods, and even individual examples or anecdotes long after the scientific field to which they are an introduction has moved on. Not infrequently introductory textbooks will carefully teach ideas, approaches, and even "facts" that have been entirely refuted at higher levels of the same discipline.

Conflict can arise from what may be termed frequency mis-tunings. Journalists, habituated to high-frequency public address, and academics, attuned to the rhythms of mid-frequency writing, find it hard to understand one another. They may decode each other's writing as if it should be operating at their own wavelength. The inevitable result is noise, communication breakdown, and bemusement or hostility. Journalists and academics literally (but simply) cannot get on each other's wavelength. If, however, their respective efforts are conceptualized as the *same enterprise* – public writing – done at *different speeds*, then here at least is cause for dialogue, if not common cause.

Public Writing and the Time-Space Axis

Besides the frequency (time) axis of public writing, it is also necessary to consider another axis, that of space. Public communication inhabits space as well as time. Just as the very notion of "the public" in contemporary political organization is customarily derived from classical antecedents, so the spatiality of public communication is conventionally associated with the polis or *the city*, which in the Western Hellenic tradition equated with *the state*. The period of political modernization inaugurated by the American and French Revolutions coincided with the first "virtualization" of a city-based notion of citizenship to the much more abstract concept of the *nation* as the "space" of citizenship.

Combining the concrete spatiality of a city with the abstract idea of national citizenship has resulted in the habitual association of the concept of "nation" with the *space* occupied by a people. Citizenship is modeled on the spatial idea of assembly in the agora, the forum, or the town square. To perform their role as citizens it seems people must be gathered together in space as well as time. A city's architectural showpieces act as a kind of permanent reminder of that role; they bring together the inhabitants, the place, and the particular ordering of political, religious, commercial, and national arrangements, as manifested through architectural, spatial, and inscribed "public writing" peculiar to that place.

Contemporary, faster modes of communication based on print and electronic media have radically textualized this association of space and nation. Once virtualized, a sense of civic or national identity is also rendered portable. It can be taken to all corners by contemporary media, which are *centrifugal*, radiating outward to find spatially dispersed addressees – the "imagined community" – at a given moment. The older, slower modes of public address based on stone and sculpture, conversely, are *centripetal* ("all roads lead to Rome"), drawing the people into the city center to be constituted as the public or as a congregation or crowd. Rather than reaching everyone simultaneously, the older modes of communication rely on many people, perhaps all, passing through them sooner or later. Thus frequency and spatiality are related to each other for both very high- and very low-frequency public communication, albeit in alternating modes.

As it evolved in Britain and France from the late eighteenth and early nineteenth centuries, modern journalism was organized most intensively around a frequency of between a day (the dailies) and a week (the periodicals). In those early days it was not uncommon for titles to be published twice or three times a week, but that intermediate frequency is now empty in the newspaper press. The Sunday paper is still one of journalism's most successful products, even if other weekly formats, especially the political magazine, are in decline. Indeed, the "Sunday" format is expanding. Saturday editions of dailies have taken on many of the characteristics of Sunday papers.

However, the traditional form of daily/weekly journalism as a whole is under attrition, and has been steadily declining for at least 50 years since World War II. Many commentators see this as evidence of changes in *spatial* arrangements. The slow decline of national broadsheet daily newspapers and of weekly political and women's magazines is taken to be a symptom of globalization of information, internationalization of trade, and the withering away of individual allegiance to the nation-state.

Questions of identity and citizenship are less easily associated with territorially bounded spatial entities – nations – than was previously taken for granted. Identity is more mobile, indeterminate, and voluntary. Citizenship is "weakened" as sovereignty is shared "upward" and "downward" from the nation-state:

- "Upward," sovereignty migrates *formally* to supra-national bodies like the UN, EU, WTO, NAFTA, APEC, NATO, and the International Court of Human Rights; *informally* to "humanity" movements such as the environmental, peace, and various religious, humanitarian, and charity movements.
- "Downward," sovereignty is devolved *formally* to sub-national regional, state, or federated parliaments; and both formally (by legislation) and *informally* (culturally) to communities based on ethnicity (first peoples), gender (women's rights), age (children's

rights), sexual orientation (gay and lesbian rights), virtuality (cyber-democracy), etc.

- Within this context, journalism as a *national* discourse, a discourse of *spatial belonging*, the modern (textualized) equivalent of the agora/forum of the city/polis, is in long, slow decline.

But journalism is no longer confined to the frequencies of the day and the week. Over the whole period of modernity – 200 to 400 years – it has tended to drift upward in frequency. Journalism that is *faster* than the day has thrived, in both broadcast and print forms. But also, perhaps counter-intuitively, journalism that is *slower* than the week, from monthly magazines to books by journalists on journalistic themes, seems to be in rude good health too.

Thus, while spatial metaphors for large-scale human organization lose their familiar landmarks as they evolve into new configurations, so it may become increasingly important to analyze the temporal axis. What may look like decline or even disaster on the spatial plane may look very different on the temporal plane. "Nations" and "regions" may simply be *changing speed*, at least in communicative terms. If this does prove to be the case, it is a significant matter, since of course nations are generally perceived to be much more than communicative units. Their culture, custom and character; law, language and learning; their very purpose and the power they hold over their citizens, are all commonly understood to be unique to each individual nation and one of the main sources of each person's sense of individual identity. There's considerable evidence that national feeling is stronger than ever, despite the decline of the classic, nineteenth-century nation-state (i.e. the self-contained sovereignty of "splendid isolation"). Certainly there are literally more nations than ever before, and the logic of self-determination lays claim to ever more locally defined nations.

In such circumstances, where spatially understood nations are the traditional site for the expression of their people's sovereignty, and where there are both "strong" and "weak" forces affecting how citizenship is legislated and lived, it is pertinent to ask what is happening to the "technologies" that hold such sites together in some sort of coherence. What, for instance, is happening to the technologies of democracy and of the public? Among such "technologies" – the mechanisms by which these "imagined communities" are brought into being and sustained – are the media, and diurnal political journalism in particular. This was one of the fundamental "technologies of democracy," being the very means by which "the public" was brought into being at the outset of political modernity in Britain, America, and continental Europe. Now, this is the form of journalism that seems most in decline. Its decline is far from catastrophic in terms of annual figures, but it is profound in the sense that sales, readers, and titles have all been trending downward for 50 years, across many countries. Does it follow that democracy is trending downward too? Many observers do in fact take this view. But what does the view look like if the changes are observed from the perspective of time rather than space?

Technologies of Democracy: "Hunters" and "Gatherers"

To consider the impact of "new technologies" on the space-time axis of public communication, it is necessary to move away from the notion of technology understood as "black boxes" (scientific and technological innovations), and instead move toward ideas like "technologies of democracy" and "technologies of the public." In other words, what are the mechanisms through which democracy and the public are created, sustained, and operated in modern societies?

In this context, black-box technology is not decisive in itself. The French Revolution, for instance, perhaps the most decisive founding moment of political modernity, was promoted and disseminated on the Gutenberg wooden press, a pre-modern technology based on agricultural machinery that was already 300 years old at the time. At the lowest frequencies, the same may be argued. The revolutionary form of the Egyptian pyramid was achieved not *sui generis* but by a novel application of the existing "mastaba" form of tomb. The internet may be pointing the way to change, but itself relies on the oldest technology of communication (writing). There might even be an argument to suggest that *new* technologies are less "revolutionary" in their uses than mature ones. It is necessary for a culture or epoch to become familiar enough with a medium to be able to break the rules with it before it can be used for seditious, incendiary, or reformist work. A technology cannot call a public into *action* before that public has been called into *being*, and the establishment of a community of readers around a new communicative technology takes time. Books weren't used effectively to spread ideas about science and Enlightenment across Europe until at least a century after Gutenberg. Agitation through the press for popular sovereignty waited centuries after print was invented; two in Britain (the Civil War and the Levelers' pamphlets), three in France, four in Russia, five in South Africa. Similarly, more recent "new" technologies such as television and the internet ought not to be heralded as revolutionary just because they've been invented. Instead, their social impact needs to be assessed according to their "use" in creating and occasionally mobilizing publics. Their impact is not as "technologies" as such, but as technologies *of the public*.

Political modernity is itself now over 200 years old. Despite the spate of bicentennial celebratory pyrotechnics (1976 in the USA, 1988 in Australia,1989 in France,) and a rather muted tercentennial in the UK in 1989 to mark the "Glorious Revolution," there is widespread concern about the effectiveness of the aging "technology of democracy." It sometimes looks as though it doesn't work any more, and not only at the technical level of voting machines and the notorious "hanging chads" of the US presidential election in 2000. Fifty years of Cold War, with its easy-to-understand oppositional structure of friend-and-foe politics, may have masked a growing uncertainty about who "we" are, whether "we" are understood as nations, as publics, or even as persons.

A combination of identity politics and entertainment media has grown up in the private sphere, and is now sustaining the most vibrant areas of media innovation and expansion, from "lad-mags" and the internet to spectator sport and sitcoms. Meanwhile the classic "technologies of democracy" – print media, political parties, parliaments – seem to be atrophying, growing further apart from the people they're supposed to represent, losing credibility and ratings in an inexorable decline that is no less remarkable for the fact that it has been happening for half a century.

It is no longer certain what the public is, or where to find it. The classic "technology" of the democratic public is the daily broadsheet newspaper (*The Times, Washington Post*) and heavyweight political weekly (*Spectator, New Yorker*). Both have given ground to competing media forms, from television to the tabloids. Meanwhile, along with so much else in contemporary, deregulating, commercial democracies, "the public" itself has been privatized. People are simultaneously addressed as publics and audiences, citizens and consumers, and the media of democracy have expanded into areas previously thought of as belonging to the private sphere and to commercial entertainment.

Citizen formation is now undertaken by chain stores – Marks & Spencer was named in March 1999 as the sponsor of the "National Identity" theme in London's Millennium Dome. The same week, on Wales's national day (March 1), Marks & Spencer's Cardiff store handed out to each customer a daffodil, Wales's national emblem, and a guide to the forthcoming elections to the new National Assembly for Wales. The £2 commemorative coin that marked the 1989 tercentenary of England's Glorious Revolution was *issued* by the Royal Mint (a privatized public corporation), but it was *circulated* as a free gift through supermarkets by the makers of Jif, Frish, and Jif Spray'n'Foam. Teenagers learn ethical comportment, neighborliness, and civic virtues from *Clarissa* and *Clueless*. They avoid the modernist "technology of democracy" like the plague. Does this mean they are living outside of the political community? Are they incomplete persons, not fully formed as citizens? Or has the "technology of democracy" migrated to the private sector? Commercial entertainment media and postmodern journalism are new "technologies of the public" – the new public sphere.

Hence *journalism*, as the forum in which "we" communities are constructed and "common knowledge" is exchanged, has migrated well beyond *news*. At the same time, news has evolved generically to accommodate to its media neighbors. Further uncertainty is caused. Doubts about what is fact and what is fiction are now pursued into the very fabric of media communication. These "television truths" are literally in the eye of the beholder (so navigate with a skeptical eye, citizen-consumer!). News photos are digitally enhanced, public access shows on TV are faked by using actors, columnists fake stories, TV documentaries feature fake people and situations. Meanwhile, over in the supposedly fictional world of commercial entertainment, you might find much more careful attention to old-fashioned truth.

How do these time frequencies intersect with spatiality? How do technologies of time interact with those of locality, region, nation, and international or global space? The highest-frequency media forms have tended toward transnational markets. Globalization is most commented upon in its commercial, high-speed, information-economy guise, even though mid-frequency forms such as science, scholarship, book publishing, and fiction have been international, indeed global, for decades or even centuries. Somehow, high-frequency technologies of public communication seem more threatening to technologies of space than do lower-frequency ones.

Traditional – modernist – journalism and broadcasting have pitched their tent, as it were, in the temporal rhythm of the day and the week. But this is the frequency that seems most under attrition in present developments. There's major investment in very high-frequency journalism, and also in mid-frequency forms such as magazines. Books too remain a significant component of public life, and are often extensions of journalism. They are being reinvented for a new generation of reader-citizens by innovative publishers like Dorling Kindersley.

There may be a challenge to traditional daily/weekly journalism and broadcasting in this scenario. But is there a threat to democracy? To public life? For those who worry about the decline of public service media, the commercialization of the public sphere, and the evacuation of the public domain, perhaps the problem is one of frequency. People are responding to different speeds of public communication, but this doesn't necessarily mean the end of democracy. It's not dumbing down but speeding up.

It may even be argued that the long-standing association of citizenship and nation with *space* rather than *time* is nothing more than a constraint on trade, a restrictive practice, a monopolization of the market by those who have trained their readerships to expect information pitched at frequencies these suppliers can accommodate. If all your eggs are in the daily-weekly basket, then you don't want customers wandering off the bandwidth to the nanosecond, the year, or the decade.

People who may suppose themselves entirely explained by spatial co-ordinates – nation, city, etc. – are nevertheless also attuned to temporal rhythms. The communicative year is divided into seasons marked by sports, TV schedules, annual holidays, weekends, Christmas Day, and a millennium once in a while. In other words "we" communities are identified temporally, via connections that cut across spatial boundaries. Humanity as a whole is in fact a time-based concept, referring to a "we" community of "everyone who is alive today."

Communications media can *gather* populations, or they can *divide* them. Some forms, such as sport, drama, and pornography, have proven to be reasonably indifferent to national boundaries. In tempo-spatial terms, they're "gatherers." They gather populations from widely separated places at one time to act as spectators. Others, especially news, seem reluctant to dissolve local, regional ,and national boundaries; they insist on differentiation of populations along territorial lines. They're "dividers." News media are "hunters" in the sense that they tend to define their "we" communities divisively – "we" are what others (especially other nations, but also criminal negativizations of "wedom") are *not*. Modern journalism thus has a long history of investment in *foe creation* and the language of conflict and violence. News media hunt out the alien and the criminal among the home population. Their clumsiness at this task in an era of migration and mobility, where "we" include ethnicities, identities, and activities routinely marked by the news media as "foreign" or "criminal," is cause for widespread debate and reformist agitation.

Perhaps this "hunter" aspect of news journalism is the very "technology of democracy" that is most in need of reform. Perhaps the higher- and lower-frequency media are establishing new "we" communities via new "technologies of the public" that are "postmodern," commercial, private, volatile, migratory, dispersed, and aimed at cultural identities not well served by the public sphere – for instance the young, women, ethnic minorities, and "foreigners" (migrants).

Modern Space, Postmodern Time?

Does a shift in perspective from space to time explain changes in journalistic content? For instance, news has drifted from a "modernist" status as a discourse of power, interested in the decision-maker, toward a "postmodern" status as a discourse of identity, interested in celebrity. Citizenship is now struggled over in the name of identity, not territory. There's a shift from discourses of rights to those of ethics, from unionism to individual responsibility. In short, people are identifying with "virtual" communities based on co-existence in time, not co-extension in space (see table 3.2).

Comparative Media Frequencies

Moving beyond journalism, it is useful to point out that many different communicative media function to create publics, and they also operate along frequency ranges. The visual arts, drama, fashion (clothing), music, and publishing are all instances of such media. They are indeed "technologies of the public." Internally, each such medium displays different frequencies (see table 3.3):

- In *drama*, soap opera and sitcoms occupy the highest frequency; the TV tele-movie or mini-series and the feature film dominate the mid-range wavelength; "classic" drama is low frequency. Soap operas operate to a much higher frequency of production than do other forms

Table 3.2   Space-time co-ordinates

Space (modern)	Time (postmodern)
(Co-extension)	(Co-existence)
Territory	Community
Actual	Virtual
Power	Identity
Decision-maker	Celebrity
Rights/duties	Ethics/practices
National unity	Individual responsibility

Table 3.3   Frequencies of various media (song, drama, apparel)

Range	Song	Drama	Apparel
High	Single	Sitcom/soap opera	T-shirt/haute couture
Mid	Album/CD	Movie	Suit/dress
Low	Symphony	Classic theater	Gown (legal, academic)

of screen drama. Many more episodes are made per year, and they are produced to a much tighter schedule (more pages per day are shot). They are circulated socially at a much higher frequency, being designed for one-pass scanning by a casual audience that is not expected to maintain an interest in the single episode. So it may be that hundreds of episodes of a major soap opera, or dozens of episodes of a sitcom, may be made in one year. During the same period, it is unusual nowadays for more than one feature film to be made by any one production team. Assuming it is successful, that movie will be seen over a longer time period than the single episode of an average TV serial, and it is more likely to extend its time frequency over several years via the video market, TV screenings, and cable-TV re-runs. At the lowest frequency, "classic" drama, whether film- or stage-based, achieves something close to immortality. People know all the words, moves, characters, and scenes of _Casablanca_, _Romeo and Juliet_, or _Citizen Kane_ (of which a new print was released in 1999, giving Orson Welles a new lease of life, though not very good ratings, for a new generation). Such drama is canonical, "law forming" (see chapter 5) in relation to its genre, and sometimes even in relation to its time and society, from *Birth of a Nation* to *Apocalypse Now*.

- Recorded *music* ranges from the pop single (high frequency) via the album (mid frequency) to the symphony (low frequency). It would be surprising to find a pop singer such as Britney Spears celebrated on a national currency, but symphonic composers can be. Sir Edward Elgar, not the Spice Girls, is pictured on the 1999 British £20 note (it was said that Sir Edward's hairy moustache would deter counterfeiters, but the same could be argued in relation to Scary Spice's hair: this was not a "technical" decision). Unlike pop, symphonic music may be taken to express low-frequency, national values. In this context high-frequency music is deemed commercial, ephemeral, global, and "unworthy." No matter how talented, popular, original, or profound a pop act might be, it won't achieve "serious" status until it has released multiple albums – until, that is, its musical frequency is lowered at least to the mid range (see also table 3.4 below).

- *Vestimentary* media (i.e. communication via apparel) range from haute couture collections and the T-shirt (both high frequency, though at opposite ends of the pop-/high-culture scale) via the suit and dress (mid frequency) to academic, religious, or legal garb (low frequency). Legal wigs and gowns are continuations of eighteenth-century costumes; academic gowns and priestly vestments are medieval. When members of the general public step out of everyday time and into a "timeless" state – as for instance during a wedding ceremony – they may signify the same by radically lowering the frequency of their vestimentary communication. The "traditional" bride's wedding dress and the groom's top hat and tails are derived from upper-class Edwardian fashion; "timelessness" is achieved by changing to low-frequency costume. Other vestimentary codes are also tied to time frequencies. For instance, the business suit of the "salaryman" is worn exclusively within the frequency of the working week; holiday fashions follow an annual rhythm; Santa Claus dons his red suit but one day a year (except in Lapland).

- In the *visual arts*, "old master" painting (high-art oils) is low frequency. Portraiture in photography or painting is mid frequency. Billboard advertising and photojournalism are high frequency (see table 3.4).

Table 3.4 Frequencies of culture

High	Popular culture
Mid	Intellectual culture
Low	High culture

- In *publishing*, the book is lower in frequency than the periodical. Within book publishing itself there's a wide range of frequencies, ranging from work that is an extension of journalism in the higher ranges to reference works such as the *OED* at the lowest. Some modes of writing such as canonical Literature tend to operate socially at a low frequency no matter what their original wavelength, including journalism of a former age (e.g. that of Samuel Johnson), or political speeches that achieve identity-forming status, from Pericles' funeral oration to Lincoln's Gettysburg address. Even fiction may be received initially as high-frequency journalistic communication, achieving canonical status later (e.g. Dickens's novels) (see tables 3.4 and 3.1 above).

The mid-range frequency is developed to the greatest extent not in journalism but in the area of fiction. The "season" or annual wavelength is occupied by new movies, TV series, novels, and comparable productions such as CDs, videos, and computer games. Moving to the lower frequencies of public communication, the so-called "serious" arts predominate – "classical" music, "classic" or canonical literature, and "fine" art.

Time and Tide: Frequency in Various Public Contexts

Temporal periodization is itself sensitive to frequency (see table 3.5, p. 58): postmodern (high frequency), modern (mid frequency), pre-modern or "classical" (low frequency). Whether or not this corresponds to more than the words used in journalism and academic colloquy to sort the concepts into coherence is a moot point (but see chapter 2). However, where distinctions are made between the modern and postmodern, for instance, an increase in frequency is clearly an issue, often a cause for concern, to the point where the very word "postmodern" is now a

Table 3.5 Frequencies of historical periods

High	Postmodern or global
Mid	Modern
Low	Pre-modern or "Classical"

Table 3.6 Frequencies of political economy

High	Commercial
Mid	Professional
Low	Public

term of abuse in culture-wars journalism, not least because modernist print journalism has a lot to lose in the current acceleration to multi-platform and mobile media.

It may be that there is an economic aspect to frequency distribution (see table 3.6): the commercial sector is characterized as high frequency (and high investment), the professional sector as mid range and the public sector as low frequency, especially toward the "dignified" part of the constitution – state occasions and courts of law, rather than state enterprises.

It follows that within such a structure, the type of information tends to vary according to frequency (see table 3.7). Rumor, "gossip," and information are "faster" than knowledge, fiction, and science; these in turn are faster than belief, myth, and religion. News, however, ranges across many of these frequencies in its *content*. News can be a textualization of high-frequency rumor, gossip, and information. But equally news can express much lower rhythms in the guise of quotidian narrative: myths and beliefs – not to mention fictions – are routinely recreated in the form of daily stories.

As we descend the frequencies from screen via page to stone, it is possible – though far from inevitable – that meanings move from volatile to stable, private to public (see table 3.8). To the extent that this may be so, it may further occur that *volatile* meanings are associated with private affairs and are about identity; meanwhile *arguable* meanings are associated with the collective life of society and are about power. At the same time, *stable* meanings are associated with public life, and aspire to the condition of the natural. Thus *frequency* seems to carry extra import

Table 3.7 Frequencies of knowledge-type

High	Rumor	"Gossip"	Information
Mid	Knowledge	Fiction	Science
Low	Belief	Myth	Religion

Table 3.8 Frequencies of meaning

Range	Durability[a]	Medium	Location	About
High	Volatile	Screen	Private	Identity
Mid	Arguable	Page	Social	Power
Low	Stable	Stone	Public	"Nature"

[a] Cf. the old Latin saw: "verba volant, scripta manent" – words fly; writing remains.

– low-frequency public communication seems closer to "nature," literally written in stone, when compared with higher-frequency messages.

As it has drifted steadily upward in frequency over the past century and more, journalism has also tended to drift in its meanings. Where it was a discourse about power, focused on the decision-maker, it is now (at least as much) a discourse of identity, and is focused on the celebrity. Its meanings are more volatile.

Conclusion

In public address, speed is of the essence. Frequency (rather than ostensible content) may be a major determinant of what a given piece of writing means. Over the *longue durée* of history, public communication has exploited differences in frequency to articulate different types of meaning. Apparently revolutionary periods may be explicable by reference to changes in communicative speed, and also by investigating changes in the balance between temporal and spatial co-ordinates of national and personal identity. To understand what is happening to journalism in the current era of change from spatial (national) to temporal (network) communication, the frequency of public writing is a crucial but somewhat neglected component. It determines what kind of public is called into being for given communicative forms, and therefore has a direct bearing on the development of democracy. Changes to "technologies of the public" have historically tended to increase speed or frequency of communication; democracy itself may be migrating from space-based technologies to faster, time-based ones.

4

Television and Globalization

The previous chapter introduced spatial co-ordinates into its discussion of time frequencies. This chapter takes the spatialization of knowledge a step further, and brings us a step closer to television as a particular object of study, by considering television in relation to globalization. Narrowly defined, globalization is the extension of cross-border economic ties, leading to greater integration of societies and economies around the world. More broadly, however, it is used as a proxy term for the market economy or as a euphemism for capitalism. In other words, a spatial term is used to express a power relationship. This also brings us closer to the mainstream of TV and media scholarship, as may be discerned from the change in tone of the writing within this chapter.

In relation to television, globalization of TV-set manufacturing and of programming, as well as the global reach of media corporations like TimeWarner, Viacom, Disney, News Corporation, Bertelsmann, and Sony, has intensified since the 1980s. Perhaps more to the point, television is one of the key sites for debate and activism in relation to the broader definition of globalization as "capitalism." TV is a convenient metaphor – and scapegoat – for many of the perceived ills of commercial democracies, particularly worries about the effect of popular media on national and cultural identity in different countries.

We would do better to think of "globalization" as a *concept* than as a description of historical *process*, because it is not in fact the case that once upon a time economic or social life was city- or nation-based and then it began to go global. We are not faced with an evolutionary or developmental change so much as a change in the history of ideas. In other words, we have begun to *conceptualize* the global dimensions of phenomena we had previously thought of or experienced only in local or national settings. This way of conceptualizing has now gained very wide currency beyond the world of intellectual specialization, as globalization has become one of the most dynamic terms in popular media and politics in recent years as well as in more formal academic theorizing.

The globalization that we hear most about results from those in-your-face outpourings of US consumer culture, e.g.:

- globalization of movies and TV ("Hollywood"; see Miller et al. 2005),
- globalization of fast food (the "McDonaldization of society"; see Ritzer 2004), and
- globalization of fashion (e.g. the four most-worn items of clothing in the world are all American – baseball hat, T-shirt, jeans, sneakers; see Tyagi 2003).

Such media, apparel, entertainment, and shopping phenomena are themselves products of globalized but still US-dominated commercial investment, internationalized production, and marketing; "global capital" to its critics.

Since the 1990s the world has experienced unprecedented levels of intensity in the international movement of investment and marketing, and also in the global reach of information, knowledge, and communications. But even among fully globalized industries, transnational movement is often only one-way. It is easier for US companies than for African and Asian countries to globalize their operations and markets, which means in practice that such Western-originated products and services as pharmaceuticals, infant milk formula, and entertainment formats find their way into African and Asian homes quite readily, while much of the agricultural, intellectual, and cultural produce of those countries is effectively blocked from entry into the US or EU. Global movement of people (labor) has also remained much less free than that of capital; again, especially migration to the affluent West from the rest of the world.

Critical analysis of corporate globalization has focused on analyzing these unequal freedoms. Critics tend not to emphasize the real advantage to be reaped from international traffic in goods and services, which, for advanced economies, principally takes the form of radically lower costs enabled by standardization and modularization of components, economies of scale, and the ability to source materials and labor wherever they are cheapest internationally. The manufacture of TV sets provides a good example:

In 1956, an RCA color TV set was sold for US$500, or US$1,300 in today's dollars. That same year, the average car sold for $2,100 and average annual salary was $5,300. In 2002, it is possible to purchase a standard, no-name 20-inch TV set for $130. That's a ten-fold decrease in price in 46 years. (Mougayar 2002)

Even while benefiting from such cheap and ubiquitous technology, critics of globalization focus on the increasing control of resources, labor, and markets by locally unaccountable international firms (McChesney 1999). Criticism has also dwelt on the feared "homogenization" (in practice the Americanization) of culture in many countries or localities, to the perceived detriment of national identity and local diversity. Television has become a potent symbol of these issues in recent years, because TV so clearly interlinks economic and cultural issues (Barker 1999; Lee 2003; Tomlinson 1999).

But the present-tenseness of entertainment and the size of American corporations should not blind us to the fact that globalization is as old as the media themselves. Printing, for example, was invented in its "modern" form, using moveable type, over half a millennium ago, during the 1450s in the city of Mainz. Printing (technology) and the publishing trade (business model) were recognizably modern and fully international from the start, not unlike like other "creative industries" of the time such as cathedral-building and acting. Firms located in Germany and the Low Countries soon supplied the entire continent with published product. Venture capitalists like Johann Fust, and his long-continuing firm Fust and Schöffer, who took over Gutenberg's firm in Mainz, or entrepreneurs like Caxton (Bruges and Westminster), Plantin (Antwerp), and later on Elzevir (Leyden), operated in different countries at once, building productive capacity, demand, and local variation across a range of markets. Printing spread very quickly from the 1460s, being distributed throughout Europe by 1490. Globally, it reached Istanbul in 1503, Morocco in 1521, Iceland in 1534, Mexico in 1539, Goa in 1556, Cairo in 1557, Russia in 1564, Palestine in 1577, Lima (Peru) in 1584, Macao in 1588 (which was also the year that the first printed Welsh translation of the Bible was published), and Japan in 1591. Content too was truly global from the outset, with an expansionist craze for maps, travel stories both fantastical and historical, and accounts of expeditions of exploration, which was at least as important as the equally transnational religious content of early printing in the West (Vervliet 1972: 356, 397–8). In case a period of just less than a century – the time it took for print to globalize – seems leisurely, it is worth noting that television itself took nearly as long to spread across the world. TV started as a practical system in the 1930s (see chapter 11 below). Thereafter it took 60 years to reach the kingdom of Bhutan.

Imaginative content has also been expansive and international for centuries. Both music and drama had been itinerant professions since the Middle Ages, and actors, singers, and acrobats crossed national boundaries long before the print and electronic media began to dominate popular culture. Many of Shakespeare's plays, for example, which premiered in London from the 1590s to the 1610s, were set in global locations including Denmark, Rome, Athens, Illyria, Egypt, France, and Bermuda. Shakespeare used cosmopolitan sources too, raiding books from across the known world. And of course Shakespeare's own work was itself quickly globalized via both print and performance. In this case most commentators were full of praise for the outcome, rather than protesting at cultural imperialism, even as the very English worldview of the Swan of Avon conquered hearts, minds, and box offices from Alma Ata to Zeffirelli (see chapter 9 below).

Factual content has also been global from the word go. News was international from the moment of the earliest newspapers in the seventeenth century, although editors had to rely on couriers who traveled no faster than horse or sail could carry them. News content that was simultaneously available across the world had to wait until the mid-nineteenth century, when the Reuters agency, founded in 1851 to send stock prices from London to Paris, pioneered the transmission of news via new telegraph cables that linked Britain to Europe, the Americas, and the Far East. Reuters scooped the world in 1865 by being the first agency outside the USA to report the assassination of President Lincoln.[1]

These examples demonstrate that the technology, organizational form, and content of media have been global for centuries, from which it is necessary to conclude that recent interest in globalization, which has burgeoned since the end of the Cold War, was not caused by new human activities. Globalization was *newly noticed* as a political and intellectual problem. Social theorists began to think of it as a condition of contemporary society, not just as a feature of economic or communicative activity. The reason globalization became a key term in the 1990s, almost entirely supplanting the by-now derided term "postmodernism," is partly *political*, partly *intellectual*.

Politically, the adversarial ideological stand-off between left and right was reconfigured at the end of the Cold War when the international communist movement collapsed as an institutional opponent to global capitalism. Marxist, anti-capitalist, and radical single-issue groups began to organize around "anti-globalization" as way of contesting the remaining superpower. Contrariwise, proponents of free trade and economic neo-liberalism promoted globalization as the key to business growth and competitiveness. This in turn provoked further critical concerns about US hegemony and the influence of corporate-controlled market forces. Opposition was voiced to US cultural power, as well as to its political, economic, and military might, often spectacularly, in street demonstrations.

It is in this cultural context that the idea of globalized *society* – understood as a mixed blessing at best – gained prominence. Journalistic and academic observers alike began to comment on the *experience* of globalization for consumers and citizens, not just on the existence of global business operations. However, it was increasingly evident that the gap between corporate performance and consumer experience was rapidly closing, because the way consumers felt began to affect the bottom line. Across the world, citizen-consumers might easily express their political opposition to US power by resisting US brands. Such sensitivities needed to be taken into account by corporate analysts as they assessed the risks to American competitive advantage:

> The danger for US companies is that they will fail to appreciate the growing self-assurance of consumers in markets such as China or India. This increasing confidence could translate into a growing tendency to take offence at cultural slights. This month, China banned a Nike advertisement that depicted US basketball star, LeBron James, defeating a kung fu master and other Chinese cultural icons in a video-game style battle. China said the advertisement was offensive. Advertising executives suggested Nike erred by not letting the home side win. BBH got a better response with a Levi's advertisement that showed an Asian man facing down a street full of mean-looking westerners. "We have to be very careful about advertising in these countries," Mr [Maurice] Levy [chief executive of Publicis] said. "We know *cultural things are very touchy.*" (Roberts 2005, my emphasis)

Intellectually, in the sciences as well as the arts and humanities, there has been a growing willingness to consider global organization as a defining property of various phenomena both natural and social. The idea of explaining things in terms of their global coherence (rather than by reducing them to their smallest units as in normal science) has an intellectual history that goes back at least as far as the late nineteenth century, when scientists began to observe and theorize various phenomena as *global systems*. Where previously there was just locally encountered air, or life, or culture, or media, now there was the atmosphere, the biosphere (or ecosystem), the semiosphere, and more recently the mediasphere (Hartley & McKee 2000).

Can we imagine something big enough to cover the planet, coherent enough such that each tiny part may interact with all the others, and small or local enough to interact with and affect each individual person? Evidently we can: global television has these characteristics, as Marshall McLuhan pointed out with his concept of the global village (McLuhan 1964; McLuhan & Fiore 1967). But before we get to that, it's worth remembering that the very same characteristics apply to other things than TV, including the physical and natural environment. For instance, take the atmosphere – what is it? It's the air each of us breathes, the weather we live under, the smog we choke on. It's about as intimate to our own personal life and as crucial to our individual comfort as anything we know or experience. At the same time the atmosphere is as big as the planet, stretching all the way around the globe and many kilometers above it. It's hard even to imagine how big that is, and yet we have relatively little trouble thinking about "the" atmosphere in the singular – it is just one object, spread thinly like skin, but like skin a coherent organ in its own right.

The fact that we can imagine the global atmosphere as a single object, while individually breathing little bits of it in and out again, has recently become a significant matter in political and public life, because of concerns about the effect of greenhouse gas emissions and global warming. In fact pollution may be one way to glimpse just how big the atmosphere is, because the sheer weight of what we pump into it each year is itself mind-boggling. During the 1990s, for instance, the countries of the European Union alone belted out about *four billion tonnes* of "greenhouse gases" (mostly carbon dioxide) into the atmosphere each year. And yet carbon dioxide comprises only about 0.035 percent of the atmosphere's volume.[2]

Turning from the physical to the natural environment, the atmosphere itself provided a model for the biologist V. I. Vernadsky to propose the concept of the *bio*sphere – comprising all the living organisms on earth, their interactions, and the conditions for the continuation of life (thus "biosphere" is a similar concept to the later term "ecosystem"). And turning from nature to culture, again following directly from the model of the atmosphere and the biosphere, the semiotician Yuri Lotman coined the useful term *semiosphere*: the "semiotic space necessary for the existence and functioning of different languages," without which neither communication nor language could exist (Lotman 1990: 123–5). Like the atmosphere and biosphere, the idea of the semiosphere is not simply that it covers the planet, but more importantly that this global organism is the *condition of existence* for all the differentiated parts and interactions that go on at local level. Life (or "biota") cannot exist in detail (species by species) without the entire biosphere, not least because any species survives only by virtue of those others that it depends upon for food. Similarly, meaning cannot exist, language by language or even speaker by speaker, without the entire semiosphere as a structuring set of conditions for relationships and interactions within which any individual communication can occur.

Using the same model, and turning from meaning to media, the term *mediasphere* was coined (Hartley 1996) to encompass the idea of something big enough to cover the planet, coherent enough such that each tiny part may interact with all the others, and small or local enough to affect each individual person. Like the semiosphere it expresses the various *forms, relationships and structural conditions for existence and interaction* of a worldwide system of media communication. The mediasphere is "multiplatform," not confined to one medium like television but encompassing the entire variety of print, photographic, audio-visual, and performative forms, which interact with each other, such that television shares technological, industrial, and semiotic forms, and audiences, with other media like radio, theater, movies, and print. It cannot be understood without the global interactive system that has shaped it and allows it to operate in any given local instance.

As noted above, the mediasphere is older than it may seem. There was an international traffic in mediated plays, poems, and stories long before the modern industrial era. But it became "visible to the naked eye," as it were, only during and following the great modern industrial and imperial expansions of the nineteenth century. This period took all manner of European media, including books and literate reading publics, newspapers, magazines, theater, news agencies (like Reuters), songs, stories, and live entertainments, across the world. What was new about this was not so much the global reach as the narrow source of media. Suddenly it wasn't just the same technology that was available across the world for producing local materials (like the printing press), it was the same *content*, expressing the desires, fears, and energies of Western commercial democracies and their military enforcers everywhere, all at once, apparently drowning out other voices. In other words, the media-sphere could now appear as unified to a single reader-consumer at a speed that had not been possible before. It was increasingly filled with the monocultural "emissions" of industrialized and imperial media.

Such a unity of content at the point of reception was only possible via a "broadcast" model of communication; one-to-many, one-way, with centralized, professional producers and dispersed, passive consumers. This was not orderly turn-taking transmission and reception by more or less equal communicative partners; it was not modeled on oral conversation but on the oratorical tradition of the preacher and performer – and their modern secularizations the impresario and publisher. The potential for both political and commercial persuasion via such global one-way medi-ation became a continuing theme not only of national politics (will our own population be adversely affected by messages from abroad or from undesirable sources?) but also of colonialism, experienced first within the countries of Africa, Asia, the Americas, and Australasia that were directly colonized by European powers in the nineteenth and early twentieth centuries, but more recently by those powers themselves as American broadcast entertainment carried all before it.

In the twentieth century the audio-visual and broadcast media – radio, cinema, and television – came of age, overtaking but not supplanting print as the most pervasive media, and in the process intensifying transatlantic rivalry as American media ascendancy grew. The global reach of radio was first demonstrated by its inventor Guglielmo Marconi, who sent the first transatlantic radio signal on December 12, 1901. He topped this feat on March 26, 1930, by using radio-telegraphy to turn on the Town Hall lights in Sydney Australia – by throwing a switch aboard his yacht *Elletra*, which at the time was moored on the other side of the planet in Genoa harbour (Marconi 1999: 44–54, 57–61). While Marconi was perfecting the global infrastructure, the BBC began to globalize content via the Empire Service (predecessor of the BBC World Service) from 1932. It broadcast via shortwave radio from Bush House in London, whose massive portico bears the BBC's globalizing motto: "Nation Shall Speak Peace Unto Nation."

But perhaps more to the point, "across the pond," Hollywood was vying for global supremacy with European film studios like Cinecittà, Mosfilm, Ealing, and Pathé, establishing a powerful but not uncontested dominance after talking pictures arrived (generally dated from Al Jolson's *The Jazz Singer* of 1927). All of these developments indicate not only that the broadcast mediasphere was understood to be global from the very start, but also that much of the current disquiet about the cultural impact of global media has its roots in European dismay at the Americanization of what until then had been "their" mediasphere from a date well before television took hold. Emblematically marking this decisive shift in strategic and semiotic power from Europe to the US was the identity of the TV show that happened to be playing when the BBC unceremoniously pulled the plug on its Television Service upon the outbreak of World War II in September 1939. It was the same show that they used to re-launch television in 1946 (after being so rudely interrupted, as it were). It was of course a Mickey Mouse cartoon from Walt Disney, although the American Mouse was soon followed by the home-grown, high-stepping Windmill Girls.[3]

Television grew up in an existing atmosphere of technological excitement and international competitiveness, but to begin with it was established very much on a national basis, especially in Germany, Britain, the USA, and the USSR. Each country tried to develop its own system under its own legislation, using its own programming. There was little chance for viewers to see programs from another country unless they visited it. International traffic was restricted to filmed materials, including newsreel footage, documentaries, and movies. Made-for-TV drama series were also exportable if they were made on film. But the special strength of television – liveness – could not be shared among the nations. Europe pioneered international television exchange via the Eurovision network in the 1950s. Eurovision's technical capabilities were popularized via the all-too-live *Eurovision Song Contest* from 1956. But international live TV didn't really take off until it could cross the Atlantic, which the launch of the Telstar satellite made possible on July 10, 1962.[4]

Meanwhile content had begun to be traded and some of the later features of globalization could be discerned, not least the business of "dumping." For example, when television was introduced into Western Australia in October 1959 the local commercial licensee needed a lot of content. What better than to buy a package from the USA. Some of it may have been of dubious aesthetic or entertainment merit and of zero relevance to the home viewer's local culture or experience, but it was incredibly cheap. Old TV westerns could go out for literally a few dollars an hour in WA, when making the program might cost hundreds of thousands of dollars per hour and require resources and talent that were simply not available to local producers. The costs of US TV shows were entirely recouped in their home market, releasing for export high-quality, easily understood, commercial entertainment that was effectively cost-free at the point of export. Sales agents could therefore set whatever price would undercut local providers. Small wonder then that global commercial TV began to rely on US programming. At the same time public TV stations were borrowing wholesale from the British, especially the BBC, for the same reason.

Commercial good sense and an international market in TV shows (which is still based in Los Angeles) thus inadvertently resulted in a distinct mismatch between popular programming and national or cultural specificities – people who had little in common with one another and even less with California all ended up watching *Hopalong Cassidy* and (later) *Dallas* (Liebes 1990). By such means, American and British TV programs were effectively global by the end of the 1950s.

The global coherence of the mediasphere as an organized system of communication was not apparent to most individual viewers until they could see it on their own screens. Two separate developments have promoted this trend: global TV channels and global TV formats (Moran 1998).

- The launch of CNN (June 1, 1980) and MTV (August 1, 1981) heralded global TV channels.
- Endemol's *Big Brother* (from 1999) and Celador's *Who Wants to Be a Millionaire?* (from 1998) are exemplary global TV formats. *Millionaire* is seen in over 100 countries; *Big Brother* in 20.[5]

The novelty of reality-format shows from the business point of view is that a single (global) concept or format can be reproduced in different (local) markets, which means that the production company can profit from global distribution, but the local audience actually sees a customized show that is to all intents and purposes their own. Contestants on Australian or Brazilian *Big Brother* are Australians and Brazilians, not Dutch. The flexibility of this concept is such that different versions of the same show can develop distinct national characteristics, for example with more sexual activity and plotting and conniving in some countries (the UK), more female winners in others (Sweden), contestants who like each other (Australia), or a different eviction regime (in the US contestants are voted out by housemates not viewers). Also, the local reproduction of global formats increases the scope for multiplatform and interactive elements, bringing phone, fast-food, and internet companies into the game, and allowing viewers greater levels of personal interactivity with the show, including attending live events.

Does the globalization of television production, technology, and content have an adverse effect on cultural identities, and does US-led media entertainment impoverish media culture in less favored countries? The early flood of publications on globalization – themselves representative of the global reach (not to say hegemony) of US left-academic activism – tended to answer both of those questions resoundingly in the affirmative. US TV companies ruled the world; US TV entertainment coca-colonized the planet. But latterly more measured judgments have come to the fore. It has been noticed that Latin American *telenovelas* are hugely popular in Eastern Europe, for instance – there's a global *counter-flow* of media content among countries as various as Brazil, India, Egypt, Japan, and increasingly China.[6] Todd Boyd has made the point that it is not just dominant US culture but specifically counter-hegemonic *black* culture, represented in music, sports, fashion, and style, that is exported around the world (Boyd 2003). And it is self-evident that even the most intense global consumption of American media does not turn the people of the world into Americans, no matter which way around they wear their baseball caps. Indeed, since the Iraq war it has become evident that prolonged exposure to US media can create aversion rather than conversion. Furthermore, identity is often felt to be more important in small, hard-pressed nations than in more populous, heterogeneous ones: e.g. Wales or Scotland rather than England (though that's changing); Norway or Croatia rather than Germany; or Indigenous people rather than settler Australians. Being "inundated" by another culture, not least via television programming, may actually provoke sharper and more defined local or indigenous cultural identity, not destroy it.

A recent tragic event has shown that positive as well as negative outcomes can result even from the *globalization of disaster*. The so-called "Asian Tsunami" (as the news-bars called it, although it also reached Africa) of December 26, 2004, and its aftermath was – among other things – a global television event. It demonstrated how television's global system of news-gathering resources, transmission networks, and audience responses could be mobilized for humanitarian and public good. It showed the full *integration* of:

- *Sources of TV images and stories:* all channels relied on amateur footage of the event, and used general internet/email traffic as a reliable news source. This disaster was reported as much by the audience/consumer as by professionals, especially in the earlier moments, integrating producer and consumer in the production process more visibly than is common in mainstream TV. It showed how the pervasion of digital cameras, mobile phones, and computers among the general population has permanently altered what can be seen and said on TV, which is no longer the only "window on the world," looking out on viewers' behalf, but an extension of their own sense-making activities.

- *Media*: the event attracted immediate blanket coverage from media across the globe, which in previous times, before global television was fully integrated, would not have occurred. Compare the international coverage of the 1976 earthquake in China, where perhaps 250,000 people also died. Access to that event was restricted by the Chinese government of the day, of course, but so was interest in the event among Western media organizations and audiences.

- *Populations*: among the enormous toll of dead and missing people were many thousands of Western tourists, including a number of prominent people and celebrities. At one point it was reported that more Swedes lost their lives that day than in World War II.[7] Every country that covered the event could focus on its own nationals as well as local victims, thereby forging instant common cause with populations that are usually not thought of as neighbors by Western audiences.

- *Response*: it quickly became clear that the tidal wave itself was being matched by a no less remarkable wave of fellow-feeling and generosity from the global viewing public. The speed and amount of donations to help the victims were themselves a major TV news story. Spontaneous acts of generosity from sports personalities like Russian tennis star Maria Sharapova (who was in Thailand at the time), and speedy responses from organizations, like the gift of £50,000 from each of Britain's Premier League football clubs, soon shamed governments and international brands into following suit. A multinational bidding war was duly reported on CNN and BBC World, with the USA, European countries, Australia, and Japan vying to outdo each other. Norway alone contributed over 1 billion kroner – the equivalent of US $40 for every person living in that country. The Chinese government (not to be outdone by Taiwan) pledged the largest aid package in that country's history. In Beijing students braved the cold to collect personal donations in Tiananmen Square.

Across the world governments, firms, organizations, and individuals were integrated in an active and practical desire to help. As so often, it took the worst of circumstances to bring out the best in a system of television production, organizations, content, and audiences. Globalized TV came of age as a part of a mediasphere where the smallest individual elements could clearly be seen to interact with all of the others, right around the planet. This was a globalization not so much of technology, economics, or even content as of humanity. And television played the central enabling role.

Notes

1 See about.reuters.com/aboutus/history.
2 See   themes.eea.eu.int/Environmental_issues/climate/indicators/Kyoto_ Protocol_targets/yir99cc5.pdf; www.statistics.gov.uk/cci/nugget.asp?id=366.
3 See www.xtvworld.com/tv/bbc/tv_is_coming_back.htm.
4 See   www.bbc.co.uk/radio2/eurovision/2003/history/60s.shtml;   www. roland.lerc.nasa.gov/~dglover/sat/telstar.html.
5 See www.endemol.com/format_descriptions.xml?id=1; www.celador.co.uk/ productions_history.php.
6 See www.apparelmag.com/bobbin/reports_analysis/article_display.jsp?vnu_ content_id=1786051.
7 See   www.smh.com.au/news/Asia-Tsunami/Sweden-braces-for-death-toll-not-seen-since-war-with-Denmark-in-1814/2005/01/03/1104601300972. html.

Part II

Is TV a Polity?
Ethics/Politics of TV

This part explores the relationship between television and citizenship. Given TV's global reach and the voluntary nature of its relations with audiences, it obviously can't be classified as a state, nation, or polity of the kind that is generally associated with citizenship. However, television is closely associated with individual conduct and the moral principles of action and self-comportment, the traditional subject of ethics in philosophy. Often television's relation to conduct is considered only in the negative and only when individual action is reduced to "behavior." TV is thought by many to precipitate or even cause certain forms of behavior in individuals, especially when it is regarded as morally reprehensible, whether "passive" (couch-potatoism, obesity), "active" (sex, violence), or "uncivil" (bad language, bad taste). To counter the influence of behavioral psychology as the preferred or default framework of explanation in media studies, many scholars, myself included, have sought to explain television's relation to individual action in terms of citizenship rather than behavior. In the social sciences citizenship is primarily conceptualized as a relationship of both rights and obligations to a state. However, in an older literary tradition, citizenship is the outcome of acculturation and may be thought of as adult membership of a given cultural community (i.e. the "nation" rather than the "state" in the "nation-state"). It is within this latter version of citizen-formation that television plays its most important part.

Chapter 5 shows how nations themselves are the outcome of "narrative accrual," and that citizenship is intimately bound up with story. Modern nations are multi-ethnic, multivalent, and conflicted polities. It is important that a sufficiently broad selection of stories finds its way into the national narrative, otherwise marginalized "subjects" will be excluded from citizenship as well as story. However, chapter 5 argues that media like television tell different kinds of story, here divided between "law-forming" and "anomalous" narratives. If a given group – here Indigenous people, but the same thing applies to other marginalized or underrepresented groups – is "narrated" only by one kind of story, in this case "anomalous" stories in the news, and not in "law-forming" narratives of cultural renewal and reproduction, then they are likely to figure in the national narrative only as problems, not as full citizens. The real problem is their unresolved national status, not their ethnic or even cultural backgrounds. In short, television plays a strong role in imagining the polity, and therefore in assigning symbolic or cultural/narrative citizenship to various types of subjectivity.

Chapter 6 extends this discussion to the question of how the television audience compares with the "reading public" established in the early years of print-literate modernity. It argues that the political public of modernity is an extension of the reading public, and that media audiences need to be understood in the way that previously applied to the "informed citizen" of the print-literate era. The idea of a "television republic" updates the idea of the "reading public," but as chapter 7 shows, various problems of representation are necessarily opened up in the process. New, interactive forms of entertainment add to the complexity, since it is now possible for audiences to influence narrative accrual directly. If it is one, TV is a strange sort of polity, where instead of democratic deliberation and will-formation there is the plebiscite. Chapter 7 explores the productivity of this development, where voting itself seems to have migrated from modernist duty to postmodern pleasure. The section as a whole shows that including media narratives and relationships within the apparatus of citizenship is both necessary and troubling. There's a long way to go before a satisfactory method of self-representation and accountability is developed. Meanwhile the long-standing division between power and pleasure still works to reduce narrative to a form of political entertainment. TV studies has its work cut out to show how narrative accrual, direct participation, and effective "semiotic process" can add democratic value to the global super-polities that are building on entertainment media and digital social networks.

5

Television, Nation, and
Indigenous Media

*That mob up north have made one bloody good movie with Ten
canoes. You are taken back into the world before Europeans, before
alcohol, before cars, before syphilis, before petrol, to the heart of the true
Australian culture: eating, rooting, taking the piss (some things
never change). This is a beautiful movie that every Aussie should see.*
Review *of* Ten Canoes *(2006), the first Australian film in an
Aboriginal language, Ganalbingu*[1]

Voluntarist Citizenship

In certain very sensitive places, where culture, identity, citizenship, and
nationhood have collided catastrophically, legislation has boldly gone where
narrative – and attendant sporadic violence – went before. The "Good
Friday" Belfast Agreement of 1998 enshrined "DIY citizenship" as a *civil
right* of people in Northern Ireland. They could *choose* their national identity. They may "identify themselves and be accepted as Irish or British,
or both, as they may so choose, and accordingly confirm that their right
to hold both British and Irish citizenships is accepted by both Governments" (Belfast agreement, quoted in Kiberd 1999: 441). As Declan
Kiberd commented, the Good Friday Agreement "offers a version of
multiple identities of a kind for which no legal language yet exists." But
even so, it "effectively sounds the death-knell for old-style constitutions"
(p. 443). It enshrined a voluntarist conception of hybrid or "DIY
citizenship" (Hartley 1999: 179–81), based on cultural identity and
choice, not on the relationship of people to territory, or even to a single
sovereign nation-state.

During television's first 50 years – the broadcast era when "nation" and "television" were frequently understood to be coterminous – popular domestic audiences went through an almost anthropological process of "transmodern teaching" (Hartley 1999: 38–47). New notions of citizenship arose during that same period that stressed culture, identity, and voluntary belonging over previous definitions based on rights and obligations to a state. These new, mediated forms of citizenship were organized around affinity and choice, and new understandings of other people's lives (i.e. difference) based on mediated contact. Mass broadcasting to national audiences remained a dominant mode of television, but it was no longer the only one. TV was moving to post-broadcast forms, from time-shifted video and the generic bundles of cable TV to the customized library system of TiVo or online video-streaming. Some TV screens became also interactive computer screens. As this re-purposing of the TV platform unfolded, so the "national" aspect of television changed, because viewers could access their choices from international websites via podcasts, video downloads, or DVDs. As the blogosphere, social networking sites, and YouTube expanded, so the kind of "media citizenship" associated with national broadcast systems began to migrate to sites based not on national identity but on communities that were more fragmented, more international, more virtual, and more voluntary than heretofore.

Already, "the" audience could be "gathered" to act as a national citizenry only with increasing difficulty. Aspects of civic life formerly strongly associated with "public life," as *opposed* to commercial enterprise, shifted to commercial or corporate contexts. The practice of democracy was increasingly undertaken by "corporate citizens," from the Bodyshop to Benetton, from Tesco to Accenture (which used the advertising tagline of "MY-DEMOCRACY.COM" in 2001), led by broadcast and print media, which were themselves habitually "for profit" and "pro patria" all at once. So, *commercial* democracy and *DIY* citizenship began to make their presence felt in contexts where "public service" and obligation had been a predominant discourse. In this context, familiar aspects of national identity were being tested, perhaps to destruction. What comprised a nation, citizenship, broadcasting, or democratic participation was, like Irish citizenship, entering an unsettling period of choice.

A practical issue for Australia at this time, perhaps of more fundamental constitutional importance than the temporarily lost republican referendum of 1999, was how to accommodate its Indigenous population. One the one hand, how to resolve the national status and aspirations of Indigenous people; on the other, how to "narrate" Australia *as* an Indigenous nation.

Both of these questions went well beyond television, but necessarily television and other media were implicated and affected in their turn. Thence, precisely because of the challenge of Indigeneity to both nation and narration in a media environment, further pressure was put upon television itself, in both content and organization. TV could not survive unchanged at such a time, not least because Indigenous people themselves were prolific media producers (Hartley & McKee 2000: 166–203). Various new technologies provided a platform on which "national identity," both Indigenous and non-Indigenous, was a customized application of media functionality.

This was a long way from the model of television as "national culture," where everyone in a nation-state was routinely presumed to be watching the same shows, sharing the same values, (and therefore) united in the same identity (Anderson 1991). That broadcast model of television suited the idea (and the period) of "mass" societies, but citizenship had evolved along with post-broadcast models of community. In this transitional phase, broadcasting evolved to post-broadcasting, citizenship evolved from "cultural" to "DIY," and nations evolved from states to states of mind. At such a time, the narration of nation was perhaps as important as any other matter on television.

Sometimes TV simply related the mundane succession of stories from day to day, which provided the various communities in a national audience with knowledge and "affect" (both positive and negative) about each other, and perhaps thence the conditions for what Richard Hoggart once called the "amelioration of manners" (see Hartley 1999: 179–81). Occasionally this routine was interrupted by staged ceremonies of contact, where TV played a more spectacular role. Corroboree 2000 witnessed sympathetic and even carnivalesque attention to various acts of reconciliation between Indigenous and non-Indigenous Australians. There was wide national and international coverage of the series of reconciliation walks over bridges in most state capitals, including one across the Sydney Harbour Bridge that attracted over 250,000 people. Even more spectacular was the Opening Ceremony of the 2000 Olympic Games. Even if "hard" political outcomes of such events – e.g. a treaty – were not immediately discernible, nevertheless a crucial *visualization* and *euphoricization* of Australia as a multinational (i.e. Aboriginal + settler) state was briefly established.

Aboriginality was dramatized in both the banal and the ceremonial modes of public narration, and thence in both the "efficient" and the "dignified" components of the constitution (as famously identified by nineteenth-century British constitutionalist Walter Bagehot).[2] Perhaps the emblematic moment of the Olympics Opening Ceremony was when "efficient" 13-year-old Nikki Webster, embodiment of the young (white) nation of Australia – of what might be called, if I may, juvenated paedocratic democratainment and DIY citizenship incarnate (see Hartley, 1999 for most of these barbarisms) – held hands with "dignified" Djakapurra Munyarryan of Bangarra Dance Theatre, representing Aboriginal Australia (see figure 5.1). They "bridged" authenticist

Figure 5.1 Nikki Webster and Djakapurra Munyarryan – Olympic opening ceremony (2000). *Weekend Australian*, September 16–17, 2000: 3. Photo: Craig Borrow, Newspix

identity and voluntarist citizenship in an act of cordialized nation-building in front of a TV audience estimated by the live TV commentators at 3.7 billion worldwide, more than half of the people then alive, including an actual majority of the Australian population (itself an amazing feat). In fact so decisive was this moment that the *Australian* newspaper managed to photograph it before it had happened – their "Opening Ceremony Souvenir" was printed using dress-rehearsal shots (*Weekend Australian*, September 16–17, 2000: 3).

When Aboriginal athlete Cathy Freeman won Australian television's highest ever rating for a 15-minute segment while running the 400 meters at the Sydney Olympics, a new form of "political" achievement was finally complete. This moment was in fact the culmination of a public narrative that had been building throughout the 1990s; the story of the "Indigenous public sphere." Instead of politics, here was sport; instead of politicians, here was Cathy Freeman; instead of sovereignty, here was a flag (see Hartley & McKee 2000: chs 7–9). Such symbolic and entertainment-based markers of identity constituted an important currency in popular politics. And the Aboriginalization of the "efficient" sphere itself was canvassed in media speculation about Freeman pursuing an elective career after the Olympics, with the Australian Labor Party at the front of the queue to welcome her aboard. In the meantime, however, she chose "celebrity" rather than "power," by signing up with an international high-status agency, the IMG management group.

It could properly be argued that the "efficient" part of politics was slow to put practical effect to these "dignified" visions of an Aboriginal nation (or national identity) within the Australian state. And it might have been noticed that cutesy Nikki Webster gained more media attention in the months following the Opening Ceremony than did the impressively talented, operatic-voiced Djakapurra Munyarryan.[3] Business as usual quickly reasserted itself in the practical outcomes of "efficiency" as opposed to "dignity."

But it should nevertheless be recognized that putting even symbolic Indigenous nationhood "above" politics, and recognizing the multiple citizenship of Indigenous people in Australia as an accomplished historical fact, was constitutionally novel. An agenda for long-term reorientation of Indigenous politics was set. By 2001 the peak Indigenous body ATSIC (the Aboriginal and Torres Strait Islander Commission, a devolved arm of government with a governance structure directly elected by Indigenous people) was calling for a change. Its elected chair,

Geoff Clarke, called for a shift from Native Title claims (which he saw as bogged down in legal process, and which had served in many instances not to empower but to distract Aboriginal self-determination) to a national treaty (*Australian*, August 3, 2001). In the meantime ATSIC also put its weight behind a campaign to launch a new National Indigenous Broadcasting Service (NIBS), in both TV and radio. NIBS was intended to complement the existing "national broadcasters" of the ABC (a publicly funded corporation on the lines of the BBC) and the SBS (a multilingual, multicultural, national TV and radio service, funded by a mixture of advertising revenue and government funding).

An Indigenous Public Sphere?

In this volatile symbolic context, the concept of the "Indigenous public sphere" (see Hartley & McKee 2000 for the full elaboration of this idea) described the highly mediated public "space" for evolving notions of Indigeneity. It was the forum for putting them to work in organizing and governing the unpredictable immediacy of everyday events. The Indigenous public sphere was hardly under the control of Indigenous people. Indeed, it was a peculiar example of a public sphere, since it preceded any "nation" that a public sphere normally "expressed," as it were. It was the "civil society" of a nation without formal borders, state institutions, or citizens.

Indigenous people were represented to their non-Indigenous co-citizens via media; possibly more often than in live, casual social contact "at the supermarket checkout" (Langton 1993: 81–4). This *communicative* association, largely unsupported by face-to-face contact, gave rise to a simultaneous over- and under-valuation of Indigenous people's claims on citizenship as compared with other Australians. The forum for such evaluation was media comment and debate. To some their conditions appeared "fourth-world" and radically below the standards of civic, political, welfare, and human rights enjoyed by other citizens. To others their claims to rights (notably land rights) based on ethnicity, culture, identity, or un-redressed deprivations seemed to be a "privilege" not enjoyed by other citizens, and therefore an example of inequality of citizenship with the advantage going to Indigenous people (see Mickler 1998). Both of these positions were *symptoms* of the structural anomalousness of Indigenous citizenship, which could be summed up very simply – they were citizens without a nation.

Because of the co-evolution of citizenship and media, this issue was of central concern to media studies. The unresolved national status of Indigenous people was of course a product of territorial, ethnic, political, and colonial history. But the outcome was a major fault-line or fracture for the contemporary Australian body politic. As such it came increasingly to preoccupy the media, both serious journalism of record and demotic expressions of emotional affinity. Indigeneity became the site around which Australian national identity in general was narrated, disputed, and thought through, in a large-scale colloquy that was several decades in the making.

This public colloquy unfolded in media that were themselves right at the center of developments in notions of citizenship that stressed culture, identity, affinity, and choice, that gathered disparate populations in a virtual or imagined "communities" where difference could be celebrated rather than eradicated. Thus many non-Aboriginal people could begin to see their own issues refracted in Indigenous ones that they encountered through television and media coverage on a daily basis.

Meanwhile, the same media that worried and tugged at the unresolved national status of Indigenous people were also, for Indigenous people themselves, the means by which they developed their own internal (but public) colloquy – the media were the public sphere for the Indigenous "nation" itself. Mainstream media produced by non-Indigenous people, Indigenous people working in the mainstream media, and specialist Indigenous media all played a part in producing and circulating "national narrative" for Indigenous people, even as they were simultaneously thinking through issues of national identity for non-Indigenous people.

So there was a peculiar sort of marbling effect in the media narration of nation. Black and white were not mixed but intermingled, circulating around each other, resulting in patterns that were explicable only by reference to the other component. An Indigenous "nation" was discernible in but not of an Australian identity. An Australian nation was at odds with Indigeneity but also obsessed by it. Dialogue was disproportionately intense. Here, in media, was where the nineteenth-century concept of the nation-state was being tested to destruction, where nation was becoming detached from state.

Historically, European narratives gave agency to Europeans, construing "natives" as passive recipients of good actions (development) and bad ones (extermination or coercive control), but only rarely and grudgingly giving agency and a "speaking part" to the "other" of their imaginings (see Miller 1995). This certainly described the history of

Indigeneity in Australia, but here too change was rapidly occurring. Indeed, the "Indigenous public sphere" was evidence that Australia was Indigenizing its narrative sense of self as a whole.

Thus, the period could be characterized as an intense dialogue between "Aboriginal" and "Australian" components of the overall Australian "semiosphere," the outcome of which was not yet resolved. Would there develop an autonomous Indigenous "nation" within an Australian state? Or would Australia indigenize its own history, politics, and community identity? There was some evidence that both of those possibilities were occurring at once. Certainly imaginative space was made for them in media stories and visualizations. But of course it was not inevitable that either of them *must* eventuate.

Nation and State, Not Race

Why was Indigeneity understood as a matter of *race*? It looked to some observers very like a matter of *nation* (Reynolds 1996). Why was Australia – and not only by a provocative political party of that name – seen as "one nation"? It looked very like one *state* (Chua 2000). Why were some "Australians" *not* understood as "ethnic"? Australia contained people from more nationalities than you could poke a stick at; but it "ethnicized" some immigrants and Indigenous people while instating its "British" or "Anglo-Celtic" component as a kind of ex-nominated Established Race (see Griffiths 1996: 229–30).

The Australian *nation* was habitually conflated with the *state*, allowing no space for several nations in one state. The solution that had more or less worked in Singapore for so long – to "ethnicize" everyone in a racially neutral state, including the majority Chinese – was difficult for Australia. In Singapore, as Chua Beng Huat has pointed out, English was the native tongue of *none* of the three recognized racial groups, Chinese, Malay, and Indian Tamil, all of which were therefore equal in having to learn it to conduct both business and the business of government:

> In the Australian and Canadian case, the Anglo groups cannot be ethnicized. Whereas in the case of Singapore, the demographically dominant Chinese group is in fact ethnicized by the state – it is just another racial group. That is to say, the interests of the state are not captured by the interest of the dominant Chinese majority. . . . If [Singapore] had

adopted Mandarin as the national language, it would have been a whole different politics. But, by insisting on the neutral English language, it allowed the ethnicization of the majority, and therefore separated state interests . . . from Chinese interests. (Chua 2000)

For a long period the White Australia policy supported a conflation of state, race, and national identity, and some conservative populists remained politically active on that ground long afterward. Despite real and popular concessions to its multicultural and Indigenous components since 1967, a powerful strand of thought continued to insist on ethnic cultural content as part of Australian identity. And because there was no unitary *Aboriginal* nation before 1788 – there were several hundred different language communities – there was skepticism even among Aboriginal people themselves about political organization at the national level. Advances in recognizing Native Title did not help in this respect. They tended not to nationalize but to Balkanize Indigenous polities around "clans." An Indigenous public sphere required a level of "national" organization of the Indigenous "polity" that had no precedent in Aboriginal and Islander history. Without a "nation," without a "state," Aboriginal people were hemmed ever further in by "race."

The recognition that there was a difference between nation, ethnicity, and state was an international development, at different stages of contestation and resolution around the world, from Palestine to Fiji, Sri Lanka to Canada.

In the UK, even the English had begun to discover that they were ethnic, compared not only to immigrants and their descendants but also to the newly decentralized "indigenous" (Celtic) "home nations" of Scotland, Wales, and Ireland, not to mention Cornwall. To the dismay of political and cultural elites, the most visible form taken by popular *English* ethnicization was chauvinism and football hooliganism. But increasingly there were calls for an English parliament. The Belfast Agreement – subversive of "old-style constitutions" on both sides of the Irish Sea – offered that vision back to the English. A paragraph discussed "devolved institutions" in Northern Ireland, Scotland, and Wales, "*and, if appropriate, elsewhere in the United Kingdom*" (quoted in Kiberd 1999: 442) – which must have referred to the possibility of a "decolonization" of the *English* nation from "British" state arrangements (Nairn 1997, 2000).

Meanwhile, English ethnicity became defensible at law, interestingly in the very field of broadcasting and national identity. In August

2001 a veteran radio broadcaster won a case against BBC Wales for wrongful dismissal. The man was (and sounded) English, and his long-running show was dropped in favor of "a strong Welsh voice." Despite the BBC's protestations that the show in question was "tired and out of touch," and that they had wanted to "reverse declining audience figures and broaden the station's appeal to the whole of Wales," the tribunal found that racial discrimination against the Englishman had occurred.[4]

In Germany, a continuing debate about "deutsche Leitkultur" (German lead or guidance culture) suggested that many in that country weren't yet prepared to separate citizenship from ethno-territorial heritage. Certainly Germany retained strong ethno-cultural content in its citizenship rules, even when this may have had negative economic effects. For instance, a scheme to attract IT specialists to Germany from India failed in 2001, not least because of language and culture requirements of immigrants that were not needed in the US, Canada, or the UK. In this context, despite its English-language environment and multicultural commitments, Australian immigration rules leant toward the German model. Immigrants were under formal and informal pressure to "identify" *with* received Australian ethno-cultural content.

Developments in Indigenous nationalism were equally international. Indigenous leaderships in many countries, from Siberia and Scandinavia to North America and New Zealand, shared the same problems both *internally*, in the extent to which they could speak on behalf of "their whole people"; and *externally*, in the degree and direction of activism needed to defend, survive, and adapt (see Jull 1994). "Ethno-nationalism" itself was fraught with dangers for indigenous peoples and others, as events attested in Chechnya, former Yugoslavia, Zimbabwe, and elsewhere. Nevertheless, it was precisely out of such hotspots where cultures collided that new notions of "the" nation, and new ways of accommodating difference within citizenship, could emerge.

Writing of Indigenous people in Siberia, Marjorie Balzer identified what she called a "form of nonchauvinist ethnonationalism, a politicized yet usually liberal ethnic consciousness born of the need to defend their cultural heritage and lands" (Balzer 1999: 221). Many Native American leaders also rejected full assimilation, she wrote, "while accommodating themselves to living with dignity in the Anglo world. On both sides of the Bering Sea, multiple identities on multiple levels, activated situationally with flexible style, have become normal for indigenous leaders, if not for all their peoples" (p. 220). She concluded that "Native consensus-style democracy (not necessarily United States majority-rule democracy) may be a means toward ensuring more liberal varieties of ethnonationalism" (p. 223).

Non-chauvinist ethno-nationalism, multiple identities, voluntarist citizenship, plus land and good lawyers, were part of a groundswell for a shift toward "multinational" states. How did people on both sides "accommodate to living with dignity" (in addition to efficiency) in each other's world? Contact and dialogue were essential, both personal and at the mediated national level. National and international media were central to the process.

"Two Domains"

Turning to the history of national narrative, the "narrative accrual" that Bain Attwood (1996) identified *as* Australian nationhood, it was clear that Indigeneity was among other things a *story* – one historically *about* rather than *by* Indigenous people. With Alan McKee I conducted a three-year research project, funded by the Australian Research Council, on the reporting of Aboriginal issues in the media (Hartley & McKee 2000). Our research found that two distinct types of story were found across the range of academic, government, and media stories about Indigenous issues in the period up to the late 1990s. Here again, an innovation in method in media studies could be claimed. Instead of identifying the "coverage" of Aboriginal issues in the media narrowly, we used a wide definition of media, to include newspapers, television, radio, magazines, and academic or policy reports; and a wide range of media forms and genres, from news and talkback to sport, lifestyle shows, and drama. The "reporting" of Indigenous affairs could not be understood without situating news media in that larger structure – "news" was a form of story-telling that performed certain narrative functions that were only comprehensible when contrasted with others. The "universe of Indigeneity" was a dialogue between differing domains within an overall "semiosphere," linking rather than separating academic, administrative, media, and political narratives of Indigeneity. We took the terms "law formation" and "anomaly" (not to mention "semiosphere") from Yuri Lotman (1990: 151–3). He distinguished between two types of structure within the "semiosphere" (see figure 5.2, p. 88).

Lotman's typology of texts brought together kinds of story that were usually so strictly separated from each other that they seemed

The semiosphere	
Law-forming texts	**Anomalous texts**
Fixed in space	Mobile – "able to cross the structural boundaries of cultural space" (infringement)
No new information (repetitious)	One-off occurrences (anomalies)
Narrative determined by nature (season, cosmos, land)	Narrative determined by succession of deeds (plot)
Identity (e.g. night/winter/death are transformations of each other)	Difference (surprises, news, accidents)
Reduce diversity of world to "invariant images"	Add to knowledge of the world
About "me" (the listener)	About the world
Cyclical time	Linear time
Function to create a picture of the world	Record chance events, crimes, disasters, violations of established order
Record principles	Record events
Give rise to law-affirming texts, both sacred and scientific	Give rise to historical texts, chronicles, records
= **Myth**	= **News**

Source: Adapted from Lotman (1990: 151–3).

Figure 5.2 News and myth within the semiosphere

unconnected: scientific inquiry and news; or traditional myths and contemporary soap opera; or fact and fiction; right down to micro-distinctions such as those that operated within a given form, such as "hard" and "soft" news, news journalism and feature journalism, the daily press and the magazine press, print journalism and broadcast journalism. These were strongly felt distinctions that could sustain entire industry sectors. But the stories produced within each specialty shared important characteristics with those from elsewhere, and could only be properly understood in a larger typology of contrasting story-types.

The maintenance of the distinction between different forms could prove more important than individual stories. Truth-seeking stories were produced by such great, overarching cultural institutions as "science," "education," and "government," and were kept radically apart from stories produced by "the media," especially those parts of the media that seemed to deal only in ephemera and entertainment. But the very

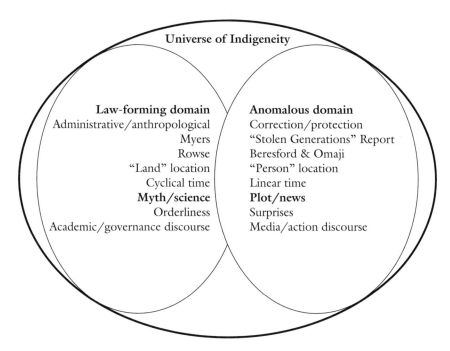

Universe of Indigeneity

Law-forming domain
Administrative/anthropological
Myers
Rowse
"Land" location
Cyclical time
Myth/science
Orderliness
Academic/governance discourse

Anomalous domain
Correction/protection
"Stolen Generations" Report
Beresford & Omaji
"Person" location
Linear time
Plot/news
Surprises
Media/action discourse

Figure 5.3   The "universe of Indigeneity" and the "two domains"

efforts made to keep different story-types separate was evidence that the different categories, organizations, and institutions were parts of a larger, common structure.

Discourses of *action* needed to be contrasted with discourses of *order* – neither could be understood without the contrasting co-presence of the other. News vied with myth. In Lotman's typology myth shared the same aims as science – reducing the world to order to understand it – and used the same techniques as soap opera. Meanwhile news was a species of history, using the same techniques as the action-hero plot. Narratives from apparently dissimilar contexts, like academic research, media information, and media entertainment, occupied the same category in the overall scheme of things in the "mediasphere."

Analyzing academic and media "inventions" of Indigeneity over the past decade, McKee and I identified "two domains" in an overall "universe of Indigeneity" (see figure 5.3):

- *Indigeneity of law-formation*. A sphere of *anthropology and administration*, exemplified by the work of Fred Myers (1991) and Tim Rowse (1992, 1993). It was centered on land, and interested in traditional forms of life, land rights, remote communities, ATSIC. It was dedicated to the reproduction of orderliness, and was conducted by academic discourses and discourses of governance. Its characteristic narrational form was myth.

- *Indigeneity of anomaly.* A sphere of *correction and protection*, exemplified by the work of the Stolen Generations Report (National Inquiry 1997), and by that of Quentin Beresford and Paul Omaji (1996). It was centered on persons, located in urban and suburban life, and interested in the impact of the welfare and justice systems, of carers or fiduciaries of Aboriginal populations, and in Aboriginal people living a non-traditional life. It was dedicated to action discourses. Its characteristic media form was news.

On the one hand was law-formation, fixed in space, where central narratives were concerned with identity, nature, reducing the world to order, and where stories were about the "we" community, recording principles. On the other hand was found mobility, infringement of boundaries, narratives about action, the world, difference, and anomalous occurrences, and where stories were about "they" identities, recording not principles but violations, crimes, and events. In short: myth and news.

But these opposing text-generating mechanisms were not capable of independent existence on their own. As Lotman said, each needed the other to exist at all. It was important to notice the implication, that the "anomalous" domain – which appears to be *the* one-and-only Aboriginal domain in much news coverage of Indigenous issues (because of the type and function of news) – was merely one side of the narrative coin, needing to be understood in relation to law-forming narratives that exist elsewhere in the "mediasphere." In other words, news was only the half of it. It was *systematically* the half.

"Narrative Accrual"

Bain Attwood discussed how a nation was constituted and became aware of itself through a process of what he called "*narrative accrual*": "a process whereby a corpus of connected and shared narratives constitute something which can be called either a myth, a history, or a tradition. Furthermore, it was only as the people came to comprehend and know this story that they came to realize and be conscious of themselves as Australians" (Attwood 1996: 101). The implication of Attwood's schema was that the "universe of Indigeneity" was itself part of the process of "narrative accrual" that constituted Australia. Together, the "anthropological/administrative" domain of "law-formation" and the "anomalous" domain of "correction and protection" made up an "Aboriginal" component of that narrative accrual. This component occurred within a larger "semiosphere," along with "British" and "Australian" components, each with its own history, and a mutual history of interactions, dialogue, and silence, more or less intense in different periods, in which Australia as a whole "accrued" narratively (see figure 5.4).

With the amendment of (British) common law by the Mabo and Wik decisions on Native Title in the early 1990s, which established that Indigenous possession of traditional lands continued after European settlement, Australia turned out to "mean" something quite new. Its

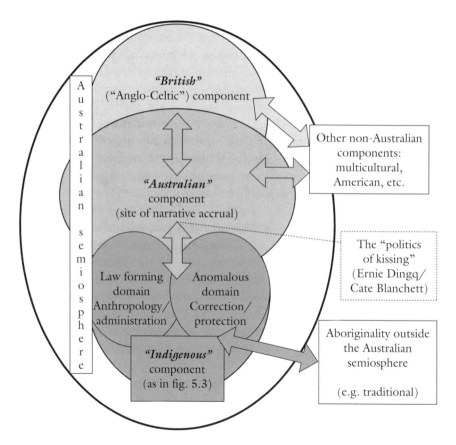

Figure 5.4 The "narrative accrual" of the Australian nation

origin as encoded into the common law doctrine of *terra nullius* ("empty land" or land without property) was overturned – it turned out to have been a *myth* of origin not a *legal* precedent. Australia's future turned on the outcome of new dialogue with Indigenous people. Aboriginal and Islander people were "discovered" by history to be separate from the Australian nation, resulting in "three nations encased within the Australian state" (Reynolds 1996: 177). They became more important than the "British" component of Australia. This, however, like the IRA (in Gerry Adams's famous phrase), didn't "go away" – as witness the referendum in November 1999, when a particular model of an Australian republic was rejected, with the result that the British crown remained the Australian head of state.

These changes occurred within an explosion of discourse right across the media (both factual and fictional), government, and the academy. The 1990s in Australia were characterized by unusually intense internal dialogue about what was at stake in the meaning of the new relationships, from Mabo to One Nation to the referendum. In 2000 the trend continued with Aboriginal Reconciliation and the Olympics. The whole structure would have been neat and tidy if it hadn't been for Aboriginal people's own politics, on the one hand, and the crisis of legitimacy precipitated by Mabo and Wik (i.e. literally "rewriting Australian history"), on the other. The orderly generation of stories in government reports and the news media about Aboriginal life and crime was radically disrupted in the 1990s. To understand media coverage of Indigenous issues during this period, then, it was necessary to:

• contrast the two different "Aboriginal domains" with each other;
• contrast the "universe of Indigeneity" thus constituted with "Australian" and "British" components of the Australian national narrative over time; and
• understand how Indigenous appropriations of the domains, of their component of the stories, and of the media themselves, were producing new patterns and relationships in the Australian "semiosphere."

It would be impossible to go into archival and analytical details here (see Hartley & McKee 2000: chs 7–9); this chapter has simply attempted to identify the Indigenous public sphere in light of these principles.

The importance of such a "dialogic" model of national narrative was confirmed by the existence of Aboriginal people's own media productiveness. The growth and vibrancy of the Indigenous media sector itself, and the number of Indigenous people working in the media and across the creative industries, meant that it was no longer wise to assume that "the media" should be understood as an alien force that did something to Indigenous people. On the contrary, they were clearly doing something to the media, both individually and collectively – or "nationally." What they were doing was having a narrative effect on Australia "as we knew it."

The Politics of Kissing

That effect – changing the meaning of "Australia" – was itself made into a scenario for some imaginative television. During the 1990s, an especially intense period of dialogue occurred between the "Aboriginal" and "Australian" components of the Australian semiosphere. It did not entirely take the form of law-formation on the one hand (Mabo, Wik, Native Title), and anomaly (care, welfare, justice) on the other. The news wasn't all "dreamtime" versus "doing time." There was something new: there was kissing.

The ABC-TV drama series *Heartland* was first broadcast in 1994. It starred the Aboriginal actor and entertainer Ernie Dingo and a very pale-skinned Cate Blanchett in her first leading role. The series was interpreted in detail by John Morton, who concluded with an argument about how it symbolized a new direction in politics, where adversarial antagonism was forced for good practical reasons to give way to more cordial mutual accommodations:

> In the absence of any foreseeable effective revolution by Aboriginal people, and any subsequent violent displacement of the Crown, it is clear that Aboriginal rights can only be secured through the liberal democratic process inherited from Britain. It follows that Aboriginal people's only prospect for getting what they want is in the Aboriginalization of that process, which, in a liberal democracy, must partially entail an effective mobilization of its discursive regimes of representation. Heartland is a case in point. (Morton 1996: 132)

Heartland was perhaps the first "nationalization" of the progress made toward the Aboriginalization of the Australian semiosphere during the period of the Keating Labor government (1992–6). Its chosen metaphor for reconciliation, a sexualized relationship between Aboriginal and non-Aboriginal Australians, took the "personal" and "boundary-crossing" elements of the "anomalous" domain and brought them into the "law-forming" domain. Here the relationship between Dingo and Blanchett established a principle, reducing the world to a new orderliness, in which the "universe of Indigeneity" joined with the "Australian" component of the Australian semiosphere. The kiss was a promise.

Heartland was classic broadcast television – a drama mini-series put out by the "national broadcaster" (the ABC). The end of Australia "as we knew it" was presaged in this fairy-tale marriage of the prince and princess from different mediated nations. Reality begun to catch up a bit afterward, with the reconciliation bridge-crossings around Australia, for instance, the "sorry" movement, and some real attempts at political cordialization on all sides, not just at the Olympics. Still the national status of Indigenous people remained unresolved, but at least the direction became clearer.

And what of "television" as we knew it? As technologies converged, as cultural content became a service industry, the greatest *product* of broadcast media – the mass, national audience of citizen-readers – could not survive intact. Instead, internally differentiated, customized, interactive, and individuated audience segments would make their own choices, would increasingly act as *producers* as well as *consumers* of mediated meanings, and would identify less with nation-states and more with constituencies of taste and affiliation that were local and international at once. The Indigenous media sector blazed the trail. It was within that context that analysts and activists alike had to look for the next episodes in both the narrative accrual of Australia, and the historical evolution of television.

The Morning After . . .

Heartland made its promises in dramatic, fictional mode. Time would tell whether the worlds of politics and news could live up to that promise. The election of a conservative federal government in 1996, the rise and fall of the One Nation anti-Aboriginal party, and the intense media coverage of Native Title and land rights, suggested that this was a kiss that might yet die on the lips. But the very intensity of the debate, the vicissitudes of a relationship between parties who felt mutually unintelligible, bespoke a "mutual attraction" between the "Aboriginal" and "Australian" components of the Australian semiosphere that was evidence not of a one-night stand but a of dialogue leading to a long-term affair, including the usual ups and downs. The terms of engagement in which that dialogue was conducted were not confined to traditional "public affairs." The personal, sexual, and private were also key components of the Indigenous public sphere, as the "Stolen Generations" saga made all too clear (see National Inquiry 1997).

Since the 1990s the political process has not kept pace with this communicative potential. As the decade unfolded it became clear that the rightist federal government was devoting considerable partisan energy to dismantling the Indigenous public sphere where it had power to do so (e.g. by abolishing ATSIC). The same government actively promoted an ideological version of national identity based on settler values and heritage, while Indigenous politics were rescaled to the local level and to welfare services. The media spotlight turned away from Indigenous initiatives toward a concerted campaign by right-wing journalists and others to challenge what they called the "black arm-band" view of history, to deny the extent of settler atrocities in the early days of the colonies, and to retreat from acts of symbolic (let alone substantive) reconciliation. Interpersonal and institutional dialogue between the Aboriginal and Australian components of the Australian semiosphere continued, as did creative Indigenous inventions of both television and other media. But for the time being the imaginative vision of two radically different stories being made intelligible to each other on national TV was quiescent at best, possibly in active retreat.

Notes

1 See thecia.com.au/reviews/t/ten-canoes.shtml.
2 Read Bagehot's *English Constitution* at www.bibliomania.com/2/1/328/2415/frameset.html.
3 See Munyarryan's bio at www.qpac.com.au/education/classroom_resources/boomerang_study_notes.pdf.
4 See news.bbc.co.uk/hi/english/uk/wales/newsid_1467000/1467534.stm.

6

A Television Republic?

The era of popular broadcast television, which reigned supreme for fifty or so years from the mid-1950s, was also the period when television studies budded off from an already hybrid knowledge tree. Treated as part of mass society, television was routinely analyzed as a bad object, blamed for social, political, cultural, and behavioral outcomes that were, *a priori* it seemed, negative. Very little progressive optimism was applied to television in a systematic way in formal academic, intellectual, and critical writing. This was in large part a symptom of twentieth-century intellectual politics, with television as merely the latest in a long line of miscreant media stretching back through movies, radio, and music hall to the gutter press, yellow press, and penny dreadfuls of previous centuries. Cultural elites were habituated to "assailing" media that in their view failed to "uplift" the masses (Carey 1992: 214–15; see also Butsch 2000: chs 10 and 15).

Television studies branched off from existing branches of social theory, social science, psychology, cultural criticism, and other academic disciplines. Its immediate purpose was not to understand but to discipline television. The term "discipline" here invoked two senses at once:

- to put TV into the supposedly orderly context of disciplinary taxonomies of knowledge;
- to "discipline" TV via rhetoric of control, prohibition, and pejorative labeling.

The disdainful mood was not confined to academics. Scholarly analysis and popular journalistic accounts seemed to agree that the right way to take television seriously as an object of study was to treat it as some sort of pathology. The successful titles were by professional critical pessimists such as Jerry Mander and Neil Postman, using arguments that had hardly changed since the 1950s (e.g. B. Rosenberg & White 1957). Even Pierre Bourdieu (1998) weighed in from left field, but with the same old story. Few influential voices took television as a force for good. People got used to thinking that watching television was *behavior*, of interest to psychologists. It was not, in other words, taken to be emancipationist or literate *communication*, of interest to democrats.

TV was routinely made to stand for society was a whole. Following from scientific method, analysis was insistently present tense, generalizing, and universal, not historical and contingent. TV was not taken as a "thing in itself." "Freedom to think of things in themselves" had been Virginia Woolf's touchstone for intellectual emancipation (1945: 34). But television was persistently treated as a symptom of something other than itself – power, usually – that was thought to be threatening to social or moral well-being (Butsch 2000: 231–4). This mental default setting not only missed the opportunity to understand television "in itself," but also inhibited "freedom to think" among critics. "Television rots your brain" became normal science.

Media Republicanism

But an alternative way of thinking was already to hand. For several centuries thinkers in various fields had written of such imaginary domains as the "republic of letters," the "republic of taste," or even a "republic of the fine arts" (Barrell 1986). This republican terminology had seemed to fizzle out with the advent of screen and electronic media; it was confined to print and painting, i.e. to political philosophy and the philosophy of art; disciplines of collection rather than diffusion. But if print and paint had democratizing tendencies, and were useful in both constituting and tutoring cultural citizenship, then it would seem appropriate to ask if the contemporary mass media might be thought of in the same way (Wark 1997; Lumby 1999; Gibson 2001).

This is the purpose of the present chapter. It seeks to restore republican terminology to television, by comparing it with the republic of letters. Did broadcast television – the "thing in itself" – constitute a republic in these terms? The most important question at stake in this thought experiment is that of the status of the audience. The republic of letters was and remains characterized by the interaction between authorial voices on the one hand and a readership, often vast, on the other. Within the textual system of print literacy, the most important product was not the commodity form as such – books, newspapers, magazines, etc. – as the readership that long before television had been formed at one and the same time into market, public, and nation. Did the television audience amount to a "cultural commons" in the same way? Television could be understood historically in comparison with print literacy and its order of reading (Hartley 1999). From such a perspective, the TV audience could be seen as an extension and reformulation of the reading public, rather than representing its demise.

An early *Dictionary of Quotations* gave the term "Respublica" as: "Lat. – 'The common weal.' – The general interest" (MacDonnel 1822: 337). Such early-modern usage was part lawyer's jargon, part literary. A telling instance of this use of the notion of a republic of letters came from Tom Paine. In *Rights of man* (1792) he praised the "representative system" of government over hereditary ones, writing as follows:

> Experience, in all ages and in all countries, has demonstrated that it is impossible to controul nature in her distribution of mental powers. She gives them as she pleases. Whatever is the rule by which she, apparently to us, scatters them among mankind, that rule remains a secret to man. It would be as ridiculous to attempt to fix the hereditaryship of human beauty as of wisdom. Whatever wisdom constituently is, it is like a seedless plant; it may be reared when it appears, but it cannot be voluntarily produced. There is always a sufficiency somewhere in the general mass of society for all purposes; but with respect to the parts of society, it is always changing its place. It rises in one to-day, in another to-morrow, and has probably visited in rotation every family of the earth, and again withdrawn. As this is in the order of nature, the order of government must necessarily follow it, or government will, as we see it does, degenerate into ignorance . . . As the republic of letters brings forward the best literary productions, by giving to genius a fair and universal chance; so the representative system of government is calculated to produce the wisest laws, by collecting wisdom from the place where it can be found. I smile to myself when I contemplate the ridiculous insignificance into which literature and all the sciences would sink, were they made hereditary; and I carry the same idea into governments. An hereditary governor is as inconsistent as an hereditary author. (Paine 1937: 148)

Paine united the three elements of a "republican" approach by bringing together:

- textuality (republic of letters),
- nation (*respublica* – the common weal), and
- citizenship (representative government).

Paine modeled his favored system of government on publication – on the republic of letters itself. He put his model into practice too. He was one of the founders of the United States of America, which, in an early and unsurpassed act of branding, he named. And he was a founder of the République française, where he was an elected Girondist deputy in the National Assembly (and imprisoned for opposing the execution of the ex-king). He had a go at reforming Britain too, via *Rights of man* and *The age of reason*, but to less immediate effect.

Paine's model of republicanism could assist television studies. It was significant that the bringing together of textuality and citizenship in the common good or general interest was done in *Rights of man*, one of the founding texts of political modernity in the West. The combination of textuality and citizenship has often been mistaken for a recent, postmodern gesture, and frequently condemned for being anti-modern and apolitical, even anti-real. The idea that it might be at the heart of modern political theory and practice was anathema to some of the very modernists who practiced that theory. However, the republic of letters had a fully documented historical basis. The reading public was literally, historically, the model for "the" public (see Altick 1957; Klancher 1987; T. Richards 1993; Lyons 1999; Hartley 1992a: chs 5–8, 1996).

Textuality and Citizenship

For a comparison between television and the republic of letters to make sense, the television audience needs to be understood as a public, in the same way that the readership of (commercially produced) newspapers has been since the nineteenth century. There were of course many technical and social differences between print and screen media, and between reading publics and media audiences. But public communication was central to any polity organized along democratic lines, where a sovereign but anonymous population governed itself via representative intermediaries. A two-way flow of information was needed to link the "imagined community" together; public affairs and decisions heading one way, public opinion and feedback heading the other. Polities adopted different mechanisms to channel this public communication, but in all cases both a literate population and truly ubiquitous media were required. Such media literally constituted the public in the act of mutually informing them and their representatives from day to day.

Ever since the advent of modernity in the West, there has been a noticeable tendency for publics to place their trust in the fastest and (compared with existing forms) least-mediated medium, which was often also the newest and most obviously technological. In the Reformation print was trusted more than sermons and homilies. There was a good reason for the public to distrust public preaching as opposed to private reading. Sermons and homilies were not, as they may intuitively have appeared to be, oral, face-to-face communication between an individual cleric and his lay congregation. With the Reformation they became a fully constituted mass medium, with a centralized, uniform message, political surveillance, and legally enforceable delivery to "the simple people." In England and Wales, for example, a manual was issued in 1574 that standardized Protestant propaganda throughout the realm. Its full title proclaimed its purpose: *The Book of Homilies: Certain sermons appointed by the Queen's Majesty to be declared and read by all parsons, vicars and curates, every Sunday and holiday in their churches; and by Her Grace's advice perused and overseen for the better understanding of the simple people* (Homilies 1850).

In the Industrial Revolution the popular daily press (both commercial and radical) was trusted more than official government information channels (see Klancher 1987; Secord 2000; Habermas 1989). In the twentieth century the public information content of cinema, which was for decades a significant competitor with newsprint via newsreels, documentary, and hybrid genres such as bio-pics, was more or less completely abandoned to television following World War II. By the 1970s television news was trusted more than print sources – a major milestone in semiotic history. By the turn of the twenty-first century, the instantaneousness and decentralized provenance of internet information was beginning to win trust in its turn.

In other words, the platform of the medium – print, screen, or interactive – was less crucial for the purposes of citizenship than its speed, its ubiquity, and the perceived trustworthiness of its information. Of course "reading" such media differed experientially depending on the nature of the platform – watching TV was not like sitting at a computer, which was not like reading a book. But at the fundamental level of constituting publics for democratic polities, this was irrelevant. "Reading" itself migrated across platforms, from sermon to print to newspaper to cinema/radio to television to interactivity, and each successive platform supplemented rather than supplanted its predecessor. Reading as a public persisted, even though the mode of literacy required did change, and the readership for a given platform was most likely to be taken as "the" public during its initial ascendancy and popularity.

Reading itself was always a multi-skilled activity. Reading print was not confined to silent decipherment of graphical marks. Print literacy involved visual (design) and pictorial (image) elements, not to mention sound (reading aloud). Similarly, both screen and interactive media, even cinema, retained major commitments to printed text, from credits, subtitles, and inter-titles to product placement and all sorts of signage within the fictional world en scene. Reading then was a varied activity at different periods and in relation to different media forms. It was sustained by graphic, aural, and visual codes that were more or less naturalistic, and thence less or more difficult to learn, but never entirely separated from each other. "Watching" television was also always "hearing" – in fact television was as much a talking medium as a visual one, and sound was often the dominant element of the television text. Soon, assisted by technology, viewers could remotely mute irritating or offensive sound content, but leave the pictures up. Like cinema, television also involved written graphics of various kinds both on and off screen – from maps and charts in news shows to *TV Guide* on the armchair.

The idea of the republic of letters had egalitarian and utopian resonance in the eighteenth century, because involvement in it was not based on property or inheritance, and could not therefore be controlled by traditional aristocratic governance. It was understood as inherently more transparent than previous modes of communication (Olson 1999: 5–6). Talent in authorship was not heritable. The ability to read was not socially exclusive. It was therefore a shadow "republic" used by polemicists such as Tom Paine to harry the inequities of the actually existing formal constitution. But in principle, the "republic of letters" was no more or less than the reading public of print literacy constituted as a modern political public and cultural consumer all at once.

The "Order of Reading"

At the turn of the twenty-first century, a book was published that provided a glimpse into the state of the republic of letters and of scholarship about it. *A history of reading in the West* (Cavallo and Chartier 1999) showcased an important strand of European thinking about publishing, the book trade, literacy, and reading publics. A concluding chapter on a future for reading was contributed by Armando Petrucci, a leading authority on writing and the social history of books in the Italian paleographic tradition (Petrucci 1995); in other words an expert in the very crucible of the republic of letters. He described the "chaos" resulting from over-capacity in that realm: it was "irrational" on both the supply (addresser) and demand (addressee) sides. On the *supply* side, publishers were "dom-inated by the terror of a market crisis continually perceived as imminent." The market had "gone mad." Publishers offered:

> *Triviallitteratur* and classics with parallel translations, journalistic "instant books" of the worst sort, books for hobbyists, philosophical or linguistic essays, collections of jokes, volumes of poetry, mysteries, science fiction, books on politics, histories of customs or of sex, and lightweight rom-ances. Neither the publisher's imprint nor the way a book is marketed nor the price discriminates among them, or brings any sort of order to the mass of texts that are produced every day. (Petrucci 1999: 356)

Publishers were hardly failing to *produce* books, which were appearing in alarming numbers. But, Petrucci argued, they were failing to produce *discrimination* within an "order of reading" shared by themselves and their readership: "For some time now, what the major publishers have been doing . . . is . . . obliterating every criterion of selection. It might be con-sidered a genuine fraud perpetrated on the reader-consumer" 1999: 356).

Petrucci saw the same indiscriminate tendencies on the *demand* side: "The reader-consumer reacts in an equally irrational manner":

> The reader behaves in a highly disorganized and unpredictable way within the market. He or she buys or does not buy, chooses or refuses to choose, prefers one type of book today and another tomorrow, is seduced on one occasion by a reduced price, on another by the graphic presentation of a book, on still another by a passing interest or by a publicity blitz. In short, the reader too begins to lose all criteria of selection, which makes it hard to programme production rationally on the basis of predictable public tastes. (1999: 356)

Petrucci contrasted the distracted, irrational, seduced consumer of this imagining with the "so-called strong readers" who had "solidly consistent tastes" but "declining numbers"; and who "in every society make up the most conservative (and hence most stable) portion of the universe of readers."

Petrucci painted a picture of what he called "reading disorders" in the republic of letters. He lamented the inauguration of an age of purposeless reading – of "reading to read." This he contrasted with reading for improvement, or for induction into a Foucauldian "order of reading," characterized by discrimination, classification, a canon, and the reduction of discursive multiplicity, authorial fertility, and potential infinity of meanings to a system with constraints, controls, and restrictions – and thereby, of course, productivity (Petrucci 1999: 349–50). He suggested that the republic of letters was in a period of decline and fall, comparable to that of another, ancient, republican empire, but this time the barbarians at the gate were electronic. Literacy itself had remained unbroken since Pharaonic Egypt and Sumerian Mesopotamia (3100 BCE or thereabouts), but during that time there had been crises of reading, almost amounting to mass extinctions, notably in the Dark Ages after the fall of the Roman empire, and in the Renaissance during the fall of the Roman church. In both periods established canons were overturned and abandoned, and new literacies put in their place (both were Romano-Latin canons giving way to Germanic and Anglo-Saxon vernaculars). It seemed that at the end of the twentieth century the same fate awaited another Roman *imperium* – that of letters. Roman script itself was feared to be giving way to visual media, its order reduced to chaos, its practice preserved in barbarous hypertext at best. But in fact the "decline and fall" scenario was evidence less of an actual historical event than of a certain historiographical attitude. The Roman empire did not "decline and fall" until Edward Gibbon said it did, for *eighteenth-century* reasons. The "decline and fall" thesis was underpinned by the principles of the Scottish Enlightenment, through which Gibbon saw Roman and Byzantine Christianization as a decline from the "public good" of the Antonine empire to "private gain" via religion and ultimately "barbarism." Similarly, television did not cause the decline and fall of the order of reading, even if it was associated with changes in literacy.

Critics, intellectuals, and academics were Petrucci's "strong readers" with established tastes and commitment to a stable canon, and therefore were the most conservative in relation to changes in reading practices. They were most likely to dismiss everything on TV as worthless, and to see in its indiscriminate publishing and reading practices the annihilation of their own order of reading. A republican TV studies would need to investigate this scenario, without assuming in advance that television was the death of knowledge, purposeless reading the end of history, and non-canonical texts the end of truth "as we know it."

Indeed, the question was: did Petrucci's excellent concept of an "order of reading" – the imposition of "discipline" in the taxonomical sense, of classification and the reduction of meaning to a system with controls and restrictions that enabled productivity – did that apply to broadcast television? Did television establish its own internal, systemic, "governmental" apparatus – an "order of viewing" amounting to a "republic of television"? If so, does that have anything to teach those for whom the crisis in the established, modernist order of reading was seen as a decline or disaster? Was "reading television" (to coin a phrase) an *extension* of the republic of letters, or its *doom*?

If the foundation of modern citizenship occurred somewhere in the interactions between the "two Rs" of *reading* and *rioting*, between journalism and politics in the streets of Paris for instance, then how might transformations in the order of reading have produced changes in citizenship? How did textuality influence citizenship in, if one can be recovered for analysis, a republic of television?

Television and the Republic of Letters

Historically, television viewing displayed characteristics that were directly comparable to developments in the history of print literacy. To the extent that this was so, television could be seen as an extension of the republic of letters, even if both letters and the republic were somewhat transformed in the process (see Wark 1997; Lumby 1999; Gibson 2001: ch 6). The "chaotic" and "irrational" "disorder" that Petrucci described in both publishing (supply) and reading (demand) applied directly both to television programming (supply) and viewing (demand). Broadcast TV appeared to be a very weakly "disciplined" medium compared with letters.

However, it was not so different from early print. In the 1500s book publishing was still organized around a practical presumption that knowledge and the knowing person were in principle coterminous, and that therefore no system of generic classification was necessary because one person could "know everything." This was the period of "univer-sal" histories, for instance, in which authors attempted or purported to write the entire history of the world – from creation to the present – often in one volume. Sir Walter Raleigh, while imprisoned in the Tower, was among the last to attempt this feat, in 1614, with his own *History of the world*. If knowledge was understood as universal and comprehensive, it didn't need to be divided into specialist branches. That was certainly the case for early television content – there was almost no evidence of specialization of audience. Even where different demographics were targeted they remained aspects of a universal "normal family" – mum, dad, teens, children. Television content and its consumer were assumed to be in principle coterminous. Both literate reading and television viewing were in principle available to everyone who shared the code, and once inside, virtually everything was on offer to virtually everyone. This is why broadcasters tended to conceptualize their regime as a "paedocracy" (Hartley 1992b: 107–10) rather than a republic – they addressed a universal, pre-specialist subject, of which the best common-sense model was not the citizen but the gratification-seeking child.

As far as content was concerned, an order of television discourse based on genre, scheduling, and channel was quickly established and widely understood. The classification of early print content in the sixteenth and seventeenth centuries was not radically different:

- Publishing required *genre*: for instance books on household or enterprise management, religion, narrative entertainment, etc.
- Reading, like TV viewing, was time-sensitive, requiring *scheduling*. Reading for different purposes – action, reflection, or passing time – would be done at different times of the day or year. Different kinds of books were produced to fulfill such various needs.
- Publisher-booksellers were the equivalent of *channels*. It was important for readers to know which supplier could be trusted – to be, for instance, Protestant. But equally, choice among a limited bundle of differentiated but nearby outlets was important. The earliest retail bookseller-publishers congregated round St Paul's churchyard in the City of London, for instance. Readers could channel-change by walking next door.

Print literacy took several centuries to evolve the complexity, scale, and professionalization that resulted in such important taxonomic innovations as the Dewey system of library classification, to render its repertoire more productive for knowledge-seeking readers. Television did not evolve an equivalent system in its broadcast era. It remained, as it were, consumptive; wasting itself away as it lived on its own tissue. Despite the brief ascendancy of commercial video libraries there was little systematic public archiving of television. This strange failure was hardly noticed in television studies, which remained silent while television companies taped over master-copies of classic series, although expensive attempts were being made at the same time to archive cinema, provoked by the chemical crisis that threatened nitrate film. Meanwhile, knowledge-seeking viewers and television researchers had to rely on their own resources to gather and archive television content. Real libraries continued to obsess about books, gathering and classifying television content only fitfully and unsystematically, as "ephemera" not "knowledge."

Television literacy was gained informally. Especially in relation to television's most popular forms, there was no school, no tutoring, no orderly progression through levels of difficulty, no homework, and no canon of required reading. Here television – differed from print literacy, which depended from the start on specialist institutions (i.e. church, state, and "dame" schools) to promote the skill of reading. Only the word "waste" could adequately describe the relationship between knowledge and the untutored watching of television (Hartley 1992b: 143–4). Masses of information were there, but there was no "search engine" to help a self-motivated viewer to find their way to and through it. Despite the large number of help shows from cooking and house makeovers to gardening and sex, little effort was made to render broadcast television itself into useful knowledge. Schools used television as they had already accommodated film. As entertainment it was banned and denigrated, but like film it was accepted into the classroom in the form of improving documentaries (often somewhat older than the students who watched them). In some US colleges, television content that had been produced for the broadcast audience could be watched for course credits as early as the 1970s, with series like Jacob Bronowski's *The ascent of man* on PBS. In the same period, the Open University in the UK began to use broadcast TV as well as correspondence for direct teaching.

Television entertainment aimed at popular audiences also started trying to be helpful, beginning with daytime shows aimed at busy housewives. Some began to offer fact sheets (later websites) to extend their utility. Others gave the phone numbers of help-lines offering further information on stories covered, from natural disasters on the news to teenage pregnancy in the TV re-version of *Clueless*. But television as a popular pastime remained most heavily committed to a "chaotic" disorder of programming in which a massive repertoire of incommensurate material was broadcast under the banners of variety, entertainment, and purposelessness. Watching TV was just that, not for anything, and in principle everything was meant to be legible to all viewers.

Whether viewers wanted a more productive, purposeful, "disciplined" order of viewing was never tested, although "public service broadcasting" in Europe came closer to recognizing that possibility than did commercial network television in the USA. The capital intensity of television production, and the need for audience maximization to achieve profit, meant that viewers were encouraged to be non-canonical, purposeless, and undisciplined – "watching to watch," as it were. This was exactly as Petrucci had characterized contemporary readers, especially younger ones. He wrote of the emergence of the "anarchical reader," quoting Hans Magnus Enzensberger on the "liberty of the reader":

> This freedom [to make whatever use of the text suits the reader] also includes the right to leaf back and forward, to skip whole passages, to read sentences against the grain, to misunderstand them, to reshape them, to spin sentences out and embroider them with every possible association, to draw conclusions from the text of which the text knows nothing, to be annoyed at it, to be happy because of it, to forget it, to plagiarise it and to throw the book in which it is printed into the corner any time s/he likes. (Enzensberger 1992: 11)

Enzensberger was evidently promoting the freedom of readers, rather than describing in any scientific detail what actually existing readers may have done in statistically significant numbers.

There was a similar debate in media studies about whether audiences had rights – "semiotics" said yes; "power" said no (Fiske 1989; Morley 1992: 29; and see Abercrombie & Longhurst 1998: 31ff). Whichever the case, readers and audiences faced essentially similar possibilities. The anarchic potential of the republic of letters was one of the most frequently noted characteristics of television usage too. But what Petrucci lamented as anarchy Enzensberger proclaimed as freedom. That freedom consisted in the openness of text to being used in ways that were aberrant from the point of view of producer-institutions. Print shared this productive capacity with television. Indeed, at the very dawn of television studies Umberto Eco had identified "aberrant decoding" as one of the defining characteristics of the "television message" (Eco 1972). Following Eco and Enzensberger, a republican media studies perhaps might promote more self-conscious and adventurous exploitation of that basic "right" than currently prevails.

"Ironclad Order" to Disciplined Order?

Stages in the establishment of television's regime of viewing could be compared with similar stages in the history of reading. Television's history as a mass medium began not with anarchy but on the contrary with what Petrucci calls "an ironclad 'order of video'" (1999: 367). This was a highly ideological form of programming, backed by both cultural control (it was produced by elites) and political regulation. It was designed to impart specific meanings from a trustworthy center to a powerless lay populace. To the limited extent that this was so, and notwithstanding the viewer freedom noted above, TV was doing no more than following in the footsteps of reading.

Reading was established in the early modern West as a tool of government, or governmentality more widely (see Miller 1998). Within ruling circles themselves, full literacy, i.e. writing as well as reading, was used as an autonomous means of communication. Beyond such circles, reading but not writing was promoted for highly ideological purposes within the most controlled environment. This work was first undertaken by religious authorities (sixteenth to seventeenth centuries). Later, state schools and public libraries (nineteenth and twentieth centuries) took over, as bearers of what Petrucci called the "democratic ideology of public reading."

The publishing industry accommodated its output to ideological requirements. For instance, popular non-fiction, especially travel and exploration, natural history and popular science, was used for directly counter-revolutionary purposes in the nineteenth century. Organizations like the Society for the Diffusion of Useful Knowledge (1826) were designed "to undermine political radicalism with rational information"; the aim was, "as some working-class readers reportedly complained, 'to stop our mouths with kangaroos'" (cited in Secord 2000: 377–8) – to silence dissent with nature study. Or as Petrucci put it: "before the advent of television, reading was the best means for diffusing values and ideologies and the one easiest to regulate, once controls had been established for the processes of production and, above all, the distribution of texts" (1999: 349).

If the early regime of broadcast viewing was "ironclad," there were long-standing and sometimes brutally enforced regulations about the content of print, with prohibitions extending from science and politics to religion and sex. People were burnt alive for what they published.

The initial ironclad order of reading was loosened if not unhinged by the effects of growth, fragmentation, competition, internal opposition, and deregulation over a long period. However, the liberty of readers was never complete. It remained confined to Enzensbergian freedom in the act of reading itself. Property and defamation laws, and restrictions relating to obscenity, national security, and community values, continued to govern what could and could not be read and by whom. Even in countries like the USA, with fully modernized First Amendment constitutions guaranteeing freedom of speech (i.e. publication), both formal regulation and informal cultural policing ensured that the much-vaunted freedoms of print literacy were constantly chaperoned, the more so in the most popular media.

The will to govern applied equally to print, television, and successor media. It was driven by the popularity of a medium, not by its platform. This was evident internationally once again as new computer-based interactive media matured into popular or mass media. The early, anarchic regime of reading/viewing on the internet and worldwide web (e.g. open source) belied its material origins in the defense industry, and in any case it was brought progressively under the control of various national legal and corporate (copyright) systems. Landmark decisions imposed governmental control over content in countries as various as France (Nazi content on Yahoo), the USA (IP law, e.g. Napster), Malaysia (Asian values), and China (national self-determination).

International cooperation in content policing was evident too, especially in the areas of security (hacking the Pentagon), finance (secure credit cards), and Western family values (child pornography). As well as national and moral considerations, commercial imperatives were at work. Massive investment in interactive technologies required equally massive numbers of users – scale was still the key to financial return. An orchestrated campaign to suburbanize the internet – to assure middle-of-the-road users that the pleasures and dangers of ungoverned street life were not "just a click away" – focused on stories about pedophiles. These almost mythical figures took over the traditional role of ogres and footpads, figures of fear of communication in its physical mode (at least until *Shrek*). They were in direct line of succession to all the weird and wonderful corruptors of youth that were said to lurk within each new medium, from popular fiction in print, through cinema and radio to television itself. Making the highways and byways of hypermedia safe for suburban pilgrims was the "moral" of these stories.

Broadcast television in its early decades may have appeared to be ideologically over-controlled in contrast to print literacy (in the contemporary West, at least), but it was simply and briefly a successor; any ironcladding that was applied to television had already been thoroughly battle-hardened in previous media from print to radio. Unwittingly or otherwise the first generation of highly literate TV producers, regulators, and critics (but not audiences, Enzensberger would argue) organized broadcasting's regime of viewing around the imposition of control, not the encouragement of innovation; it was compliance before performance. Perhaps it was inevitable that those schooled in the disciplinary apparatus of print literacy should seek both government over the new medium and the maintenance of strictly enforced distinctions between it and the established order of reading. But the eventual and inevitable failure of those controls and distinctions did not have to be seen as disaster or decline. It was just history repeating itself.

The New Three Rs: Reading, Writing, and Redaction

Just as there had been in print, in early television there were very general and extensive forms of prohibition, from banning to bowdlerization, designed to make television knowledge unharmful. There was a radical separation of "reading" from "writing" TV. There was a regulatory presumption of television's disorderliness and the potentially disruptive effect of that on viewers and cultures. Television was praised only when it was being used to teach the most conservative or law-affirming cultural and political values, associated with patriotism and wise consumption. But it was prevented from trying to stimulate viewers too much, in fictional as well as factual output. The only effect television was allowed to have without questions being asked by populist politicians in Parliament or Congress was on sales of toothpaste, and only then if they increased.

The curious (or perhaps merely Foucauldian) situation arose where print reading was widely praised because it seemed orderly and well governed (schools, libraries, disciplines) but its value was said to reside in the freedom it bestowed on readers. Meanwhile television watching was criticized for disorderliness, even though TV's regime of viewing could not be satisfactorily controlled. Governmentality was inevitable. Regulation of any textual system is necessary for its productive capacity to develop, but nevertheless the early history of television regulation was governmental in an oppressive, not a fully productive sense. It was characterized by general and uncomprehending attempts to discipline its potential unruliness; not to develop its own regime of viewing, or semiotic and informational productiveness, so much as to minimize its effect on other people, print, and politics. There were voices that promoted the educative and enlarging potential of television in democratic countries (Hartley 1999). But the prevailing discourse was dedicated to keeping the new medium as distinct as possible from the existing order of reading, not to welcome it as an extension and democratization of the same.

Meanwhile, even under such "ironclad" regulatory pressure, television did in thirty years what the republic of letters took three hundred to achieve: it established its own transnational and society-wide "order of viewing." That order displayed features that seemed contradictory when considered from the point of view of contemporary book reading. Anarchic freedoms co-existed with ironclad ideologies. What was the relation between addresser (text) and addressee (citizen) in this context – was it more "anarchic," or more "ironclad"? Television studies explored this relation almost exclusively in terms of power; i.e. presuming that the order of viewing was ironclad. But two concepts derived from the republic of letters were available to help to identify how the order of television operated, and how comparable it was with the order of reading. One was "authorship," the other was "writing."

Much has been written about the nature of authorship, from its omniscience to its death. But, as a central component of the republic of letters, authorship has rarely been associated with television and other electronic media, although it achieved limited purchase in cinema studies via auteur theory. Conversely, the characteristic modes of text production in television, where authorship is dispersed and dissolved, have rarely been applied to print. Television was from the start a team sport. Authorship was diffused among many individuals, and may more properly have been claimed by a studio, company, or channel than by a person, as creative IP increasingly was. In television, authorial originality of imagination or expression, or of research and information-gathering, or of a shaping artistic vision, emerged as much from direction as from scripting, from producers as much as from performers, and more from the corporate resources of giant organizations (Fox, Viacom, BBC) than from individual creative genius (which was nevertheless both valued and necessary throughout the whole enterprise). Did this suggest a chalk-and-cheese distinction between TV and book authorship? Did corporate authorship entail more ironclad control as opposed to anarchic individual talent? Not really.

Apart from the banal fact that literary authors often worked in TV, and vice versa, there was more to authorship in practice than the ideology of the creative individual allowed. Within the republic of letters itself, for instance:

> There is another anomalous and potentially "anarchical" figure who corresponds to the new readers and their innovative reading practices. It is the consumeristic writer who produces texts of para-literature, rewrites other people's texts, churns out lightweight romantic fiction and mysteries, or patches together articles for second-tier periodicals, often anonymously or as a member of an editorial team. (Petrucci 1999: 366)

This very interesting figure, Petrucci suggested, had "surfaced" in previous "times of crisis in book production, of a suddenly expanded reading public, or of widely divergent levels in the product." But Petrucci's historical observation was clouded by his prejudicial language – "consumeristic," "para-literature," "churns out," "lightweight," "patches together," "second-tier."

A more neutral term to identify this type of writer is required in order to advance understanding of the interconnectedness of corporate authorship, popular media, and servicing the needs of users, whether they were readers or viewers. Corporate authorship in the context of public communication was first established in journalism. It is in that context that I have identified the emergent figure of the redactor: one who produced new material by a process of editing existing content. Redaction is a form of *production* not *reduction* of text (which is why the more familiar term "editing" is not adequate). Indeed, the current period could be characterized as a redactional society, indicating a time when there is too much instantly available information for anyone to see the world whole, resulting in a society that is characterized by its editorial practices, by how it uses the processes of corporate and governmental shaping of existing materials to make sense of the world. Individual authorship itself is increasingly redactional in mode. The most trusted and most visited sources of truth are not individuals but organizations, from CNN to the Guardian Unlimited website, depending on your preferences. It is redaction, not original writing (authorship) as such, that determines what is taken to be true, and what policies and beliefs should follow from that.

The republic of letters and the television republic are both represented by redactors. It is no longer accurate to draw a distinction between print and media literacy, or between literary authorship and media production. In any textual system undergoing massive expansion, a major priority is for someone to sort out order from the chaos. This was what the redactor does. Everywhere in the republic of letters, from Dorling Kindersley to textbooks, pulp fiction to journalism, there was a diffusion of authorship into redaction. Petrucci's distinction between original and "para-" literature was untenable. In television, the redactional form of authorship was standard practice. There was major overlap between the most popular and expansive parts of the republic of letters and that of television. The redactor brought together information, images, "matter of reasoning," and discourse not only within but also between the apparently distinct republics of letters and television.

The anonymous and unknown population – the reading public – that has gathered together into some sort of relationship with all this material made some use of it. Attention needed to shift from studying TV's impact upon individuals and societies, toward the use made of it by such. Watching television needed to be thought of more as a literacy than as a behavior. If, however, television were ever to claim literate status then it would have to include "writing" as well as "reading." The stakes in shifting the conception of TV literacy from "read only" to "read and write" were, it transpired, high. Petrucci wrote: "Writing is instead [of reading] an individual skill and is totally free; it can be done in any fashion, anywhere and to produce anything the writer wants; it is beyond the reach of any control or, at the limit, of any censorship" (1999: 349). Petrucci contrasted the individual freedom of writing with his ironclad order of video: "in the electronic mass media, television in particular . . . a 'canon' of programmes is rapidly becoming uniform throughout the world, and . . . the viewing public (of all cultural traditions) is just as rapidly being levelled" (p. 349).

In fact, such a radical distinction between the freedom of writing and constraint of reading could not be sustained even within the republic of letters, where written literacy was routinely conventional, instrumental, coercive, and dull. But even so, writing was evidently more active and individuated than watching TV purposelessly as part of a "levelled" public was reputed to be. So did TV literacy begin to extend writing to those who were formerly restricted to reading? The evidence suggested that it did:

- At the most basic level, viewers with remote control devices could countermand the flow of television sequence by zapping, slaloming, and muting. This demotic form of redaction was apparently highly valued in some contexts (competitive zapping in US fraternity-house TV lounges), and highly irritating in others (homes where dad controlled the control).

  Much more sophisticated forms of writing and rewriting of television textuality were evident in the fan cultures that have been extensively studied by Henry Jenkins and others (e.g. Jenkins 2006; Hills 2002; Gwenllian-Jones & Pearson 2004).[1]

- Extending slowly from art-college, avant-garde, and political advocacy groups, the redactional skills of scratch video and image/sound manipulation were extended to those who could do clever things with computers. These included websites that made cult TV characters participate in viewer-created narratives, dance routines, or even other worlds.

- Even within the TV industry as established, the distinction between viewer and maker was dissolving: weakly in various audience-participation shows; strongly in such "access" series as the wonderful *Video Nation*, broadcast by the BBC.

- The public became the star of reality TV formats, from *Popstars/ Idol* to *Big Brother*. Audience interaction was central to such formats, and extended to non-TV platforms including the internet, telephone, and SMS. Successful broadcast shows like *Dawson's Creek* began to introduce interactive element on the web, such as Sony's "Dawson's Desk" and "Rachel's Room" sites, encouraging audiences literally to write themselves into the narrative.

- The invidious distinctions between "amateur," "connoisseur," and "professional" remained forceful, but were blurred. "Home video" was used for an increasingly sophisticated range of activities – from cannily faked accidents for submission to "Funniest Home Video" shows, to the "Jenni-cam" or "cam-girl" phenomenon where private individuals set up webcams in their domestic space and shared their lives with up to millions of fellow netizens (see chapter 8; and Turner 2004: 63–9). TV channels experimented with shows that resulted from giving young people cheap digital cameras and an arduous, amusing, or audacious task.

- Social groups ranging from Indigenous people to migrants and expatriates, including advocates for movements arising from various identities based on gender, ethnicity, sexual orientation, region, or age, increasingly used both broadcast TV and non-broadcast video to communicate to their own communities, and to communicate about themselves to larger publics.

- Home video, community video, corporate video, promotional video, music video: all extended television "writing" beyond broadcasting, across the spectrum from amateur to avant garde.

After decades of patiently taking their turn as receivers of television discourse, it seemed, viewers were being transformed and transforming themselves into transmitters or "vidders" in increasing numbers, well beyond the control of any ironclad "videologues."

Political and Semiotic Economy: Who Rules?

A republican television studies would be interested in ordinariness; in the extension of cultural and semiotic resources into everyday life. It follows that the primary object of study need not be the ownership and control of television stations. The ownership of publishing houses had an important bearing on book production but did not explain the republic of letters. Similarly, media ownership did not explain the semiotic, social, or even political productivity of the textual system of television – only how it could be exploited by certain state or commercial forces.

A republic of television, if there were one, would not be sustainable if it was an absolute monarchy, at the whim and disposal of the inter-locking royal families of big corporations like News International, Viacom, and Disney. Some of these did in fact display monarchical tendencies, including a desire for hereditary succession. Despite the best efforts of long-serving CEOs like Rupert Murdoch and Kerry Packer on behalf of their offspring, they were rarely successful in that aim. Tom Paine could rest easy. Television as a textual system was an invention of commercial culture and could not be done without corporate organization. Part of the project of republican television studies would be to investigate the extent to which any potential television republic could be realized in that corporate, baronial context.

The viewing public of ordinary viewers had very little direct financial or managerial stake in TV production, but viewers did make a high semiotic or cultural (and temporal) investment in television's textual and social form. In other words, the familiar feudal language of "media moguls," "press barons," and "literary lords" was at odds with the much more modern structure of the television republic as it developed into a textual system on a society-wide scale. The growth, diversification, and use of media textuality were not in the control of the feudalists; nor were viewers ever mere serfs of the semiotic economy.

The political economy approach to television focused on ownership, control, finance, and regulation, and often had very little to say about, and no way of measuring, the productivity of the system in terms of meaning, knowledge, communication, information, and culture. This approach was associated with writers like Herb Schiller, Nick Garnham, Peter Golding, and Graham Murdock, even Naomi Klein and the "culture-jammers." But that cultural, non-instrumental use of the media, human rather than economic, was its use-value for the viewing public that television called into being (and that was the extent of its purposelessness). The interests of commercial producers did not extend very much further than enlarging the potential viewing public and stimulating reconsumption, which of course explained why TV encouraged reading over writing for so long.

But the viewing public could not be confined to such a subsistence economy. The system was too large, complex, and diverse to remain under the control of any one power, no matter how powerful some individuals appeared to be. A republican television studies would be interested in the relations between different powers within its commonwealth, but would not need to assume, *a priori*, that only one of those powers could explain everything else in the system. The golden eggs gathered so spectacularly by Rupert Murdoch and his media-baron cousins were actually laid by the rather unglamorous goose of the viewing public. Each needed the other in a commercial democracy. And as Richard Caves argued in his economic analysis of the creative industries, innovation – the very use-value that made these industries viable – was in the gift of the consumer, not the producer: "It is almost appropriate to say that innovation in creative industries need involve nothing more than consumers changing their minds about what they like" (Caves 2000: 202). Meanwhile it was increasingly evident that the existing representative apparatuses of old democracies allowed little room for direct self-representation by media citizens, except as such relationships were already heavily mediated via the marketplace and government offices. A republican television studies would be useful, therefore, to identify ways in which the ordinary public could be better represented within a developing television republic.

Media Citizenship

The concept of citizenship was the subject of widespread reflection during the era of broadcast television, and not only in the field of political science. Citizenship was no longer simply a matter of civic rights and duties. The concept shifted from law to history. Following the classic work of T. H. Marshall, it could be argued that the history of citizenship in modernizing countries was one of extension of rights and reduction of duties. But more importantly, citizenship evolved increasingly from the political toward the cultural domain, and from obligations to a state toward self-determination by individuals.

In that context it was important to understand what form "media citizenship" might take. Marshall suggested that from its Enlightenment base in civil or individual rights, citizenship extended from there to political (voting) rights during the nineteenth century, thence to social (welfare, employment) rights up to 1950 (Marshall 1963). During the second half of the twentieth century in advanced modern countries, it extended to cultural (identity) rights, and most recently to "DIY citizenship" (Hartley 1999: 162–3).

With extension came also dissolution – as James Holston and Arjun Appadurai pointed out, the rights of citizens were increasingly claimed by non-citizens (welfare rights, for instance), while the duties (jury and military service, taxation) seemed increasingly onerous and apt to be evaded (1996: 190). Attempts to revive citizenship led to "perverse outcomes." Attempts to make it more exclusive and local led to xenophobic violence; the alternative attempt to make it more inclusive and transnational "tends to preclude active participation in the business of rule." Holston and Appadurai wrote of the "replacement" of the "civic ideal with a more passive sense of entitlement to benefits which seem to derive from remote sources. Far from renewing citizenship, violence and passivity further erode its foundations" (pp. 190–1).

Violence and passivity as an outcome of evolving senses of citizenship? Violence and passivity were the very effects that watching a lot of television was said to produce. Once again the connection between textuality and citizenship needed investigation, although here in a negative form. Television may have added to xenophobia, remoteness, violence, and passivity. But television's textuality may also have been a site for new forms of cultural engagement and even civic participation through which emergent forms of citizenship could be discerned.

In the modern era no citizenship evolved anywhere without citizen-readers. The evolution of citizenship began with the inauguration of civil, individual rights, followed by political rights; both of these were achieved among communities, such as the Parisian poor, whose civic and political emancipation followed their mobilization as readers of, for example, scandalous journalism, political pamphlets, and revolutionary philosophy. The Enlightenment, in short, was written down, diffused by reading, and established by those who made up the reading public. As Holston and Appadurai argued: "The extension of the shared beyond the local and homogenous is, of course, an essential part of citizenship's revolutionary and democratic promise. This extension of citizenship is corrosive of other notions of the shared precisely because its concept of allegiance is, ultimately, volitional and consensual rather than natural" (1996: 191–2). Writing, specifically journalism, was the medium by means of which "the shared" was extended in an ultimately volitional, consensual way. The "democratic ideals of commonwealth, participation and equality" (Holston & Appadurai 1996: 192) were the core values of the republic of letters.

Holston and Appadurai discussed the politics of identity in the context of citizenship. Noting that feminism had taken a lead in critiquing a liberal notion of citizenship that relegated prior differences of gender, for instance, or race to the private sphere, they pointed to a current problem of democracy: "The politics of difference becomes more important and potentially incompatible with that of universal equality as the real basis for citizenship. For example, this politics argues that although different treatment (e.g. with regard to gender) can produce inequality, equal treatment, when it means sameness, can discriminate against just the kinds of values and identities people find most meaningful" (1996: 194).

A polity that was "indifferent" in both senses, with the indifference of impartial law (and impartial media), and the indifference of uncaring inequality, fueled criticisms of what became known as the "democratic deficit" of otherwise egalitarian, modern, secular countries. The demand for cultural citizenship based on identity, and for recognition and respect for identity based on authenticity or essential qualities such as ethnicity or sex, extended (perhaps to breaking point) conceptualizations of equal citizenship based on civil, political, and welfare/employment rights. Holston and Appadurai argued that:

> The argument from authenticity leads to a politics of difference rather than to a politics of universalism or equalization of rights. . . . Although this kind of demand would seem contradictory and incompatible with citizenship

as an ideology of equality, there is nevertheless a growing sense that it changes the meaning of equality itself. . . . Thus, it would define citizenship on the basis of rights to different treatment with equal opportunity. (1996: 194–5)

In the context of growing demands for difference within universalizing polities, what was the role of television? One version of its history, which I offered in *Uses of television* (1999), was that the population-gathering and popularizing imperatives of commercial television had a part to play in this process. As communities became more virtualized, and consent more volitional, television was able to provide a means of "cross-demographic communication" unrivalled by any other means in history. Within that context, it was one mechanism for the actual process of sharing difference. It was possible to extend the "notion of the shared" without that entailing the erasure of difference. Thus while television was routinely accused of provoking violence or encouraging passivity among its vast audiences, the possibility that television played a role in reconstituting citizenship on the site of virtualized identities of various kinds needed to be further explored.

Citizenship and Identity

Holston and Appadurai sought to relocate citizenship in the world's major cities, and of course they were right to do that. But citizenship was never a spatial belonging alone. Increasingly media critics and commentators have looked for ways in which the symbolic if not the juridical element of citizenship might be shared through media that were not available when citizenship first extended from urban centers to the vast and virtual "imagined communities" of nations. Cities were of course the strategic site for the early development of citizenship, but the new media, including television, played a part in "virtualizing" what had already been "nationalized" and thereby abstracted.

The possibility that television was a component of "communicative democracy" has not gone unnoticed by other critics. Writing from a feminist perspective, for instance, Joke Hermes argued that:

Popular culture is typically unorderly and unattractive from a modernist point of view; creative and inspiring, however, seen from a post-modern orientation – especially when democratic government and community-building are seen as endeavours that benefit by, nay, even need central fictions. Thus, even though popular culture is never the domain of administrative politics, of voting and decision-making, it may provide the grounding for a citizen identity. (Hermes 1998: 160)

From this perspective (and see Hermes 2005 for a fuller discussion), Hermes concluded that "women's crime writing offers elements of a feminist utopia and ongoing criticism of the hurdles women face in their march towards full social and civic participation." These popular books "contribute to building a sense of what is needed where sex, justice, humour, and professionality are concerned" (1998: 164). Such cultural citizenship – a community of readers in this case, gathered in the name of pleasure, fiction, "commitment and engagement" – needed to be understood in new ways: "Citizenship also needs to be understood as intrinsically mediated practices . . . Individuals can be competent participants in different communities fully aware that codes or ideologies clash but not particularly concerned about this – since we are all adept to 'do in Rome as the Romans do'" (1998: 160).

Hermes was at pains to point out that the participation she described was not reading only, but extended to writing: "The women's movement is a case in point. Many types of media content have been generated by feminists, ranging from flyers and political tracts to songs, autobiographies and literary novels" (1998: 166). In short, popular media in general (not just books) not only produced a "reading public" that used them to ground its own commitment to citizenship, but they were also modes of "writing" available to groups who wished to share their identity or difference among their own or wider communities, as writers like Nancy Fraser and Rita Felski pointed out about the "feminist public sphere" (Felski 1989).

Not just for individual citizens themselves, but for "specific social groups" based on identity and difference, it was increasingly the case that "membership" was no longer of "the" public but of many different "publics" at once; public spheres became public "sphericules" (Cunningham 2001). Groups and movements pursuing goals related to identity via cultural politics needed internal communication for the adherents to the cause, and external communication to address wider publics. One place where such group-based communicative practices jostled and co-existed was of course television, which remained the "cultural forum" Horace Newcomb and Paul Hirsch said it was many years ago (Newcomb & Hirsch 2000), the more so as it moved into the post-broadcast era of subscription-based viewing.

In relation to ethnic communities this could produce what Herman Gray called "complexity in an age of racial and cultural politics where the sign of blackness labors in the service of many different interests at once" (1995: 84). Gray identified three kinds of discursive practice on American television that anchored contemporary images of African Americans: these were:

- assimilationist (invisibility),
- pluralist (separate but equal), and
- multiculturalist (diversity) (1995: 84).

Of these co-existent forms, the multiculturalist one was the most interesting, certainly for Gray, who reported that in such TV shows: "black life and culture are constantly made, remade, modified, and extended. ... In these shows, differences that originate from within African American social and cultural experiences have been not just acknowledged, but interrogated, even parodied as subjects of television" (1995: 84). Gray showed in detail how textuality and citizenship intersected in black television:

> In Living Color and A Different World, for instance, have used drama, humor, parody, and satire to examine subjects as diverse as Caribbean immigrants, black fraternities, beauty contests, gay black men, the Nation of Islam, Louis Farrakhan, Jesse Jackson, Marion Barry, racial attitudes, hip-hop culture, and white guilt. The richness of African American cultural and social life as well as the experience of otherness that derives from subordinate status and social inequality are recognized, critiqued, and commented on. The racial politics that helps to structure and define U.S. society is never far from the surface. (1995: 91)

Such shows, in short, addressed African American viewers as part of a "complex and diverse" culture marked by internal difference (p. 111), rather than addressing the "hegemonic gaze of whiteness." But of course those same images were available for anyone to see, "creating a space for this slice of black life in the weekly clutter of network television" (p. 112).

While Herman Gray (unusually for a media scholar) cheerfully admitted that some of the appeal of the shows he analyzed was that as a TV viewer he liked them, he was also trying to draw more impersonal lessons from thinking about blackness in the context of television:

Cultural struggles, including those over the representation of blackness in our present, help us to prepare the groundwork, to create spaces for how we think about our highly charged racial past and possibilities for our different and yet contested future. Commercial television is central to this cultural struggle. In the 1980s, claims and representations of African Americans were waged in the glare of television. Those representations and the cultural struggles that produced them will, no doubt, continue to shape the democratic and multiracial future of the United States. (1995: 173)

Cultural struggles went on within television, between it and its audiences, and between TV and critics from various complicit but more or less hostile groups. One such struggle was about the effort to have representatives from significant identity groups develop as writers, not simply as readers, or at best on-screen symbols. Gray made a point of naming the black professionals and production companies working in the industry who were having a material impact on the representation of African American culture on American TV – as writers. This was still a struggle, since half a century of audience maximization and an obsession with promoting reconsumption had not done much to encourage diverse writers, least of all from minorities. But Gray demonstrated that things were changing historically.

Television: Teaching Good Citizenship

As the market has matured, and as new communication technologies began to allow "television" to be studied in the past tense, some of the gains and losses of the early strategy of audience maximization and recon-sumption could be assessed. It was of course conventional to criticize broadcast television for universalizing the viewing subject, and for making too little allowance for difference. TV was also frequently criticized for ideology, populism, "dumbing down," and all that. The losses involved were obsessively catalogued in TV studies.

Have there been any gains? Chief among them was surely the creation of the viewing public. Just as the popular press of the nineteenth century was responsible for the creation of the mass reading public and thence "the" public, so TV became the place where and the means by which, a century later, most people got to know about most other people, and about publicly important events or issues. Located in the heart of civil society, private life, and everyday culture, television occupied the very place from where the most important new political movements of the current period arose, from feminism to the green movement. Even the most sober critics believed it could promote new forms of citizenship; for instance Peter Dahlgren:

> Television can also engage and mobilise. . . . The question is whether television can . . . make a social difference. I would maintain that the medium has not yet lost this potential, limited though it may be. Television is a tricky medium and can do many things, including, perhaps – given the right circumstances – generating societal involvement and conveying a sense of citizenship. (1998: 93; see also Dahlgren 1995: 146)

Here Dahlgren was recognizing, albeit cautiously and belatedly, that popular TV is part of the public sphere. Such recognition implied that television could "engage and mobilise" its vast cross-cultural audiences in ways that modernist critics were reluctant to admit. I argued in *Uses of television* (1999) that broadcast television did indeed function to generate "societal involvement and a sense of citizenship." The means by which it achieved that were not at the margins as Dahlgren suggests, with a well-meaning charity appeal here or consumer campaign there, but in its very structure as a popular medium of communicative entertainment. Television not only created the largest imagined community the world has ever seen (the TV audience), but it functioned as a teacher of cultural citizenship over several decades. That was the outcome or productivity of its literacy.

More recently, and as the medium itself evolved into post-broadcast forms with fragmented programming and user-choice options, television began to contribute to "do-it-yourself" or "DIY" citizenship. But the routine form of analysis of the relation between TV and its audiences, i.e. via concepts of power, hegemony, ideology, and populism, contrived to dismiss, downplay, or set aside the role of television as a teacher, and the creative and autonomous uses to which those who are literate in its order of viewing could put it.

A re-reading of some of the founding theorists of cultural studies, especially Richard Hoggart, suggested that popular television was understood from the start at least partly in terms of a pedagogic or teaching role (Hartley 1999: chs 10 and 11). The positive potential of such a role has been somewhat forgotten in subsequent work in cultural studies. But television continued into the "postmodern" period various teaching functions inherited both from modernity and from pre-modern (medieval) cultural formations. It behaved anthropologically in this respect, not like a pedagogical institution. It taught in a *trans-modern* mode, promoting, among audiences who were not instrumentally purposeful in their learning, the construction of selves, semiotic self-determination, and a sophisticated understanding of (literacy in) the mediasphere. I apologize for the neologism, but I called this function of television "democratainment" (Hartley 1999: chs 12 and 14).

Democratainment – Why it's like Irish Dancing

Television was busy creating the viewing public and teaching new forms of citizenship based on population-gathering within a recognition of different identities. Meanwhile, what were the "uses" of academic criticism of television? TV studies as a disciplinary discourse had one direct effect on television itself that was not helpful. The new medium was launched into a hostile critical climate in the period between the 1930s and 1950s. Subsequently, TV studies evolved in the hyper-politicized and advers-arialist intellectual environment in the 1970s. Throughout, academic and a good deal of journalistic criticism of television was dedicated to "disciplining" the new medium as if it were a disorderly child. The response of TV was to make itself as safe as possible, not to be too adventurous, to be disciplined in the way that a boarding school is supposed to be disciplined – by prohibition and uniformity.

Such discipline produced a characteristically peculiar action in the televisual body politic. It ended up looking like an Irish dancer: all buttoned up, stiff, and po-faced at the top, legs going like the clappers underneath, control and creativity co-present but not on speaking terms, the rational expression held impassively aloft by the wildly energetic but skillfully choreographed emotional legs, which were studiously ignored even as they skipped between the athletic and the erotic. That's democratainment: a suitably "republican" image, perhaps, to suggest that television was working, indeed dancing, upon the ground of democratization throughout its broadcast history. During the same period, for many intellectual critics, the extension and celebration of democracy were seen not as a desirable goal but as a defeat of more revolutionary-utopian aims.

Television became old when the desires and fears it used to attract as the latest, most popular, all-singing, all-dancing attraction were transferred to newer media such as the internet. This is perhaps a good time to reassess the legacy of both television and television studies. One plausible judgment is that TV itself has less to be embarrassed about than do its critics. The teacher's report on TV studies itself might even read "Must try harder"; for instance to help make TV more varied, publics more literate, and the relations between the established republic of letters and the emerging media republic less hostile. The technology is there, thanks to post-broadcast media providers and a media-literate population, but the software – the critical discourse itself – is very conservative, prejudicial, and nostalgic. Television studies has much to learn, from the citizens of media and media themselves, as it explores the next phase of development of the republic of television.

Note

1   And see www.henryjenkins.org/aboutme.html.

7

Reality and the Plebiscite

At the root of democratic politics is the vote. Voting has an instrumental purpose – expressing the popular will – but it is also pleasurable. People *like* to vote; including people who don't often do it. In a recent survey in California, "92 percent of infrequent voters say they like to vote. 62 percent strongly agree with the statement, 'I like to vote,' while 30 percent agree somewhat" (California Voter Foundation 2005: 7). Even 48 percent of *non-voters* agreed with the statement (pp. 27–8)! This chapter shows how the vote is faring in *entertainment* formats, especially in reality television, where it seems to be thriving, as if someone had pressed the refresh button on one of the oldest technologies of democracy.

I argue that the yoking together of politics and entertainment is as old as democracy itself. What is new is a shift from "modern" democratic processes to a new paradigm based not on representation but on direct participation; a shift led from consumer rather than from political culture. I want to identify a new form of intermediary that has grown up in the interface between consumers and popular media, which I call the "plebiscitary industries." These may be defined as those agencies, production companies, and technical service providers whose business it is to commercialize the popular vote by turning it into an entertainment format. They have evolved from existing ratings, polling, marketing, and production agencies, which themselves grew out of an earlier "representative" rather than "direct" model of mediation. But the "plebiscitary industries" are not the same as "pollsters," in just the way that the "creative industries" differ from the "cultural industries" – they belong to a new paradigm of business practice that values consumers for what they *do* rather than for how they can be made to *behave*. During the modern era of "mass" communication, the preferences of consumers and audiences were "represented" in media only indirectly, notably via ratings. Now it is possible for individuals to express their views and votes directly, and the evidence suggests that they're having a ball while doing so. The plebiscitary industries have caught the digital wave and are using new interactive technologies and software for what Stephen Coleman calls "conversational democracy" (Coleman 2005). Part of its appeal is the straightforward fun to be had from making public, by voting, the personal act of choice.

Many reality TV formats use the plebiscite as part of the entertainment, especially talent shows in fashion and music. Such plebiscitary *formats* may be distinguished from plebiscitary *industries* in the same way that *Big Brother* can be distinguished from Endemol (which makes it), the aggregators who collect the votes, and the various TV networks that screen the show. Plebiscitary formats have proven very popular internationally in recent years. For the industry they are a live experiment in different ways to incorporate voting into existing light entertainment. The plebiscitary format is sometimes "about" politics (*American Candidate*) but more often the formal world of politics is the last thing on its mind (*Idol, Big Brother*). However, the political and the escapist ends of the reality spectrum are both expressions of something new – a widespread popular desire for participation in a direct open network rather than control by closed expert systems. In fact, plebiscitary formats in reality TV may be seen as *transitional forms* through which the plebiscitary industries are conducting R&D to see how far they can maintain the scale of modern "behavioral" or "mass" communication while accommodating new demand for personal choice and direct participation in large-scale communicative interaction. In some of these formats "democratic" progress is minimal. Viewers do little more than vote, and the vote is rigged. But even among these early and hesitant experiments, the "medium is the message" – the plebiscitary format *is* an experience of democracy; the demos is *doing* something *together*, not just being told what to do or how it has behaved. Despite these shortcomings, plebiscitary television is exerting pressure to reform upon "representative" models of both media and politics, in order to make space for the desire for direct active participation by consumers in the very human process of choosing their own representations. This process has not yet reached maturity by any means, but in the meantime the plebiscitary industries (not formal politics) are the place to look for both technical and imaginative progress.

Politics and Entertainment

Crash-merging politics and media – the story of modernity?

The plebiscitary industries and plebiscitary reality formats, taken together, are acting as a catalyst for the mutual modification of politics (democratic deliberation, policy decisions, national identity, security) and entertainment (engagement/affect, narrative, personal identity, conflict). The admixture of power and pleasure, decision-making and celebrity, reason and "affect," democratic deliberation and individual identity, citizenship and consumption, war and drama has long been at the center of attention in cultural and media studies, especially those emanating from an interest in popular culture and the everyday life and audience-hood of ordinary people.

But political science has been much slower to accept that mediated entertainment is at the center of the political process. Political scientists are generally trained in the formal operations of the democratic process and government, such as deliberative debate, lobbyism, political parties and elections, government agencies and NGOs, policy formation and participation, and also public opinion (seen as a science of measurement). The nearest they get to mediated popular culture is "the news media," on the model or ideal type of political coverage in newspapers of record. While political scientists are well aware that the media are a crucial component of politics, it is to CNN, Fox, and the electronic or latterly internet-based *news* media that they turn to see what's going on. This is natural enough, but it ignores two crucial truths about the media: first, that news is a small and declining component of the overall media mix (some media like cinema have learnt to do without it altogether); and second, that what attracts and holds popular media audiences is not news, never mind politics. In short, political science has a skewed image of the media. From that blinkered perspective, most of what people do with and like about their TV usage is invisible. And so the antics of reality TV formats must seem very foreign, a continuation of what has long been seen as a contamination of the political process by demagogic mass spectacle or populist manipulation by corporate interests. But the political process has never been pure (as media theorists have long been arguing). Indeed it must be mediated, using the rhetorical arts and media technologies of its time. Politics depends on the arts of persuasion and on the power of emotion; these need to be communicated to vast, cross-demographic publics in real time.

Meanwhile, using the same means of communication, the world of "escapist" entertainment is often able to use dramatic conflict and narrative, character and action, not least via celebrity personifications, to get very close indeed to fundamental human, social, cultural (and political) dilemmas in ways that may capture and fire up the popular imagination for straightforwardly political purposes. Think back to popular drama from Greek tragedy to Shakespeare or popular literature from Dickens to Orwell; children's fantasy from *The Wizard of Oz* to *Lord of the Rings*; or how a single TV show might directly challenge government policy (e.g. *Cathy Come Home* in the 1960s or *Death of a Princess* in the 1980s); or how a movie like *Apocalypse Now* summed up a war for a generation; or how black music from the blues onward expressed minority experience and carried new political consciousness across the world; or how the counterculture learned its politics and ethics from songs by Bob Dylan; or how Band Aid and its successors Live Aid and Live8 conjoined pop music and global foreign policy (see also Spigel & Curtin 1997; Curtin 1995; Torres 2003).

The con-fusion of politics and entertainment can be traced back to any originating moment of any contemporary polity that you care to name, including the great modernizing political "revolutions" of the USA in 1776 and France in 1789. The same applies to Russia in 1917 and China in 1949, not to mention Italy in 1922 and Germany in 1933 – whose totalitarian visions of mass politics as emotion-laden entertainment and spectacle served as a dreadful warning of just how potent the mixture could be in unscrupulous hands.

Despite the warnings of Frankfurt-School critics against the aestheticization of politics, those of Hannah Arendt against populist demagoguery, or those of Susan Sontag against "fascinating fascism," there is no type of popular political participation ancient or modern that is not also mediated, spectacular, irrational, and emotion-laden. Democratic polities as well as totalitarian ones are served by entertainment both routinely in the daily news-round and at crucial times of heightened political risk, such as elections, wars, scandals, and economic downturns. Semiotic as well as social leadership has always been needed to capture the popular imagination, alongside or even in advance of reasoned argument. Democracy was fanned and disseminated by popular journalism as well as (as much as) by political activism. Good journalism has always prioritized a clear story, dramatic conflict, and latterly compelling visuals as the means by which it must address the information- and enlightenment-seeking citizen. Michael Schudson (1999; see also Schudson 1998) has pointed out that when the idea of the rational "informed citizen" took over in the USA in the 1880s from the previous model of political participation based on spectacular partisanship, actual voting numbers dropped. People had to be brought back to the ballot box by showbiz razzamatazz and campaigning chutzpah.

But the use of entertainment techniques to reach the popular voter was not a corruption of previously pure political communication. It was constitutionally required by the very form of modern representative democracy. Political modernity is inaugurated in any country when the source of sovereignty shifts from the monarch (think Charles I of England, Louis XVI of France, Nicholas II of Russia, or Cixi, Dowager Empress of China), as the personification of divine authority and thus in a real sense the "author" of his or her people, to "the people" (think Congress, Parliament, Soviet). In this shift "the people" remained a *representation* – there are no *direct* democracies in mass-scale societies. In his *Politics*, Aristotle (350 BCE: 7.4) confined the size of a state governed by direct democracy to "the largest number which suffices for the purposes of life, and can be taken in at a single view." Some representative democracies do retain elements of direct democracy – contemporary examples include the State of California and the Confederation of Switzerland, both of which use plebiscites to decide specific issues of policy on a regular basis. Many other countries use referenda as well as general elections. But for routine government, the overwhelming majority of nation-states use representation; direct plebiscites are the exception.

Instead, "the people" themselves are "textualized" via a series of mechanisms both directly political (e.g. foundational "representation of the people" acts) and mediated; i.e. "the press" as both representative and representation of the public ("the fourth estate"). The further that suffrage was extended – eventually to become more or less universal – the more a democratic polity needed a universal medium of communication that linked *rule* with *rights* – active political representatives and economic leaders with the formally sovereign voters, and vice versa. The only mechanisms to come anywhere near this ideal were the pulpit and the press; and in an era of secular, scientific empiricism where truth was held to reside in objective facts rather than revealed faith, and where in any case competition among religious sects meant that there was never a time when just one sect could prevail over all the others, the fact-hungry press quickly attained universal supremacy as the intermediary between "the people" and their representatives in politics, government, and business.

Nevertheless, sovereign citizens were not directly involved in the arts of business and government, and the daily run of news events was often of little intrinsic interest to the general population. It was therefore necessary for the press to find reliable techniques for getting lay people to attend to them and to follow issues that bored or repelled them. The trick of getting uncommitted non-professionals to read things they don't want to know about should not be underestimated, but success in achieving it is a precondition for media power. It always must come first. As Lord Beaverbrook pointed out to the Royal Commission on the Press in the 1940s, there was no point in owning a newspaper, even if one's intention was to use it for proprietorial propaganda, as was the case with his *Daily Express*, unless it was in a "thoroughly good financial position": he said, "in order to make the propaganda effective the paper had to be successful" (Royal Commission 1948: para. 8660). Such success was at least partly in the hands of the readers themselves, who did not put up with everything that was thrown at them, no matter how powerful and manipulative the "regime" of ownership and control. It became imperative to know what sovereign citizens *liked*, what they thought, and how they would act. Three great questions of commercial democracies needed answers, every day anew:

- *Will they vote* (for me)?
- *Will they buy* (this product or message)?
- *Will they riot* (against what)?

A range of intermediate agencies developed, including pollsters, circulation auditors and media monitors, publicists and marketing firms, whose purpose was to gauge public opinion and advise both commercial and political clients on how (and whether) their campaigns were "playing in Peoria." From political propaganda to celebrity endorsement, they were on hand to monitor and manage the risky interface between popular entertainment and public affairs. As can be gauged by the wealth and influence of the sector and the prominence of its successful practitioners, these intermediaries remain at the heart of the democratic process. They produce the polls, ratings, circulation figures, charts – and now the direct votes – that take the daily temperature of the demos; what's hot, and what's not.

Consumption and Citizenship

If "democratainment" (Hartley 1999) can be found in sitcoms, then public participation in the democratic process is not confined to TV "election specials" with entertaining pedagogic devices like Bob McKenzie's cardboard "swingometer," introduced in 1955 and still in use in UK elections, now wielded electronically by Peter Snow.[1] It extends through to the deep bedrock of television entertainment, linking the top of society with the bottom; right down to children's shows that teach citizenly values – my example was Nickelodeon's *Clarissa Explains It All*, but the whole point about that show is that there's nothing special about it: check out *Daria* or *The Simpsons* in the animated format; or *Dead Like Me* and *What I Like About You* in live comedy-drama.

Perhaps the reason that political science remained skeptical about the civic attributes of television entertainment was that the latter was seen as "mere" consumption. Modernist politics was never very comfortable with "the consumer" as opposed to "the citizen" – perversely hanging on to the idea that the consumer was an *effect* of commercial or political manipulation while the citizen was a *cause* of the political process, despite the fact that consumers and citizens were sited within the same corporeal persons. Throughout the modern period that contradiction was masked by gendering it. Citizens were imagined as activist (read masculine), rational individuals participating in the democratic process, guided by the press and political parties, while consumers were feminized as housewives at home who read "lifestyle" magazines for purposeless private pleasure, which nevertheless guided their choices in the supermarket. Out of the blokey mate-ship of citizenship were forged such heroic attributes as national identity and the public sphere, with "civil society" represented by news media that militantly mythologized their own status as watchdogs of the democratic process. This was the ground cultivated by political science. The private and feminized world of consumption was seen as *behavior* not *action*. It was barely recognized as part of the political process at all. Instead it was seen as the effect of manipulation by marketing; of "government" by private enterprise not public institutions. But it was here in this unworthy place that media studies pitched its analytical tent. Small wonder that there's little interdisciplinary traffic between political science and media studies, although the idea has grown that public communication requires engagement and "affect" as well as information and evidence, as participation in the formal mechanism of politics has dropped, especially in the USA.

Plebiscitary Industries – A Paradigm Shift

Modern expertise: reducing culture to number

The statistical and marketing experts serving the cultural industries have long learnt how to convert *consumer preferences* into *measurable scale* via TV ratings (there are also ratings agencies for non-broadcast media like outdoor advertising), audited circulation figures (for newspapers and magazines), or sales (of theatrical and cinema admissions, recorded music charts, software, and games). Popularity being the key to advertising dollars, sophisticated mechanisms have evolved to measure the number of eyeballs in front of which a given bit of content may have passed, down to the minute or less.

Some of these techniques of measurement have become established as general currency among competing distributors and network providers. In countries where consumer choice is well established as a market principle it is important to establish a yardstick by which to measure success, otherwise companies have no agreed mark against which to compete with each other. This is especially the case in the creative industries such as broadcasting and publishing where consumer choice is essentially arbitrary. The "use-value" of cultural commodities is novelty, so the economic value of a given title or product can change from bomb to blockbuster (and vice versa), sometimes overnight. "Modern" consumers drive innovation indirectly but essentially unpredictably – simply by changing their minds about what they like. Agreed measurement techniques reduce unpredictability and therefore assist creative producers and distributors to manage risk.

In countries or periods where agencies dedicated to the neutral measurement of consumer choice do not exist or are poorly developed (historically in the West; currently in China) or are not agreed among competitors, the consumer market may be corrupted by false circulation claims, by confusion, or by the intervention of non-market values such as official approval for products that consumers don't actually like (and disapproval for things they do like). So these agencies are vital to level the playing field for a "free market" to perform fairly. But it does need to be emphasized that this is exactly what they are for. The expert agencies that measure consumer preferences in modernity work for industry, not for consumers directly. They cluster around the media of distribution, not the audience. In short the modern cultural industries have managed to turn consumer choice into a representation for their own purposes – a textual form upon which interested parties can agree in order to compete with each other.

Representative ratings

Given that audiences don't directly purchase a good deal of cultural content such as TV programs, "the bottom line" is not sales but *ratings* – the textual form taken by consumers in the creative and cultural sphere. In order to be able to claim accuracy ratings agencies must turn culture into numbers. Individual people fill in diaries of their media use, or they answer survey questions, or they express preferences in test screenings, or they talk in focus groups. These are all "textual" activities that, by the use of complex not to say arcane methods (the more "sophisticated" the better, because the *method* is the agency's intellectual property or IP), are turned into ratings. Technological developments like the PeopleMeter seek to reduce culture to numbers even further, and to make the role of the consumer yet more passive, but as soon as digital media took off the PeopleMeter was found to be inadequate even by its inventor TNS (Taylor Nelson Sofres). Its numbers "missed" much of the consumer's desirable culture and activity, like internet use.

Ratings agencies must persuade interested parties, from governments to TV networks, that their numbers "count." They must have the power to command those whose very livelihoods, share price, and companies depend on them. Such power has been achieved by borrowing scientific methods, to reduce the built-in ambivalence of culture and textuality as much as possible by representing them numerically. The widespread trust that is placed in quantitative methods is itself a symptom of the modern scientific paradigm. But it only goes so far, because while the *method* must be quantitative the actual *numbers* need to be kept within practical and affordable limits. So quantity meets its opposite in the concept of the "generalizable sample" (where generality = large number; sample = small number). Ratings samples are surprisingly small – Nielsen TV ratings are based on the viewing practices of around 5,000 households in the USA. Samples are typically only 1,000 elsewhere. Despite the sophisticated efforts of ratings agencies and social scientists to ensure the statistical accuracy of such samples, faith in their truthfulness to cultural life has badly eroded, even among academic experts (see Mittell 2005; J. Gray 2005, quoted at the end of this chapter).

During a modern era of representative democracy, such methods may have appeared democratic; certainly they aroused no widespread opposition, even though a constant low-level warfare continued among rival ratings systems and technologies, and between broadcasters and those among their audiences who didn't feel themselves to be represented (including perhaps many academics and intellectuals). They worked because they were useful to high-investment players in government and business, and were accepted by broadcasters and advertisers whose profits and costs rose and fell with the numbers.

Among consumers themselves, ratings can only work when everyone accepts the logic of the regime of "representative democracy." We must all be able to say: "This show is crud but I can see why it is on TV if n-million people like it (even though I don't know anyone personally who does)." Or in the immortal words of Australia's federal communications minister, senator Bob Collins (Labor), during the run-up to the launch of pay-TV in Australia: "If people want to pay to watch crud, that is what will be broadcast to them. I'm not going to put myself in a position of telling them they cannot have crud if crud is what they want . . . If pay TV doesn't provide consumers with what they want, it will go broke" (*Green Left Weekly* 1992). Such acceptance requires quite a few acts of faith, including the restriction of what is meant by "consumers" to "people in this country and timeslot," and a willingness to be governed by the "will of the national majority" in matters of taste.

As the epoch of modern representative media segues into the era of direct digital participation, both of these preconditions are now fatally undermined. Ever since BitTorrent inaugurated what Mark Pesce calls "hyperdistribution" (Pesce 2005), TV content is increasingly available beyond the confines of broadcasting, and beyond the domestic market. Consumers may avoid (other people's) "crud" altogether. This opens TV up to new business plans not based on "mass" communication to passive consumers but on niche marketing, the "long tail," and customization for consumers who aren't just active but activist.

Even where such action is minimal, such as clicking a computer mouse, it can be traced. Agencies can convert the "clickstream" of myriad users into what they call "robust data" – making the mechanical act of choice into a "plebiscite." Combine what is already known about consumer choice at the "representative" or expert level – via *surveys* – with what can now be known directly – via *servers* – and you have the conditions of existence for the plebiscitary industries.

Most of the organizations in the plebiscitary industries are also active in some other capacity – commercializing voting is not all that they do. They are forming on the site of the agencies they are in the processes of supplanting, popping up *ad hoc* as technological opportunity or entrepreneurial instincts allow. They combine all three "new economy" levels of infrastructure, connectivity, and content. They range across the fields of telecommunications, broadcasting, and broadband. They use the skills – the dark arts, some might say – of marketing, publicity, surveying, and opinion polling, as well as those of production and broadcasting, applied to the global market in entertainment media. It is from among these existing "representative" agencies that internet-savvy "early adopters" have developed new plebiscitary possibilities using digital platforms. So the new plebiscitary industries are forming around technical and professional innovators who can exploit globally connected networks, massive computational power and software wizardry. Their products and services range from data mining and mobile aggregating to electronic polling, multinational participant TV to pop charts. While most of these skills and professions were honed in the "analog" era of representative politics and mass entertainment, the plebiscitary industries extend them to the internet, mobile platforms, and e-democracy.

Behind all this apparently random activity and opportunism, something more patterned can be discerned. The contemporary era is dedicated to the proposition that sovereignty is evenly distributed among a population (that's what the universal franchise and even "the free market" is meant to express). No longer can an expert determine on "our" behalf what is good, right, beautiful, or true. Those decisions belong to the populace. It follows that truth itself can only assume its traditional power to command once it has been sampled, bundled, scaled up, processed, and re-presented in the form of a plebiscite.

If it is the case that a paradigm shift is under way that sources sovereignty, meaning, and even truth to myriad consumers rather than to god-like author-producers or to modernist scientific-age experts, then it is imperative to develop reliable measures to find out what they mean. The numbers of people involved mean that you can't collect individual choices one by one, so you have to bundle them up. It's a specialist job, and it is only now becoming a practical possibility with computational power measured by the petabyte.

Reality TV with voting as entertainment is a symptom of the shift to the plebiscite as the preferred methodology of our era for revealing what anything might mean. So are the endlessly proliferating charts telling us what is best and worst of a given category. These judgments are not based on the god-like taste of a judge or the intrinsic qualities of an object as revealed by scientific or professional expertise, but on the vote of the punters.

Plebiscitary Formats – Reality TV

Reality TV – a matter of talent, mostly: America's Next Top Model

Not all reality TV formats are plebiscitary (yet). A good example of one that is not is *America's Next Top Model* (*ANTM*), created, produced, and hosted by Tyra Banks. The reality aspect is that the contestants must perform various modeling-related tasks throughout the series, where they – and viewers – are introduced to the real world of fashion shows and commercial photography.

Tyra Banks enjoyed a successful career as a top international model, which lent credibility to the format, but fashion values were not in fact ascendant on *ANTM*. Despite the "top model" tagline, it was not primarily looking for a contestant who would win acceptance in the international fashion world. The appeal of the show rested heavily on its qualities as "good television." Compare the *real* "next top model" during the same period (2003–5): Australian teenager Gemma Ward. She was discovered in the audience for the Perth heats of *Search for a Supermodel* in 2002, aged 15, where she'd gone to support a friend. She was persuaded to enter the competition herself, but went no further than her hometown heats, where she was one of 20 finalists. She didn't make it to the national finals or on to the international competition for Ford Models' *Supermodel of the World*. However, a photograph of her taken in Perth ended up on a desk at IMG in New York and her career took off. Described by the scout who spotted her as "surreal, beautiful, very European, wide-set eyes, angelic, not a skerrick of make-up," there has never been a contestant like her on *America's Next Top Model*.[2] Instead, contestants of non-standard height or build (compared with the look favored by "directional designers") were overrepresented among finalists, as were women of color, either because Tyra wanted to make a point about their aptitude and beauty, or because such contestants were thought to represent aspirations among the target audience demographic, or both.

America's Next Top Model is a perhaps a late example of reality TV as a *closed expert system*. The role of the audience is merely to like it or lump it; take it or leave it. Each week the young woman chosen for elimination, and also the eventual winner, was selected by an expert panel in a process not shown to viewers, although it seemed to have been heavily influenced by Tyra herself. Neither the viewer nor the fashion world played any direct part in deciding the outcome. Not surprisingly then, finalists and winners tended to emerge from reality (or soap-opera) values: authentic self-expression, overcoming adversity, personal growth during the series, eye candy, coping with tests and with the competitive dynamics and dramas of the group, willingness to confess the self. Human values and personal conflict were foregrounded, as was the upstaging dominance of Tyra Banks herself, who was simultaneously the contestants' role-model, soul-sister, and executioner, the best moments being when she enfolds someone whom she has just excoriated and eliminated in a motherly, teary hug. Not surprisingly as the series went through further "cycles" it focused ever more obsessively on the real TV "expert" – Tyra – who launched a daytime chat show along the way. *ANTM*'s eventual winners gravitated toward US-based TV careers, not to international fashion, where young Gemma Ward (among innumerable Eastern European and Brazilian teenagers) blithely reigned supreme.

Plebiscitary TV: Eurovision Song Contest

Plebiscitary TV shows are those that find a way to make voting and viewers' choices a part of the show, influencing the outcome of stories or events like a character in the plot. The plebiscite has shifted from industry tool to creative content and become a prominent feature of the entertainment package itself, notably (although not only) in reality formats, from *Big Brother* to *Mongolian Cow Sour Yoghurt Super Voice Girl*.

Plebiscitary television was kick-started by the wide availability of mobile phones and the cheap cost of SMS messaging. Previously, "representative" voting (by panels) had played its part in variety entertainment, for instance in *Juke Box Jury* (BBC, 1959–67) and *Thank Your Lucky Stars* (ITV, 1961–6). The former used celebrity panelists to vote a song a hit or a miss. The latter went a step further by introducing representatives of the target demographic, in the shape of guest teenagers who rated recent singles on a scale of one to five. Most famous was Midlands schoolgirl Janice Nicholls, "a 16 year old Black Country lass," who "became a star overnight when she uttered the immortal words 'Oi'll give it foive'. She remained on the panel for three years and the phrase became part of British colloquial language."[3]

While most such shows have long since disappeared, the *Eurovision Song Contest* has carried on for over 50 years (since 1955). One of its principal attractions is the vote, where a panel from each participant country (they have grown from 10 to 39) scores all of the others from "nul points" to 12.[4] This practice is prey to nationalist sentiment among other biases; for instance, Cyprus was notorious for always awarding maximum points to Greece and the minimum to Turkey (who both returned the favor). The Benelux, Nordic, and Eastern European countries were suspected of voting *en bloc* too. Germany never wins (except once in 1982), despite being Europe's largest country with the most enthusiastic voters (see table 7.1, pp. 140–1). And some progressive countries like Sweden criticized the "backward" musical tastes of New European countries across the Baltic Sea. Under the Eurovision kitsch there always simmered political, or rather national, rivalries (for instance when Great Britain awarded Abba "nul points" for "Waterloo" in 1974). The voting system was constantly modified to minimize them.

Thus Eurovision adopted interactive and audience-participation technologies as they became available. In 1998, as soon as it was technically feasible (though not all participant countries had the infrastructure for it), "televoting" was introduced as a complement to panel voting.[5] That year, though not necessarily as a result, the contest was won by Israeli transsexual diva Dana International. The contest was streamed over the internet from 2000, and by 2004 "centralized televoting" was installed, resulting in over four million votes being cast during 10-minute live windows in the semi-final and final. The plebiscite had become the pleasure.

Talent shows as presidential election campaigns:
American/Australian/Pop Idol

Talent contests like the *Eurovision Song Contest* are a hybrid between the true plebiscite and previous "representative" or "expert systems" formats, because they combine viewer voting with judging panels. The latter can occasionally override the popular vote, just as the Electoral College sometimes does in US presidential elections, most recently in 2000. (It also happened in the Australian version of *Dancing with the Stars*. The event sparked widespread press controversy; see chapter 10 below.)

The *Idol* family of shows marks a definite shift away from traditional musical talent shows like *Pot of Gold*, *New Faces*, and *Young Talent Time*. Comments by professional judges about the aesthetic, commercial, and talent aspects of contestants' performance are designed to guide viewer choice: like others, this is (as they used to say about authoritarian regimes in South East Asia) a "guided democracy" where "leadership"

Table 7.1 The pleasure of the plebiscite: Eurovision televoting (2004–6)
(a) Televotes for the 2004 Eurovision Song Contest by country

Country	Calls made[a]	Overall place
Germany	1,061,049	8
Switzerland	503,627	Semi-final
Great Britain (UK)	415,558	16
Sweden	294,828	6
Austria	284,902	21
Greece	192,564	3
Netherlands	158,559	20
Denmark	136,769	Semi-final
Turkey	121,008	4
Cyprus	117,751	5
Russia	96,955	11
Bosnia and Herzegovina	95,062	9
Norway	81,278	24
Belgium	76,123	22
Poland	72,295	17
Slovenia	61,844	Semi-final
France	54,495	15
FYR Macedonia	47,599	14
Iceland	46,310	19
Finland	45,952	Semi-final
Latvia	40,453	Semi-final
Croatia	40,220	13
Spain	39,005	10
Ireland	36,998	23
Estonia	34,615	Semi-final
Serbia and Montenegro	20,909	2
Lithuania	19,627	Semi-final
Belarus	16,204	Semi-final
Israel	14,297	Semi-final
Malta	12,392	12
Romania	11,698	18
Portugal	8,597	Semi-final
Ukraine	4,323	1
Andorra	3,003	Semi-final
Albania	812	7
Monaco	110	Semi-final
Total calls[a]	4,267,791	

Source: www.eurovision.tv/english/1182.html; see also en.wikipedia.org/wiki/
Eurovision_Song_Contest_2004.
[a] Not including SMS votes.

Table 7.1 (*cont'd*)

(b) Eurovision Song Contest: televoting by year

	2004	2005	2006
Calls	4,551,698[a]	3,892,330	4,312,155
SMS	2,631,177	2,662,975	4,228,169
Total votes	7,182,875	6,555,305	8,540,324

Source: www.eurovision.tv/content/view/174/155.

[a] Figure does not tally with total by country, but both were listed on the Eurovision site.

plays a strong role. Expert advice is still seen as necessary, not least perhaps because the successful contestant wins a recording contract, so attention needs to be paid to commercial realities. However, the relative autonomy of the viewing experience (human values) from the commercial imperative (musical appeal) is demonstrated by the fact that several *Idol* losers have gone on to more successful recording careers than their season's winners.

Effectively, each *Idol* series is a 12- or 13-week election campaign. The rhythm of the campaign follows that of an American presidential election. Early rounds parallel the open primaries, where devoted fans (like registered party members) whittle down the candidates to two. These contest the ultimate goal via a large-scale, national election in the final episode. If all goes well the finale will attract a much larger audience than the "primaries," and all "citizens of media" within this population are able to vote (putting aside questions of literacy and access that plague all elections), whether they are "party members" (loyal viewers) or not.

The perception that the winner of *Idol* is the contestant with the most votes is integral to the *Idol* format. Plebiscitary service providers have sprung up to conduct the vote and keep it clean. For instance, a company called Telescope Inc. managed the mechanics of the SMS voting for *American Idol* on behalf of FremantleMedia (producer) and Fox (broadcaster).[6]

As in presidential elections, hanging chads notwithstanding,[7] the process itself is subjected to close scrutiny. Indeed, viewers grew cynical about the legitimacy of *Idol*'s voting process:

- Fans were concerned about phone-line congestion – in the 2003 season phone companies recorded 100 million+ calls, Fox recorded 24 million votes.
- Auto-diallers potentially skewed the vote by enabling some viewers to find an open line to vote through, while simultaneously contributing to line congestion.
- There was evidence AT&T digital text-message votes had a greater chance of getting through than landline phone votes (Higgins & Seibel 2004: 1).

The latter issue seemed to indicate phone-company opportunism, because phone lines were tariff free while SMS voting was charged at 10c a message.[8] Deborah Starr Seibel argued that the phone-line problems reduced the democratic nature of *Idol*. The winner was chosen only by those who could get through, not all those who wanted to vote. Fan discontent was registered in discussions online and in complaints to the FCC (Federal Communications Commission) and Fox:

> The FCC has received more than a thousand complaints (69 emails sent to the FCC directly, 1,140 sent to Fox and copied to the FCC) about legitimate *Idol* voting. Most of them are from last season and center on the inability of Aiken fans to get through. The agency doesn't make public whether it is considering a formal investigation. But the trigger for such an investigation, according to the FCC's Rosemary Kimball, would be clear evidence of the show's intentionally "fixing" the numbers. (Seibel 2004: 1)

The *Idol* format "enacts" the process of democratic choice by following the rhythms of real election campaigns, but it also introduces a new character into broadcast entertainment – "the vote." This is like the old anarchist slogan: "it doesn't matter who you vote for, the government gets in." In this case it doesn't matter which contestant you vote for, or even what motivates your choice. What matters is that the show cannot come to a conclusion without a vote, and the viewer "at home" (or on the mobile) is complicit in that vote even if they don't exercise it. Viewers become "actors" on one side of the screen, while contestants (as viewers' proxies) are "actors" on the other. The vote itself is a *narrative force* – like a traditional fairy godmother or *deus ex machina*. Without it the wish-fulfillment elements, which are largely the point of the show, can't be fulfilled. *Idol*'s format insists that the fame and celebrity enjoyed by winners belongs to the consumer, because it is the *act* of the scaled-up viewer that produces both plot development and narrative closure.

More votes than the president: Mongolian Cow Sour Yoghurt
Super Voice Girl

The *Mongolian Cow Sour Yoghurt Super Voice Girl Contest*, produced
by Hunan Satellite TV in South Central Hunan Province for their
Entertainment Channel, was an open singing contest.[9] The 2005 version was one of the most-viewed programs in the history of Chinese
television. The *International Herald Tribune* reported more than 400
million tuned in for the finals in August (Barboza 2005). *The Times*
reported that the figure exceeded the estimated 400 million who
watched the *Chinese New Year Festival Gala* on CCTV, but pointed out
that no official figures were available. However, it was able to show
how greatly *Super Voice Girl* outstripped Western audiences:

- Australia: 3.3 million watched *Australian Idol* (2003 final)
- UK: *Pop Idol* topped 12 million (2003 final)
- US: Nearly 48 million watched *American Idol* (2004 final)
- India: *Indian Idol* hit 48 million. (Macartney 2005)

The plebiscitary element of the show was unprecedented in China. Over
eight million votes (or "messages of support" – the term "vote" was
avoided) were cast by mobile phone for the three finalists (Marquand
2005). These participatory statistics were widely reported, as were the
economic implications of the show. Danwei.org, for instance, carried
a commentary by Li Yu:

> *Supergirl* is a money game. Income from mobile phone SMS topped
> 30 million yuan (US$3.7 million); naming rights took 1.4 million yuan
> (US$173,000); the seven commercial spots during the finals pushed 20
> million (US$2.47 million); and printing pictures of "supergirls" on T-shirts,
> accessories, toys and other items had immense potential – production ended
> up somewhere north of several million yuan. Experts have calculated that
> the *Supergirl* brand by itself is worth at least 100 million yuan (US$12.3
> million). When a *Super Voice Girl* can bring in this sort of cash, how can
> we not submit? (Li 2005)

One of the things that appealed to viewers about *Super Voice Girl* was
that anyone (except boys) could go on the show, regardless of talent,
looks, or aptitude. The initial number of hopeful contestants topped
150,000. Many were ordinary girls without singing skills who just
wanted their "15 minutes of fame" on TV. The whole thing *felt* democratic to participants and viewers alike. The eventual winner, Li Yuchun

Figure 7.1 Li Yuchun – *Mongolian Cow Sour Yoghurt Super Girl* (2005).
Photo: Getty Images

(see figure 7.1), was a surprising alternative to the beauty-school types
and Canto-popettes who are generally endorsed as pop singers in China
(Marquand 2005; Yardley 2005). *The Economist* opined: "*Super Girl*
. . . appealed mainly because of its racy format . . . and the pleasure that many
enjoy from watching amateur singers embarrass themselves. Rebellious
young women apparently identified with the self-confident and boyish-
looking winner, Li Yuchun" (*Economist* 2005). *Time Asia* reported:

> The Li Yuchun phenomenon, however, goes far beyond her voice, which
> even the most ardent fans admit is pretty weak: her vocal range drifts between
> Cher territory and that place your little brother's voice went the summer
> before seventh grade. As a dancer, she's not much better. . . . What Li
> did possess was attitude, originality and a proud androgyny that defied
> Chinese norms. . . . For an audience reared on the bubble-gum, lip-gloss
> standards of Chinese girl pop, Li's disregard for the rule book produced
> an unfamiliar knee-weakening. Her fans wept openly and frantically
> shrieked when Li took the stage. (Jakes 2005)

The *Age* also commented on the winner's appearance in emancipationist terms, reporting that Li's "transgender appeal" suggested to some

Chinese observers that her win: "signalled that men could no longer dictate how women should dress and look. Li Yinhe, China's best-known researcher on gender issues, likened her appeal to that of Boy George or Michael Jackson" (McDonald 2005a).

One of Li Yuchun's winnings was to be invited to London to join the lord mayor, "Red" Ken Livingstone, to celebrate Chinese New Year 2005. As the *People's Daily* put it, she inaugurated "the largest celebration of Chinese culture" in London and performed to a "large crowd" of shoppers.[10]

The degree to which *Super Voice Girl* resonated with people was reported to have unsettled the government's propaganda leaders. Fans crowded shopping centers holding posters of their favorite contestant in an attempt to raise votes. Unruly fans caused security guards to be called into one shopping center. Some songs were "raunchy" in early rounds, although song choice in the finals bowed to official sensibilities: they included "folk songs, communist favorites and Western numbers such as *The Colour of My Love* by Celine Dion, and Ricky Martin's *Maria*" (*Economist*, October 9, 2005). Apparently the show's appeal was not confined to the masses. The *Christian Science Monitor* reported: "Even older Chinese have been caught up in the show. One high-ranking minister who was hosting a lengthy business reception scheduled to last until 9 p.m. was suddenly missing at 8 p.m. on Friday night. Sources close to the minister noted that *Super Girl* started at 8:30 p.m." (Marquand 2005). As soon as the popular success of the series became apparent, speculation surfaced that future series would be cancelled. Officials criticized the show for being too "worldly," for being vulgar, boorish, "and lacking social responsibility" (Macartney 2005). CCTV, the main state-run TV network, was particularly critical. "Technically, CCTV officials can shut down *Super Girl*, since they hold a monopoly position on broadcast decisions." But a rat was smelt: "Many ordinary Chinese say that it won't be worldliness that prompts any shutdown, but the fact that CCTV's advertising revenue on Friday night was lower than that of its modest Hunan competitor. A pilot of an official version of *Super Girl* produced by CCTV reportedly failed" (Marquand 2005).

Western media like the *New York Times* noted that "Unlike China's leader, Hu Jintao, Ms. Li was popularly elected" (Yardley 2005), celebrating the program as a democratic incursion into China. As *Time Asia* put it: "like *American Idol*, but unlike China itself, *Super Girl's Voice* is run democratically." The *Economist* reported as "frank" a front-page headline in *Beijing Today* that read: "Is *Super Girl* a Force for Democracy?"

An article circulating on official websites in China suggested the contest had caused Chinese intellectuals to "fantasise about arrangements for democratic elections and notice the awakening of democratic consciousness among the younger generation" (*Economist* 2005). Australian papers labeled the program "cultural democracy":

> The country's media experts have been transfixed as much by the program's formula as by the outcome. Some labeled the show "vulgar" and called for more classical shows of culture on TV, but the well known critic Zhu Dake said the show had "blazed a trail for cultural democracy." It showed the public breaking loose from the "elitist aesthetics" strangling China's entertainment industry, he told the *China Daily*. (McDonald 2005b)

But in Danwei.org, Li Yu remained skeptical about its democratic potential:

> Some people have said that Chinese people have poured their enthusiasm for voting into *Super Voice Girl*. Commentaries with titles like *The Civic Awareness in the Supergirl Selection Process*, *Super Voice Girl and Civil Society*, *Super Voice Girl and the Construction of a Democratic System*, and *Rays of Idealism in the Super Voice Girl Selection Process* have poured forth. *Super Voice Girl* has become "the dawn of civic society." But can *Super Voice Girl* really carry such a large burden? (Li 2005)

The *China Daily* pondered: "How come an imitation of a democratic system ends up selecting the singer who has the least ability to carry a tune?" The *Economist* (2005) had a ready reply: "That, of course, is democracy."

Reality president: American Candidate

Eventually reality entertainment and real politics had to collide, which they did via *American Candidate*. The original idea for the show (by FX) was to make a documentary that followed a young candidate who hoped to run for president in 2012. In the reality version it became a political *American Idol*, where viewers were to choose a candidate who would then enter into the upcoming presidential election. The plan was for a candidate to be chosen and then left to run for office with their own cash, but that idea was dumped. The concept was picked up by Showtime, who ran it as a fake presidential election (Franklin 2004).

However, *American Candidate* was not democratically run, even by reality TV standards:

The winner receives $200,000 and what host Montel Williams vaguely calls "a chance to address the nation." Too bad viewers don't get to vote till the series' last two weeks. Up to that point, each episode includes some sort of campaign challenge (a straw poll here, a focus group there), and the two competitors who perform least impressively must face off in an "elimination debate." The loser is determined by a vote of the other candidates. Sad to say, that makes *American Candidate* less democratic than *American Idol.* (*People* 2004)

A Christian lobby group got behind the eventual winner, as has been known in real political elections. Nevertheless, *American Candidate* attracted the support of some activists because it went where real politicians feared to tread. The *Advocate* described it as "part civics lesson, part *Survivor*," praising it for "reserving spots in the cast for an openly gay man and a lesbian." The article explored some of the intersections between the program and formal politics in the US:

Showtime has placed its bets on *American Candidate* because the American electorate is extremely polarized and attentive to anything political at the moment – even if it is a fictional reality show. Gephardt and Boykin [gay/lesbian candidates on the show] both say they probably wouldn't run for the real presidency because candidates are placed in fishbowls and every detail of their lives are picked apart. However, the 2004 Bush–Kerry race is never far from their minds. Like most politically active gay men and lesbians, they are pained by the attempts by George W. Bush and the Republican Party to gaybait voters. Meanwhile, they are not pleased that Democratic presidential nominee John Kerry does not support marriage rights for same-sex couples. (Graham 2004)

Chrissy Gephardt, a lesbian "American Candidate" interviewed in the *Advocate* article, said that the show made politics interesting by adding a *Survivor* edge to it:

They put an entertainment factor in it – sort of like a *Survivor*-type elimination process, and it combines entertainment and politics. If it was just politics, it would be CNN or C-SPAN. They've made it interesting with character development, which makes for a good story. We're more than just candidates; they do a bio on us and talk about who we are as people. The audience becomes engaged by our life stories. (quoted in Graham 2004: 49–50)

Reality TV – and its audience – have still to confront the problems associated with getting what you wanted, including a "democratic process" that produces "unworthy" winners like singers who can't sing or candidates with reprehensible views. However, for just this reason, the same urge that drives activists to make the real political process as transparent and open as possible also motivates the plebiscitary format on television. In the long run it's an urge to introduce something like "direct representation" (Coleman 2005); in the meantime it drives the demand (on pain of ratings) that producers make the voting process as least as fair as it is in *American Idol*, or in the state of Florida, come to that.

Mirror, mirror on the wall, which is the purest plebiscite of them all? Big Brother

Big Brother, now venerable in television terms, remains the purest of the reality TV plebiscites, because viewers vote for (or rather against) contestants on the basis of what Martin Luther King Jr called "the content of their character." Musical or other talents, no matter how dubious, are not the criteria for survival or success. In short, *Big Brother* is a polity.

Claims of "political disengagement" are frequently made by political scientists in the language of crisis, and it is usually said to be the voters, particularly younger citizens, who are disengaged from politics. People are blamed for failing in their civic obligations. But Stephen Coleman (2003) suggests that an alternative perspective would put the boot on the other foot. Political elites and agencies have distanced themselves from the citizen, who is nevertheless still the root of democracy. In this scenario it would be very unwise to assume that "the demos" is disengaged from democracy. Instead, the formal apparatus of politics and government has disengaged from the demos.

Coleman identified a decline in voting rates; a decline in participation in broader political activities such as joining political parties; and a decline in watching news and reading newspapers, especially political commentary. He also found that people trust politicians less to represent the public interest ahead of party interest. Most respondents, particularly those under 30, showed decreasing faith in the efficacy of the legal or formal aspects of government (Coleman 2003).

While these figures seem to suggest a drift away from politics, they may equally indicate that people want to participate but are averse to the available "technologies" of participation, including elections. One indicator that people are willing to vote – and even to pay for the privilege

– is plebiscitary television. The numbers do not suggest disengagement from *voting*, only from *politics*.

Does it follow that those who do vote in reality TV shows are interested only in mundane or trivial things? No; Coleman's study demonstrates quite forcefully that fans are interested in mainstream political issues without participating in political processes. Their participation in *Big Brother* votes is driven by a different mode of engagement. Coleman suggests that those who vote in *Big Brother* employ a form of emotional intelligence to assess candidates. Four general features were admired:

- honesty,
- the ability to get on in the world,
- cleverness, and
- the ability to be witty and amusing.

Honesty emerged as a predictive quality, especially when it related to perceived authenticity: those who were seen as honest were generally considered to possess an authenticity and they were usually not voted out. The qualities of politicians were compared against the same scale. The same hierarchy applied to them. Again, consistency of values was not as important as honesty.

In a study of the 2005 UK general election, Coleman came to the radical conclusion that the decline in political voting is itself a political act, and that if anyone is to rectify this democratic deficit they need to learn from *Big Brother* – literally:

> The irony of contemporary democracy is the dependence of the *demos* upon ventriloquized forms of representation. As politics becomes more technocratic and instrumental it has less to do with contested values and becomes more like an ongoing audition of competing management teams. The public find this uninspiring. They vote less, watch less and join in less. They are not just politically disengaged; they disengage as a political act.
>
> Occasionally, however, the public see flashes of themselves: on phone-in shows; in home-made films; talking to one another in web fora; and in reality TV formats. The public are not so naïve as to imagine that these glimpses encapsulate the whole picture of who they are and how they live. But even limited self-recognition is appreciated. . . . The immense popularity of reality TV formats of many kinds is linked to this desire of the public to witness themselves as a central actor in their own drama. Such witnessing, and being witnessed, is the key missing ingredient of contemporary democracy, and it is here that political communication

could derive its most interesting lessons from *Big Brother's* relationship with its audience. (Coleman 2006: 476)

Voting in *Big Brother* measures contestants' achievement on an emotional scale, rather than by assessing natural talents, as in programs such as *Idol* or *Dancing with the Stars*, where the relative merits of an individual performance can be judged against others. However, one of the attractions of *Dancing with the Stars* is to follow the embarrassments and improvements of those who – like many of the audience at home – can't dance very well. Thus good dancers are often eliminated before celebrities who can't dance but are "up for it" when it comes to trying. In other words, emotional attachment, authenticity, and honesty pay off even in talent-based plebiscites.

The thrill of voting has been claimed as part of the appeal of successful shows. Discussing the short window of opportunity *American Idol* voters have to cast their vote, Fox Networks Group president Tony Vinciquerra argued the window "increases the excitement for the show" by offering participation in "the most democratic way – it's first come, first served" (Higgins & Seibel 2004).

"So what if he wore a leotard?" Celebrity Big Brother

Politics and reality TV were literally "con-fused" when a British Member of Parliament entered the *Big Brother* house for the fourth series of *Celebrity Big Brother* in January 2006. George Galloway, serving MP for Bethnal Green and Bow in London, already had a colorful reputation as a politician, having been a Labour MP in his native Scotland. He was expelled from the Labour Party in 2003 for his opposition to the Iraq war, but won in 2005 the London seat for "Respect" (an alliance based on the Socialist Workers Party), defeating high-profile Blairite MP Oona King (one of the UK's few black MPs) by 800 votes. Galloway was a long-term supporter of the Palestinian cause and had a strong track record as a firebrand speaker "on the anti-imperialist left," supporting Pakistani claims in Kashmir and taking an interest in Libya and the Arab–Israeli conflict. His notoriety became global when he was accused of benefiting from the UN oil-for-food program in Iraq and he appeared in front of a US Senate committee in 2005 to deny the corruption allegations (to considerable "critical acclaim" from the blogosphere). Video of him meeting Saddam Hussein and his son Uday also circulated around the world.

Meanwhile, Galloway's performance as a voting parliamentarian was minimal. As Respect MP since 2005 he had the lowest possible voting record, being placed 634th out of 645 MPs. The 11 with lower voting records than himself were five Sinn Fein members (who don't take their seats), the speaker and his two deputies (who are ineligible to vote), two members who had died, and the prime minister.[11] During *Celebrity Big Brother* his sequestration in the BB house meant that he missed at least one vote in the House of Commons that directly concerned his own constituency.

It is clear from his views, his career, and his voting record that George Galloway retained little respect for traditional politics. He claimed that his sojourn in the BB house was an attempt to reach young people who were otherwise disengaged from politics, to speak up for Palestinian people, and to raise funds for a Palestinian charity. But it was not George Galloway the politician and philanthropist that viewers saw on *Celebrity Big Brother*, it was Galloway the narcissist and egoist. As with any other version of *Big Brother*, it was not his views or his intentions that interested viewers, it was his conduct and interaction with the housemates, which the newspapers agreed was "gripping and appalling in equal measure." His housemates variously described him as a "manipulative bully"; "two-faced"; "unworthy of respect"; "a wicked, wicked, wicked man"; and "as democratic as a Nazi" (*Independent*, January 26, 2006: 3).

Galloway's antics included various fancy-dress charades, provoking not only astonished reactions among viewers but also apoplectic articles (and sensational pictures) in the following day's newspapers. He dressed up as Dracula and Elvis, did an impression of a cat lapping pretend milk from actress Rula Lenska's hand, and donned a scarlet leotard to complete a task set by Big Brother: Galloway and transvestite singer Pete Burns (of 1980s band Dead or Alive) were told to express "the emotions of bewilderment when a small puppy won't come to you" through the medium of robotic dance (see figure 7.2, p. 152).

Soon after this, real voting took over: Galloway was evicted. The *Sun* was gleeful; vengeful: "Is this most hated man in Britain?" it asked (January 26, 2006), and sought to answer its own question in the affirmative:

Galloway . . . was last night booted out of the house to a chorus of jeers as:

- Young viewers he had hoped to attract by his participation in the show railed against him.

Figure 7.2   George Galloway MP and friend, *Celebrity Big Brother* (2006).
Photo: WENN

- A Radio 1 poll about his antics showed 92.5% of listeners despised him.
- Hordes of his constituents in Bethnal Green and Bow, East London, said they regretted backing him. . . .
- More than 25,000 Sun readers have now signed our petition calling for Galloway to be suspended from the Commons. (*Sun*, January 26, 2006: 4–5)

Notice how everyone was getting in on the plebiscitary act: Here were subsidiary plebiscites in the press and on radio to supplement the vote on *Celebrity Big Brother*. But note also that the latter had all too evidently been taken more seriously in straightforwardly political terms than Galloway's own parliamentary vote or his own constituency voters.

Was this a gain for democracy? Writing in the *Observer*, Nick Cohen lambasted the "liberals who think it's worse to appear on a TV show than in the court of a fascist tyrant" (January 15, 2006: 11). Tim Gardam, former director of television at Channel Four, wrote in the *Evening Standard*: "Big Brother is the great leveller; and Celebrity Big Brother has shown once again its true democratic virtues; one might argue that it is one of the most effective current affairs programmes on television" (January 19, 2006: 39). As former head of current affairs for the BBC and controller of news for Channel Five, Gardam was in a position to judge. He wrote:

In its first series, more people voted for the housemates than had just voted in the Scottish, Welsh and London mayoral elections combined. In 2002, class war broke out as the house was segregated into rich and poor. Last year, as the housemates divided along ethnic lines, it laid bare the incipient racism that lies not too far from the surface of modern Britain. And now it has succeeded where the Labour Government, the US Congress and the Daily Telegraph have all failed. It has allowed George Galloway to destroy himself. (*Evening Standard*, January 19, 2006: 39)

Galloway felt it necessary to "conduct a highly orchestrated media offensive" to restore his standing with his constituents. The *Independent* reported that "despite an avalanche of negative publicity and polls suggesting plummeting popularity in his constituency, the Bangladeshi community of Whitechapel appeared fairly unperturbed by the politician's three-week stint on *Celebrity Big Brother*" (January 27, 2006: 5). Even so, asked "if he was glad he had done the show, Galloway replied: 'Well not after I've seen those press cuttings'" (*Independent*, January 26, 2006: 3).

The power of the plebiscite was felt among the parliamentary and pundit classes, but its real achievement in this series of *Celebrity Big Brother* had nothing to do with George Galloway. The eventual winner was not a celebrity at all but, in a stunning *coup de théâtre*, a *fake celebrity*: a "once unknown Essex girl" called Chantelle Houghton who had been planted in the house by Big Brother (at the urging of PR genius Max Clifford) to con the housemates that she was a celebrity too. In this she succeeded, so she was allowed to stay, surviving eviction when Galloway himself was voted out. During the show, on hearing that George was an MP, she asked him: "does that mean you work in that big room with the green seats?"; and she referred to his political party Respect as his "band" (see under her name in Wikipedia). At the end she outpolled all the real celebrities, and naturally became one herself the instant she emerged from the house. The *Guardian* commented: "Though nobody in the crowd dared say it, they knew they were taking part in a new peak for reality TV. When storylines emerge like Chantelle's everyone must see why the master dramatists . . . number among Big Brother's more vocal fans" (January 28, 2006: front page).

Reality TV had reduced real playwrights to mere fans; the plebiscite had made a celebrity where there was not one before. But wait! There's more! Soon a Chantelle lookalike (a copy of a fake) was on the prowl.[12] Channel Four basked in ratings glory:

> The fourth series of *Celebrity Big Brother* proved to be a ratings success, with Friday's show attracting 7.5 million viewers, not to mention enormous media coverage. Sharon Powers, executive producer of the show, said: "This series has had everything – moments of jaw-dropping amazement, moments where you wanted to scream at the television, moments of high drama and utter hilarity."[13]

Scaling Up – The Plebiscitary Industries

That obscure object of choice

Across the world various pay-TV operators have included a plebiscitary button on the remote control. Shows like *Sky News* run instant polls every day on some topical issue, and the results become part of the show they're watching. The pleasure of the vote is now a business plan in its own right. Opinion.com.au (Australia) offers people a place to vote, on pretty much anything: "Did you see the Jude Law penis photos before they were censored?" and "What is ur opinion of brazillian ppl? [*sic*]" – for which the two voting options are: "never met one" and "their ok" [*sic*]. The purpose of the site seems to be merely to vote.[14] Other voting sites are more traditional in their political focus; for instance Vote.com (USA). Meanwhile, online petition sites like Petitiononline.com encourage petitions on politics and government, entertainment and media, environment, religion, and technology and business. The most active sites include those petitioning to bring back loved but cancelled TV shows, like *Arrested Development* and *Dead Like Me*.

There is a new format of TV reality show based on the plebiscite, where viewers can choose the "greatest" person or "favorite" object in a category. The BBC seems to be a lead player in this game. In 2002 they ran a series of TV documentaries on the *Top Ten Great Britons*, a list that was itself derived from a top 100 nominations by 30,000 people. Each episode of the series was introduced by a celebrity "champion" of the nominee. Viewers were then invited to vote on "the greatest" of them

Table 7.2 Top 10 great Britons

Nominee	Number of votes	Percentage of votes	Champion
Winston Churchill	456,498	28.1	Mo Mowlam
Isambard Kingdom Brunel	398,526	24.6	Jeremy Clarkson
Diana, Princess of Wales	225,584	13.9	Rosie Boycott
Charles Darwin	112,496	6.9	Andrew Marr
William Shakespeare	109,919	6.8	Fiona Shaw
Isaac Newton	84,628	5.2	Tristram Hunt
Queen Elizabeth I	71,928	4.4	Michael Portillo
John Lennon	68,445	4.2	Alan Davies
Horatio Nelson	49,171	3.0	Lucy Moore
Oliver Cromwell	45,053	2.8	Richard Holmes
Total votes	**1,622,248**		

Source: www.bbc.co.uk/history/programmes/greatbritons.shtml.

all. The top 10 "Great Britons" (and their champions) are shown in table 7.2.

The format has proven to be both portable and versatile. Discovery Channel shortlisted the 25 greatest Americans.[15] No surprises there, but an online poll conducted for BBC TV's *What the World Thinks of America* (June 2003) received over 37,000 votes – nearly half of them for Homer Simpson. The BBC felt constrained to warn viewers: "Results are indicative and may not reflect public opinion." Here they are anyway (see table 7.3, p. 156).

The BBC ran an egghead version of the same idea, receiving over a million website hits during a radio poll to discover the "greatest philosopher of all time" (see table 7.4, p. 156). The poll generated considerable press comment – the *Economist* supported Hume while the *Guardian* supported Kant and the *Independent* Wittgenstein. The top 10 featured four Germans (plus an anglicized Austrian), three ancient Greeks, an Italian, and a Scottish economist (no women; no French; no one from outside Europe).

This was fun! Elsewhere in the world, you could vote for the best PM of India or find out who was "elected" as the greatest Czech of all time (Charles IV). In Canada, CBC received 1.2 million votes in 2004

Table 7.3 Top 10 great Americans

Nominee	Percentage of votes
Homer Simpson	47.17
Abraham Lincoln	9.67
Martin Luther King Jnr	8.54
Mr T	7.83
Thomas Jefferson	5.68
George Washington	5.12
Bob Dylan	4.71
Benjamin Franklin	4.10
Franklin D Roosevelt	3.65
Bill Clinton	3.53
Total votes	**37,102**

Source: news.bbc.co.uk/1/hi/programmes/wtwta/2997144.stm.

Table 7.4 Top 10 great philosophers

Nominee	Percentage of votes[a]
Karl Marx	27.93
David Hume	12.67
Ludwig Wittgenstein	6.80
Friedrich Nietzsche	6.49
Plato	5.65
Immanuel Kant	5.61
Thomas Aquinas	4.83
Socrates	4.82
Aristotle	4.52
Karl Popper	4.20
Total votes	**34,000**

[a] Percentages do not total 100 because more than 10 philosophers attracted votes.
Source: www.bbc.co.uk/pressoffice/pressreleases/stories/2005/07_july/13/radio4.shtml;
www.bbc.co.uk/radio4/history/inourtime/greatest_philosopher_vote_result.shtml.

for the "greatest Canadian" (someone called Tommy Douglas).[16] In Australia the ABC ran a TV special in December 2004 called *My Favourite Book*, featuring both a National Top 100 and a Kids' Top 10. The BBC had already aired *The Big Read*. The same book topped all three charts: J. R. R. Tolkien's *Lord of the Rings*. However, there was press criticism of the Australian show, demonstrating common responses to the plebiscite, relating to the scrupulousness of the method, the size and composition of the "electorate," and the height of its collective brow.[17]

But the BBC at least was not to be put off. It is a plebiscitary serial offender. Without even mentioning sport, you can vote for:

- the best opening and closing sequences from a cult show;
- your favorite sitcom;
- your favorite Top Screen Scientist;
- the best *Blackadder* episode; and
- the hottest burning issue on *EastEnders*.[18]

All of this activity suggests that voting is something of a craze. The idea that there might be such a thing as purposeless voting, voting for pleasure, does not go down well in political science, where it is generally seen as a sort of work, or at least a duty, rather than play. However, the plebiscitary industries have discovered that people like to vote, and are providing them with plenty of opportunities to do so. Scorning that as pointless is perhaps to miss the point. It is doubtful whether people really expect instrumental outcomes, for instance, to a petition to bring back a favorite show, but that doesn't stop tens of thousands of them going online and voting – often leaving detailed comments about why they're doing it. So just as people use magazines, television, and even the news itself as an accompaniment to the rhythms of everyday life, so they're using the plebiscite to put on public record what they think about this and that. It's quite possible that as time goes on the craze will decline, although places with the most people – China and India – seem the least jaded in this respect.

But in the meantime, it is important not to dismiss voting for pleasure as inconsequential or worse, without first trying to identify why such activities are popular. An example of counter-intuitive meanings in this regard might help. Nobody in their right minds would claim go-karting or paintball battles as "democratic practices." However, a news report from Iran showed how young people in that country are using these pastimes precisely to get away from its heavily regulated "public sphere." Go-karting is popular, for instance, because it allows the sexes to mix, and this is seen as "defiance of the religious men who run the country" (Woodruff 2006). Bearing this in mind, beware critical complaints that people doing what they like doesn't amount to democracy. At best, they say, it's merely demotic (see Turner 2006); at worst it is a simulacrum that authoritarian regimes seek to install in place of the real thing (Victor S. 2005). Despite such criticism, it is still a good idea to ask what it is that people like to do, just in case they're on to something. It's politics, Jim; but not as we know it.

Toward direct DIY participation in reality

The *human appeal* of voting in the digital age has been developed first not by political but by marketing and media specialists. They have both popularized and monetized it via various plebiscitary formats in reality TV and elsewhere for their own commercial purposes, by the use of interactive media that can instantly convert individual choice into measurable scale. So the "plebiscitary industries" have stolen a march on many more directly political uses of the same technologies, which tend to be supply-driven, top-down, earnest, and unpopular.

However, commentators from the political side of the fence have begun to take notice, and are seeking to re-import the human element back into the democratic process itself. Popular politics has something to learn from popular media. E-democracy advocates seek new ways to engage citizens and gauge public opinion via interactive media (Coleman 2003). The relationship between the plebiscitary industries and the democratic process is now the subject of intense interest on both sides of the political/entertainment divide.

The democratic credentials of content distribution based on a mere *representation* of the audience (no matter how scientifically achieved) may now be questioned and even rejected. Jason Mittell, stung by the cancellation of his favorite show, writes:

> Ratings are seen by many in the industry as the site of viewer democracy, as people vote with their eyeballs what shows they want to watch and what they avoid. But Nielsen ratings are less like voting than like exit polling (and if exit polls were the measure of democracy, hello President Kerry!) – people cannot choose to participate in Nielsen ratings, and Nielsen only measures a miniscule fragment of the television viewing population.

Unless you're in one of the 5,000 households who comprise the bulk of Nielsen's sample, your viewing habits (along with 99.995% of all other viewers!) simply do not register within the media economy – hardly a participatory democracy. (Mittell 2005)

Mittell's vision of the future is to invoke the idea of the *passionate* consumer rather than the *passive* (but numerous) one, suggesting that advertisers will want to reach opinion leaders and early adopters in the field of content (including educators such as himself), just as they do in technology. The end-point is for consumers to become the producers not only of content but also of programming:

A sizable, motivated, and demographically desirable audience . . . awaits the advertisers and distributors who are willing to buck the centrality of ratings as determinant of television's hits and misses . . . By only investing in the traditional currency of ratings, networks ignore the multitude of ways that viewers are already actively engaging with their programs, and forego the option for people to actually participate in the selection of television programming that they want to see. (Mittell 2005)

Jonathan Gray (2005) commented on this issue:

I find it amazing and sad, too, that while the networks, cable channels, and cable and satellite companies constantly try to convince us that what they offer is democracy in action (the logic being that the choice of what to watch is the choice over human destiny), there is so little consumer outrage about the crudeness of this supposed democracy's voting system.

This is where the plebiscite comes into its own. It can be both a response by traditional broadcasters to the challenge of consumer activism and passionate choice, and a potential way forward for the reform of "consumer democracy" in the creative industries. Do you like the idea? Vote now!

Notes

1 See en.wikipedia.org/wiki/Swingometer.
2 See www.theage.com.au/articles/2004/10/29/1098992287790.html?from=storyrhs.
3 See www.nostalgiacentral.com/tv/variety/thankyourluckystars.htm; see also

members.lycos.co.uk/foive (Janice's website); www.retrosellers.com/features26.htm (interview); and www.nostalgiacentral.com/tv/variety/jukeboxjury.htm.

4 See www.eurovision.tv/english/611.htm; and see www.nul-points.net/.

5 See www.digame.de (in German) – the service provider for Eurovision televoting; and see www.redwoodtech.com/applications/televoting.asp.

6 See www.telescope.tv/americanIdol2.html for details.

7 See for instance archives.cnn.com/2000/ALLPOLITICS/stories/11/16/recount.chads.

8 See www.telescope.tv/americanIdol2.html.

9 See www.chinadaily.com.cn/english/doc/2005-08/12/content_468543.htm.

10 See english.people.com.cn/200601/27/eng20060127_238672.html.

11 See en.wikipedia.org/wiki/George_Galloway.

12 See www.thisishertfordshire.co.uk/display.var.687334.0.0.php.

13 See www.thisishertfordshire.co.uk/news/borehamwood/display.var.683353.0.big_brother_mania_strikes.php.

14 See also Hottest On TV: www.hottestontv.com.au.

15 See dsc.discovery.com/convergence/greatestamerican/greatestamerican.html

16 See sify.com/itihaas/top10.php?cid=13385804; www.radio.cz/en/article/67495; www.cbc.ca/greatest.

17 See www.abc.net.au/myfavouritebook/default.htm; www.crikey.com.au/articles/2004/12/10-0001.html; www.bbc.co.uk/arts/bigread/top100.shtml.

18 See www.bbc.co.uk/cult/classic/titles/best/vote.shtml?configfile=vote/best/votecontrol.xml; www.bbc.co.uk/sitcom/winner.shtml; ww.bbc.co.uk/cult/scientists/beakerhoneydew.shtml; www.bbc.co.uk/comedy/blackadder/vote; www.bbc.co.uk/eastenders/haveyoursay/vote/vote_hub.shtml.

Part III

Is TV Beautiful?
Aesthetics of TV

This section analyzes television in terms of its content, taking some of its own distinctive features as the criteria for its aesthetic appeal: liveness (chapter 8); transparency or "reality" (chapter 9); and the feminized staging of competition (chapter 10). Is TV beautiful? To answer that question you must decide if it tells truths in its own way.

Hence this section does not seek to determine *a priori* whether TV is art; a judgment that may safely be left to history since it cannot be determined by the intentions of the producer or by the form of expression. "Art" is never an *input* into any creative endeavor; it is sometimes an *output* (received as art by an observer or a later age) and always contextual. Chapter 8 pursues the history of TV liveness; what many see as television's unique "aesthetic" compared with other media. Liveness clearly possesses aesthetic value for our anxious species, and TV has found elaborate ways to represent it. But – as if to demonstrate how aesthetic values may lie where you least expect them – the chapter ends up in a field of cows.

Nor does this section measure TV programming against received aesthetic standards in order to find television wanting in comparison to icons of the past. On the contrary, chapter 9 compares reality TV to Shakespeare's comedies of marriageability, finding that human interaction may be staged with varying degrees of artifice but that what everyone craves is a *"code" for transparency* through which we may grasp some truths about the human condition. *Big Brother* does this just as well as did the Swan of Avon, although with less emphasis on the arts of language. What this does for audiences is to democratize the arts of "playing" – performing the self for public consumption.

Is aesthetic experience rational or emotional; objective or subjective? Chapter 10 pursues that awkward question by showing how the objective achievements of competitive sport have been supplanted by the subjective judgment of bodily beauty in various novel sports, of which synchronized swimming is but one example. The chapter argues that the values of sport have shifted from Mars to Venus, from objective power and control to subjective comportment of the self and "the judgment of Paris." Meanwhile, popular media have also participated in that shift, pioneering new sporting competitions where (Hobbesian) modernist control has given way to the values of the plebiscite. *Dancing with the Stars* is only the beginning. Its aesthetic is an objective representation of the contemporary knowledge paradigm, even as its winners are produced by the subjective judgment of the voting public.

8

From a "Wandering Booby" to a Field of Cows

The Television Live Event

The Day of the Booby

In its early years TV was transmitted live as it was produced across all genres. This was a technical requirement for all programming except film inserts, at least until the invention of videotape in 1956. Thereafter, live television gradually shrank back from drama, comedy, and variety acts, continuing most strongly in presentation, studio-based shows, news, and "OB" – outside broadcasts of sport and public or entertainment events. Counter-intuitively for later generations of viewers, in the beginning drama was live but news was not. When it launched the world's first broadcast TV in November 1936, the BBC transmitted live variety acts and tele-plays from their studios at the "Ally Pally," but for news they made do with tele-cine of *British Movietone News*, which were newsreels made for cinema exhibition.

By comparison with cinema, television's ability to do fiction and light entertainment from the studio in real time was remarkable. But its achievement was also the reason why it was doomed. A flavor of the vicissitudes of live drama transmission can be had from this passage by Nigel Kneale, legendary writer of the *Quatermass* "science fiction" series of the 1950s:

> Control . . . precision. These are the elements that until recently were always unpleasantly lacking in live television. Weeks of rehearsal would culminate in the studio on transmission day. Now the filmed and live scenes would join for the first time. All the actual sets, props, effects were there at last. Now and only now could the actual effect of the play be assessed – when it was too late to alter anything. Not only that, but disaster could strike in many forms. Your leading man could fall sick or drop dead. It's only

remarkable that more haven't done so . . . Most destructive of all, to the production and the author's intentions, was the wandering booby. Appearing in his dust-coat at the court of Henry VIII, or outside a 40th-floor window of a skyscraper. One play of mine had what was intended as a tense, penultimate scene in a Himalayan ice cave at 22,000 feet. Two heavily clad actors were acting hard on transmission when a figure appeared outside the cave. It wore a dust-coat and was busily sweeping up the eternal snows. A booby, it turned out, who was in a hurry to get home and thought he would clear up early. In those days plays were repeated live a few days later, so at the second transmission he was firmly warned. To make sure, the cave was rendered booby-proof with a black sky-cloth and a large stack of boxes. But with a waywardness that had something wonderful in it, he managed to appear again. They should put up a statue to him at the Television Centre, a monument to the old days. Now video tape enables the whole production to be pre-recorded. . . . The day of the booby is almost done. (Kneale 1959: 86–8)

Live drama gave way to pre-recorded performances, in order for directors and producers, not to mention the hapless actors, to establish the kind of "control and precision" that was already familiar in film. So *unfamiliar* did the spectacle of actors making a mess of things in front of cameras become that eventually it spawned an entirely new genre of television entertainment, the out-take "blooper" shows done as comedy, such as *It'll Be Alright On The Night* and *Auntie's Bloomers*. The "wayward booby" was back, starring in its own format.

"Liveness" as a Ritual of Improvable Community

But even as live transmission gave way to videotaping, a myth of "liveness" was assiduously cultivated within the TV industry itself. "Liveness" was a marketing advantage; a property of the new technology that could be used to encourage *governments* to liberalize the licensing of TV stations, *investors* to support TV's very costly infrastructural development, and *viewers* to buy or rent the expensive decoding apparatus.

Nevertheless, even in actuality and the "OB" or outside broadcast, television was not really all that "live." OB was expensive and required major planning. It was reserved for events that were themselves major exercises in live presentation. It seemed obvious that OB trucks (one for the scanner, one for the transmitter, one for the generator) would be sent to places where something was guaranteed not only to occur but also to be of existing interest to a large number of ordinary people. OB was not sent to shops, streets, beaches, private dwellings, or other haunts of "the" people themselves; nor was it seen in the public sphere, at local government meetings, in the boardrooms or factories of industry, in classrooms, laboratories, churches, or ports. TV took a long while to relax sufficiently to go out and about into an unrehearsed, unstaged version of live reality. TV's "liveness" was that of the theater – the performative kind. Compared with radio (even patrician BBC radio), live television actuality was overproduced and unspontaneous.

But what made the "liveness" of television more than a delusion of critics habituated to the oedipal dark of a movie theater, or a self-serving marketing slogan for commercial exploitation, was that television as a medium eventually crossed the boundary from technology or industry to become a *cultural* form. As "culture" (rather than invention or investment) television had a combination of characteristics that other media couldn't match. It was public unlike telephony, and visual unlike radio. Unlike cinema, television's public visualizations could appear *now*. This lent them an "unauthored" quality – if something is live, it may not simply represent the intentions of the broadcaster, be they commercial, political, or ideological (never mind artistic). Viewers could imagine that "television" wasn't a creation of the television institution itself. Film and television addressed their "readers" in different *tenses* – film discourse was done in the past-perfect tense; TV narrated in the present tense. Film was literally a *fait accompli*; TV could nudge up against "nextness." No one, neither producer nor audience, knew what would happen next. This was what made "liveness" appealing for the audience.

Furthermore, these unauthored public visualizations of the "here and now" appeared in the domestic environment of the private home, to be seen in the context and perhaps even the company of intimate family. In 1952, British documentarist Michael Clarke suggested how this combination of characteristics might improve society. He thought that television could be "an influence which would help to abolish the atomic concept of society which grows more and more powerful and seductive." "Atomisation" was "a potentially appalling situation; for our culture encourages individualism, and our political and economic behavior in the mass is inevitably conditioned by appeals to individual, not group, self-interest." TV could lessen the "isolation of the individual. . . . For the television set in hundreds of thousands of homes ought to be a tremendous influence to make us better informed about the fascinating detail of the complex, modern world" (Clarke 1952: 184–5).

What's more, TV could exercise this benign "influence" "in our homes, where we are least vulnerable to the illusions to which, in the group, we might succumb." Television was hailed as something *less* ideological, because less produced, than other media. It would signal the end of "mass" political persuasion and the baleful influence of the demagogue (a quite proper nightmare for mid-twentieth-century imaginations). Instead, thought Clarke, "we all need the easy, informal education that television can provide" (1952: 186). For him, the positive potential of television was its ability to bring "isolated" or "atomised" individuals together, in their homes (away from undue influence), as a community, to experience live events that would inform, educate, and improve the whole society.

Here was a "theory" of the "live event" that went on to be put into practice. The television live event was developed and used around the world as a secular ritual of community-building. What made all this important was broadcast television's eventual popularity – its ability not simply to bring live events into "the" home, but into *everyone's* home, linking a nation together in front of one event, or one show. It wasn't long before television could link people from different nations together as well; it was able to domesticate a sense of global belonging, and equate its audience with *humanity*, never mind "our country." Clarke's optimistically imagined "hundreds of thousands of homes" became . . . billions.

TV could *visualize* people's sense of "imagined community" – the confident sense most people had of belonging to a country, even though they had not met and never would meet more than an infinitesimal proportion of its actual inhabitants, their co-citizens (Anderson 1991). Such a sense of community was nurtured via:

- *institutions*: e.g. national sporting bodies and teams, schools, government, national arts and cultural organizations;
- *discourses*: e.g. nationalism, a national language, patriotic rhetoric and images, celebrity; and
- *rituals*, traditionally associated with collective religious observance, but modernized into rituals of secular "communion" with others inside a specific time/space context; e.g. watching on TV the same event that millions of others were "known" to be seeing simultaneously.

TV combined all three of these:

- *Institutionally*, in Britain and Australia, legislation produced the "national broadcaster," the BBC and ABC. This pattern was common throughout the Commonwealth, e.g. Doordarshan in India, SABC in South Africa, CBC in Canada, and STV in Singapore. In free-enterprise America, the institutional form of television was established across the nation not as a monopoly, but dominated by the big three commercial networks (NBC, CBS, ABC), with a "long tail" of local affiliates, independents, and "narrowcast" stations in various languages; overall a stable arrangement that survived unchallenged for nearly 50 years.

- *Discursively*, television excelled in a national mode of address within daily programming such as news, sport, and weather forecasting. In this context the myth of "liveness" was particularly strong. News was always presented as if live (see chapter 3), even when it contained film from foreign parts that might have taken three days to be flown to the TV station, processed, edited, and voice-overed. The important thing was not the news-gathering but the population-gathering: news *presentation* was live, and the nation was gathered around the act of disclosure, not origination. News was *discursively* if not temporally live because the "liveness" allowed something that was not literally true to be understood, accepted, and acted upon as if it were true, namely, that "the nation" was self-conscious.

- *Ritually*, like radio before it (and alongside it), television proved ideal as a site for daily private family rituals of reconsumption, via fanship for given genres, especially news, drama series, and soap opera. The "TV altar" may have been public, but observances at it were private. The connection between them was "the nation." In its broadcast heyday (1950s to the 1990s), television also exceeded the reach of any prior communications technology. Watching TV became the most popular pastime the world had ever known. Thus TV was ritualized as an institutionalized discourse of national togetherness. TV became *seriously* popular, and its visual capacity within a domestic environment made it ideal for ritualized acts of imagining, organized around the symbolic connectivity between person, home (i.e. family), and country.

National Identity Crisis (Live, on TV)

TV performed the feat of bringing together an imagined community for many modern and modernizing nations during a period when it was getting less and less obvious what that community was. With migration, multiculturalism, and globalization, and with the fragmentation of national identity away from ethnic and territorial markers, it became harder to answer with confidence the question "how – by what evidence – do I know I'm Australian (or British or American)?" at a personal level. And at a collective level, with the emergence of new identities based on gender, non-indigenous ethnicities, sexual orientation, age, religion, even taste, it became difficult to specify definitively what counted as Englishness, Australianness, Americanness. What had once seemed "natural" – e.g. that the "normal citizen" was a male, white, Anglo-Saxon Protestant or WASP – came to be seen as sexist, racist, sectarian, and exclusionary. National communities included people of color, migrants, Indigenous people, and sub-national ethnic minorities. It was not safe to extrapolate from any particular lifestyle to pronounce on what was appropriate for anyone else. Indeed, terms that had once seemed full of meaning – like "Englishness" – became a joke, conjuring up not common images but caricatures.

At best what they meant was contested. In the 1960s and 1970s "Englishness" was a site of struggle between a traditional "officer class" image and a subcultural, Carnaby-Street version (The Who, skinheads, "swinging London") that started out as a piss-take and went on to become a commercial life-saver, outliving the "authentic" national iconography on which it was initially a kitsch ironic comment. This unequal contest between "substance" and "style" even had its own TV show – *The Avengers* (style "won"). In the same period, "Americanness" became as much a term of horror as of patriotism for some of its own citizens because of the Vietnam War and the growth of various countercultures. For a time there was a vogue for altering the very spelling of the country's name to "Amerika" to signify the alienation of the younger generation from the aggressive expansionism of the "military-industrial complex."

People from within its own core community were ridiculing or rebelling against the very idea of "national identity" and turning to cultural identities associated with personal characteristics (age, gender, sexuality, ethnicity) or even "do-it-yourself" identities associated with taste constituencies (music, clothing, lifestyle). "Subcultures" became more prominent than the "parent" culture from which they were nominally derived. At such a time, if national communities were to avoid balkanization into internally warring and segregated "tribes," they needed to identify themselves with something completely different from the traditional markers of nationality, i.e. territory and common ethnic descent. They needed to "virtualize" the idea of a national community, making the name of the country completely devoid of any "intrinsic" meaning, and able to bear whatever meaning anyone from any group wanted to ascribe to it.

National identity shifted from unity based on land and blood, to diversity based on difference. It was vital, in such circumstances, to settle on *symbolic* markers of nationality, derived from *institutions* rather than land, from *discourses* rather than ethnicity, and from *rituals* not neighborhoods. People had to be brought together by *doing* things together rather than *being* something in particular. This was where TV scored highly.

TV was a good barometer for these variations in the political and cultural climate. Comedy shows, sitcoms, and drama serials were able to use their story lines, gags, and situations to discuss seasonal hot topics, to bring conflicts into the open, to explore and expand the sense of difference among the variegated audience. TV took identity out of the political arena – of contestation for rights or competition for resources – and into the cultural arena. It communicated difference across demographic groups, but simultaneously gathered populations together rather than splitting them into their constituent groups.

TV news, current affairs, chat shows, and sport became vehicles for quite disproportionate attention to the tension between "we" and "they" identities. These "live" genres were used as mechanisms for thinking through the question of "how do I know I'm . . . Australian, American, British (etc.)?" Factual television addressed that question negatively, most of the time. "Our" national identity was confirmed by being contrasted with a series of "they" identities, usually in some kind of conflict or competition. "We" were identified by negativization: "we are what others are not." In this context the live event became a kind of collective cultural calculator, thinking though the question of national identity and personal citizenship in a positive way.

"Liveness" as Ideology

During the era of broadcast television, critics on both sides of the Atlantic began to argue that so great was television's *ideological* investment in "liveness" that the idea colored everything that was broadcast, not just live segments or shows. In other words, and particularly from the point of view of the viewer's experience, broadcast television as a whole came across – or was promoted – as live, no matter how it was shot or transmitted.

This idea gained critical-theoretical credence in the screen theory of the 1970s, oddly enough just after the time when transmissions had ceased to be live for most purposes. Screen theorists Stephen Heath and Gillian Skirrow set out what might be regarded as a paranoid version of the "liveness" myth. They noted that: "Transmission 'live,' 'as it happens,' unrecorded, *en direct* (the French expression)," was "very far indeed from representing the bulk of the television seen." Nevertheless, within what they called "normal assumptions," live TV was "taken as the television norm, as the very definition of television." They argued that "within the terms of those [normal] assumptions, *the television programme is then effectively identified with the 'live' television programme*" (Heath & Skirrow 1977: 53). Most of what was seen on TV was not live, but Heath and Skirrow argued that "liveness" was a "generalised fantasy of the television institution," that "the image" was "*direct*, and direct *for me*." Through this effect of immediacy, an effect that belonged to broadcast television as an institution rather than to any particular image on screen, all sorts of heterogeneous material could be ordered into a "present continuous" sequence. "Liveness" infected, as it were, the whole shebang.

Meanwhile, the "me" for whom "live broadcasting" was "direct," said Heath and Skirrow, was "a citizen in the world of communication" – television was "here and now, for me personally, for me as the unity of everyone" (1977: 56). For Heath and Skirrow, this was the general "ideology" of television.

Applying this generalized (paranoid) perspective to the American context, Jane Feuer analyzed the "ideology of liveness" in ABC's *Good Morning America* show, anchored at the time by David Hartman. She wrote:

> *Good Morning America* is constructed around the most extreme fragmentation – a mosaic of film, video and "live" segments emanating from New York, Washington, and Chicago, with features on how to clean fireplaces and how to use an electric blanket, news of the Iranian crisis and the Olympics, ads for Sears soft contact lenses and Lucky's pinto beans, not to mention Rona Barrett's review of *Cruising*, Joan Baez' visit to Cambodia, and the last in a series of "great romances." (Feuer 1983: 16–17)

All this in one morning; there have been many mornings since 1980. Feuer identified two forces that worked to unify this "variety of content" and the "extreme spatial fragmentation" of the show across the

USA. First, patriarchy: "All this is unified by the presence of David Hartman – the ultimate father figure – in the anchor chair." Second: "the show is obsessed with its own liveness. . . . David acts as custodian of flow and regularity, the personification of a force which creates unity out of fragmentation" (p. 17). For Feuer, the anchor united both time and space in the service of "family unity": "Television, in its liveness, its immediacy, its reality, can create families where none exist" (p. 20). In all this the "event" was TV itself.

No Sooner Done than Said – Live Historical Memory

Many commentators have noticed the difference between different kinds of time, not only on TV but "anthropologically," as it were. Everyday time can be measured incrementally as a "banal," "profane," or ordinary sequence. Special time, on the other hand, is marked by the interruption of "fatal," "sacred," and extraordinary events. Weekdays are differentiated from weekends; Sundays are secularized "holy-days." In people's lives, some events are of "lifelong" significance rather than belonging to ordinary time. Births, weddings, and funerals are obvious examples.

At a wedding, people observe strange rituals clearly marked off from ordinary life, and make great efforts to slow time down to a standstill (see the discussion of vestimentary frequencies in chapter 3). They dress in special costumes, with clothes from a bygone (Edwardian) age. The "event" is out of time (not much "happens" but it is "the day of a lifetime"). The wedding is compulsively photographed to make a permanent record, although people stop what they are doing to assemble in timeless immobility for this purpose. The formal ceremony and informal goings-on both display elements going back hundreds of years. People gather from among families, friends, and neighbors who might otherwise never meet or barely be on speaking terms. The community becomes self-conscious, for an instant.

Like people, television needs both types of time. Normally, it babbles away happily in "present continuous," banal, profane, everyday time. But sometimes it switches to fatal, sacred time. This is where the live event comes into its own. Weddings, funerals, anything – so long as they are on a national scale or greater.

The "big" live event has had a bad press from critics. Aesthetically it is criticized for taking a very long time to say very little. It seems to be characterized generically by distended semiotic excess. Ideologically it is prone to other kinds of excess – the political evils of populism and nationalism, the commercial exploitation of culture, the commodification of identity. It has even been seen as contributing to "the death of history." Meaghan Morris has written about the excesses of a typical four-hour "live event" show broadcast on Australian television to mark the bicentennial celebrations in 1988 – the show *Australia Live: Celebration of a Nation* (Morris 1993). Morris argued that *Australia Live* "produced a landscape without *shadows*," in which "capital (mobility) was the basic theme" rather than historical analysis, despite the historical pretext for the whole event. But she warned against "paranoid" conclusions: "An event like *Australia Live* is no more representative of a mythic 'television-in-general' than it was reflective of life in Australia" (Morris 1993: 20, 26).

A more difficult problem for analysis, she argued, was what might be meant by "live" in live-event TV:

> The "live," in this frame of reference, has a rather peculiar meaning. Live television is an operation guaranteed, and yet contested, not by an opposite or a negation (the not-live: the prerecorded, the archival, the simulacrum, the ghostly, the "dead") but an array of vague possibilities associated with *life*: unprogrammed events, breaks in continuity, accidents, missed connections, random occurrences, unforeseen human and technical recalcitrance. (Morris 1993: 52–3)

The interruption of "the live" by "the living" was nothing less than the return of Nigel Kneale's "wandering booby," except that now the "ghost in the machine" (Koestler 1967) is a representation of "living" – disruptive – rather than *ordered* reality. This has the effect of making contemporary television into an uncanny update of Jeffrey Sconce's (2000) "haunted media," because now the disruptive presence animating an otherwise "programmed" reality is *life* itself.

Morris made the recalcitrant liveness of the wandering booby not a symptom of the death of history, or of the collapse of critical distance, but a precondition of the live genre, and in fact a reprieve for history:

> The ceremonial "present" became, for the official script on the day [of *Australia Live*], a field of suspense and evasion. Speech after speech from the dais skipped hastily from the "mistakes of the past" to expressions of faith in "the future." The *significant* present was elsewhere: with people lying in the sun, having picnics, watching boats and milling about, but

above all with the insistent critical accompaniment of the Aboriginal protest. Audible and visible in most telecasts on the day, extending later into media commentary, news items, current affairs shows and the television archive of future Aboriginal images – that protest effectively historicised, on Aboriginal terms, an entrepreneurial "national" event. (Morris 1993: 54–5)

Morris concluded: "only by beginning to think of media as accompanying experience, and as time (not just 'space') for action, can criticism respond to an event" (p. 54). The live event had not supplanted history, but in its relations with a "significant present" that was "elsewhere" it allowed criticism, both activist and reflective, to become "live."

"Produced" and "Natural" Events

During television history, there have been broadcasts of many live events. Although each one was unique, the "TV live event" displayed generic regularities that can be typified. They have tended to be of two kinds. These can be characterized as "produced" and "natural" respectively.

The "produced" category approximated anthropologically to a wedding. "Produced" live events included actual celebrity weddings, but they also included a genre unique to television, the live coverage of temporal markers of national (sometimes super-national) history: anniversaries, centenaries, millennia. This seasonal stepping out of banal time into holiday time has achieved global status at the peal of midnight each New Year's Eve, as news shows around the world relay each city's pyrotechnic excesses to the next, westward leading, still proceeding, following time-zones from Sydney Harbour to Times Square. In countries with modern constitutions, there has been a vogue for elaborate celebrations of bicentennials, primarily as TV-produced events: the USA in 1976, Australia in 1988, France in 1989. Not wanting to wait a hundred years, the People's Republic of China pulled out all the plugs for its fiftieth in October 1999, as did India and Pakistan in 1997. Countries with pre-modern constitutions had to make do with royal weddings – Britain liked to have one or two of these every decade – or royal birthdays: Thailand and Japan are good at these.

The "produced" type of "live event," like early live TV, could seem a bit of a con. So heavily stage-managed was the "liveness" that the best the audience could hope for was interruption by a "wandering booby." More interesting in many ways is the other type of live event; the "natural" variety. These are live transmission of events that are actually happening. It would be too much to claim that they would have occurred even without the TV camera, although this could be the case, but they could not be *reduced to* their television presentation alone. However, what makes them interesting is that their "natural" qualities are precisely what makes them memorable television, so they enter social memory (if not history) as *television* events, not as "natural" ones. Such events could be characterized as "fatal" as opposed to "banal" in Baudrillardian terms (see McKee 1997: 192). They approximate anthropologically not to the "produced" wedding but to "natural" birth and death events, especially death.

The No. 1 event in this category happened to be a "birth." The moon landing of July 1969 was certainly hailed as the harbinger of a new era in human history. Gregor Goethals provided a classical comparison:

> We saw images "live from the moon" and heard the voice of the astronaut as he lowered himself onto the moon's surface. Television transformed the human heroism and scientific success of those memorable, fleeting moments into public, symbolic records for all citizens to witness.
>
> In recalling these moments it is important to remember that political and economic institutions have always been conscious of symbolism. One comparison that comes to mind is the building of the Parthenon in fifth-century Athens. In the years after the defeat of the Persians, Athens was the most powerful and influential city-state. What better way to celebrate and underscore that position than to construct a magnificent temple? No matter how much disorder was manifested at the time, citizens could see tangible evidence of Athens' grandeur embodied in the Parthenon. (Goethals 1981: 83–4)

The citizens were gathered to the "magnificent temple" of the moon-landings by television. Using the most expensive and convincing empirical evidence, the Apollo program live on TV, it was possible to *imagine* human order, power, and progress as a "giant leap for mankind," done by means of the "one small step for a man."

People remembered the moonwalk "out of time," as it were – if it was a "real" or "historical" event, it was as much a television one. McKenzie Wark recorded various Australian writers' recollections of their experience as part of "generation moonwalk." One recalled being aged 10 when " 'the world' watched with bated breath, fuzzy grainy pictures in which very little happened over what seemed like hours and hours cramped five in a double desk in the grade five and six classroom." Another remembered: "we had a portable TV set brought into the class especially . . . There was a very strong sense of occasion about it, that we were watching something very special . . . There was a sense that it was a television event, as much as a historical one." Another confessed: "It was a real bonding moment for me and dad. He sat there with a glass of beer and affected a suitable silent *gravitas* while the whole damn thing took place. I admit I was impressed too . . . That it was happening live, right at that very minute, it was real impressive" (Wark 1999: 235–7).

But "natural" events were perhaps typified more frequently by *interrupting* normal programming with live coverage of negative, literally "fatal" events. Interruptive live coverage requires high-status victims in high-status countries, e.g. the assassination of Americans John and Robert Kennedy and Martin Luther King (but not Norwegian Olof Palme). It extends to the live aftermath of certain disasters, like coverage of bombings in Oklahoma (but not in Algeria or Angola) or earthquakes in California (but not Pakistan). It includes celebrity crashes – JFK Jr and Diana, Princess of Wales (but not Macedonia's president Boris Trajkovski). The "live-event" format colonized entire battles, like those of the Gulf War (see Wark 1994: 3–46) (but not Chechnya). Many other incidents of socially sacralized violence (newsworthy conflict) have turned into live-event spectacle, from the SAS storming the Iranian Embassy in London in 1979, up to the aftermath of massacres such as Port Arthur in 1996 or Columbine and Beslan Schools in 1999 and 2004 and Virginia Tech (VT) in 2007. The death of 33 people at VT displaced Iraq from the top of the news agenda for several days, even though the body-count was many times higher in Baghdad than Blacksburg that week (with 233 deaths on one day),[1] obeying the grim but inexorable law of cultural proximity: few close-by fatalities are more newsworthy than many from afar. Even VT students' objection to the "exploitative" media circus on their campus was duly reported at the top of the bulletin (BBC *10 O'Clock News*, April 19, 2007). In a class of its own was live coverage of the entire OJ Simpson trial, lasting a full year and provoking intense internal and indeed global meditation on what "America" might mean now.

It was pretty clear from these examples that fatality was a compelling pretext for live-event TV. Normally the "natural" event emanated from or went to the national agenda of the United States of America. The

US seemed less sure-footed about blowing its own trumpet in the "produced" category. The five-hundredth anniversary of Columbus's "discovery" of "America" (1992) was embarrassing even to the participants, provoking the "wrong" sort of national self-consciousness (see Stam 1995). National togetherness and self-reflection have seemed more readily sparked by "natural" events in the US, especially if they were literally "fatal" to a suitably high-status celebrity. The connection between such life-and-death issues and a more uncanny understanding of the "liveness" of US media from the telegraph to television, i.e. the idea that they don't just manifest electrical liveness but are literally alive, has been explored by Jeffrey Sconce (2000).

Liveness was American

The American live event on TV became everyone else's live event. There was a very important consequence to this; one that has been noted in relation to American national fictions by Scott Olson, writing primarily about movies and TV drama. He argued that the Hollywood mode of narration is "transparent." Audiences around the world don't see movies as being heavily coded with Americanness; instead they "are able to project their own narratives, values, myths, and meanings into the American iconic media, making those texts resonate with the same meanings they might have if they were indigenous" (Olson 1999: 5–6).

Olson used this insight not to trot out the well-worn accusations of American domination of the world via media-colonialism, but to argue something that was very nearly the opposite:

> Transparency allows such narratives to become stealthy, to be foreign myths that surreptitiously act like indigenous ones, Greek gifts to Troy, but with Trojan citizens inside the horse. . . . The process [of cultural change] is causally the reverse of what is generally assumed – the indigenous culture actively reaches out, haggles, and does not merely absorb in hypodermic needle, magic-bullet fashion some set of injected cultural values. The readings of indigenous text are indigenous, but the images and sounds are transplanted. (Olson 1999: 6; see also Lotman 1990 and O'Regan 1996: 213–26 for the transmitter–receiver relations of import–export cultures)

"Perhaps," Olson argued, "despite alarms to the contrary, the world is not being melted down into a single, hegemonic, more-or-less American monoculture, even though American cultural products dominate the world" (1999: 5). The "Greek gifts to Troy" turned out to be a Parthenon after all, and everyone inside the horse was a Trojan (even the Americans).

These issues applied not only to US fictions but also to those "foreign myths" that came in factual form, whether as news or as more expansive "live events." When people from middling or small countries watch their own national television they *see* a great deal of American programming. Viewer participation in or identification with "live events," whether "natural" or "produced," is very likely indeed to entail participation in or identification with *American* events. But the identification would not necessarily be as an American; the participation would not be within the polity of the US (see Wark 1994: 14).

Australian critic Graeme Turner has described his own "first contact" with American live coverage via CNN. He found its Americanness and its liveness both strangely liberating. The 1997 British general election on CNN was "visually dull," minimally edited, "poorly structured, repetitive and predictable." But that was the point: as a result of its very liveness, "it seemed to have moved slightly beyond the reach of the discursive conventions of television news" (the booby was wandering close by . . .). And Americanness offered a dual benefit. Contact with it, from suburban Brisbane, provided a "metropolitanising buzz," but the "Indigene" who watched from outside the US also experienced "exemption from complicity" in the national ideologies encoded into CNN's "discursive regime" (Turner 1997: 116–17). Seeing the moon-landings, the death of a Kennedy, or any other ceremonies of American national television, including *British* elections followed in *Australian* homes, did not make people from around the world into Americans. It may not even have made American citizens themselves into "Americans."

The "transparency" Olson analyzed allowed citizens of all countries to become what I have called "citizens of media" (Hartley 1996: ch 3, 1999: chs 12–14). The live event was one of the most important devices for gathering those citizens together out of their "normal" everyday time and space. When "we" watched the ecstasies of lunar landings we were fleetingly human, not national; when "we" saw the agonies of assassination, or even the lunacies of the Monica Lewinsky saga, we were "haggling" for meanings about ourselves however construed, not about our relation to the USA.

Fatal Banalities

"Suicide is painless, it brings on many changes." So said the title song of the American hit comedy series *M*A*S*H*. One of the changes it may have introduced among competing US TV executives, at least moment-arily, was doubt about their uncritical enthusiasm for the live television event. The cause for concern was the death of Daniel V. Jones just before 4 p.m. on Thursday April 30, 1998.

The problem posed by Mr Jones was apparently editorial. It wasn't the fact that he blew his brains out on a Los Angeles freeway, but that he did this while a number of competing news helicopters were follow-ing his every move, two of them in especially tight close-up at that moment. These pictures were broadcast live, following the chase of a deranged person with a gun, "OJ-style," and reporting on the traffic gridlock the chase had caused. Thus, there was no time for newsroom debate about whether or not to broadcast the act of suicide itself. In the words of Howard Rosenberg, TV critic for the *Los Angeles Times*, "No time to ponder. No safeguards. In an age valuing media speed over reflection, the Jones shooting happened and was transmitted simultaneously" (Rosenberg 1999: 70).

A banal suicide could assume world-historical significance if it happened in America. For Rosenberg this was just such an occasion: "The TV shot heard throughout much of the world was a seminal moment in news-casting excess, one representing the ultimate horror of knee-jerk live coverage that in recent years had been careening across the television-scape like fugitives fleeing police in those familiar Southern California police chases" (H. Rosenberg 1999: 70). Interestingly, Rosenberg's dis-cussion of this "seminal moment" was part of a special issue on the "future of journalism," portentously entitled *What's Next?*, in the house journal of the Freedom Forum. If "Man commits suicide – LIVE!" was indeed "what's next," then Rosenberg found himself wondering "whether some of the authority of journalism died that day in Los Angeles along with Jones."

The professional doubt turned on whether "viewers should have been shown" Jones's suicide. But this case represented more than the familiar debate about public-interest news vs. private-gratification entertainment. It even went beyond the more technical problem of live production/transmission, which was to remove editorial decision-making powers from editors. The deeper disquiet felt by journalists suggested that here was a perceived limit of what the "live event" was supposed to do. The whole point was that the death of an anonymous man was not "the ultimate horror" at all. Suicide may be fatal to the perpetrator, but it is nevertheless a banal, private, everyday, profane matter. Here it seems the real issue was professional squeamishness about using *broadcast television* for this kind of "live event."

Live Online – and in a Field of Cows

But it was already too late for such worries. *Broadcast* television may increasingly have concentrated on the "fatal" and sacral live event, as opposed to the "banal" and secular. There may well have been a glut of community-building, population-gathering, citizen-calling live spectaculars, from the Millennium to Olympic opening and closing ceremonies. And these may indeed have become more international and more global (based on the "Olson" formula that American = the universal subject position). But none of this meant that such live events as the Jones suicide had gone away. Everyday liveness was only "fugitive" as it migrated away from broadcast television, first to non-broadcast forms such as cable TV, but perhaps more decisively to the internet.

It was never clear what "live television" encompassed; now it was no longer easy to be sure what was meant by "television" either. "Television" without qualification tended to refer to the era of national network broadcasting. But television was already passing out of this era. Multi-channel cable, satellite, and digital TV meant that it was increasingly hard to gather whole populations to witness and parti-cipate in any one ritual of national togetherness. The internet, with "JenniCAMs" proliferating in their thousands, meant that the "live event" could be private, not public.[2]

One of the internet's more popular innovations was the camera sited in someone's bedroom, allowing users to check out domestic banalities (with a promise of intimacies normally banned from broadcast TV) in real time, all done for nothing by private individuals in their own homes. As well, "live" could also be interactive, a feature exploited by the porn industry to allow clients to specify exactly what they'd like a model to do, and to share their fantasy with its object. Of course, different kinds of interactive liveness could be combined: a net-search for JENNYCAM yielded, among others, "Young Voyeur Jennycam Cams Nude Girls," on the one hand and "Navigating the Image of Woman Online – A feminist approach to the JenniCAM," on the other. Then ("for the voyeur of discriminating taste") there was The Peeping Moes' JenniCAM Fan Page:

> Jennifer has graciously allowed us a live, 24 hour-a-day portal into her life . . . In one sense, Jenni is a pioneer. Since her debut, many more have followed the trail she blazed. . . . Somehow she answers a ton of email, and still keeps her sanity. Her live presence cannot last forever, but maybe the lesson of her open and unassuming sharing of it, will. – The Peeping Moes.[3]

"The nation" was fragmented, "liveness" was privatized. This posed quite a challenge to the very idea of an "event" – someone in a bedroom, whether or not engaged in activities designed to arouse sexual excitement, was not *doing* enough to qualify the proceedings as an "event" by the definition established over the previous 40 years of broadcasting. In short, "liveness" was shifting from "sacred" to "profane" time/space and participation. However, what Jenni was *not doing* nevertheless became international news: she was interviewed on the *Late Show with David Letterman*, on *E! Entertainment News*, and in a *Penthouse* "Women of the Net" story. Subsequently "she" became a banal, distributed figure, proliferating into thousands of examples of the same as teens and 20-somethings proclaimed their own liveness, if not the eventfulness of their lives, wherever webcams were sold.

Because it was rich and full of creative people, broadcast television could still reflect on and even play with these developments. One inspired example was shown on BBC television in Britain, in the days leading up to the 1999 Glastonbury music festival, an annual event which regularly attracts over a hundred thousand people. As part of their nightly continuity (i.e. the TV that is broadcast between programs, often taking the form of a station ID or an announcement about an up-coming show) the BBC sited a camera in a field with a "Live from Glastonbury" caption. For several nights the picture showed nothing more (but also, bizarrely, nothing less) than a few cattle nuzzling the herbage in the darkening hues of the long northern summer evening. Only as the festival itself took place did this unwonted vision of "liveness" (where nothing was happening) transform into its spectacular, festive, teeming, sacred opposite, filling the same field.

"Liveness," "television," and "event" were all, it transpired, doubtful terms. In the gloom of the Somerset farmland they went beyond doubt and skepticism to achieve witty self-reflexivity. Meaghan Morris thought that "the live and the living" (live TV event and living people) "interact in a mode of hostile complicity" (Morris 1993: 54), which may certainly be the case. But the BBC's Glastonbury joke – a "trailer" for a "live" event (impossible, if you think about it . . . and was the trailer *really* live?) – relied on viewer literacy about both television continuity and the accompanying "living" world. It showed that "complicity" could be post-paranoid and mutually playful too. In fact, the live and the living were connected not by either hostility or playfulness only, but also by what's now called "convergence," whether or not they supported a personal netcam site.

Or as Nigel Kneale (1959: 88) presciently put it, understanding in the language of the 1950s the integration of technology, narration, and life: "I don't like the term 'science fiction,' but if we're going to bandy it about, it could be applied just as well to the world we live in."

Notes

1 See Associated Press report for the figures from Iraq: www. suburbanchicagonews.com/heraldnews/news/348251,4_1_JO19_IRAQ_S1. article.
2 See http://www.jennicam.org.
3 See peepingmoe.com/netcams/jennicam.

9

Shakespeare, *Big Brother,* and the Taming of the Self

The Value, *or* WORTH *of a man is . . . not absolute; but a thing dependent on the need and judgement of another . . . And as in other things, so in men, not the seller, but the buyer determines the Price. For let a man (as most men do) rate themselves as the highest Value they can; yet their true Value is no more than it is esteemed by others.*
Thomas Hobbes, 1651 (1968: 151–2)

This chapter is about the democratization of playing. The performance of the self is now done by citizens for themselves and for each other, not by representative actors. The source of meaning is now located in the consumer, not the producer. The creation of meaning is now an editorial or "redactional" act, not an authorial one. *Big Brother* is a latter-day version of Shakespeare's "taming of the shrew." Shakespearean plays are "in character" while *Big Brother*'s housemates "play themselves." But both sets of players have to endure the schemes and stratagems of their peers, as well as tests set by their dramaturge. Both Shakespeare and *Big Brother* have been criticized for sexism in the way they deal with the "battle of the sexes," but both conduct their audience through the tension and uncertainties of governing or "taming" the self while being watched. In *The Taming of the Shrew* the end in mind is advantageous marriage; in the "reality" format it is to win the contest (although in terms of available social rewards these may amount to the same thing). Both characters and contestants must "tame" their inner "shrew" if they want to gain the applause of the spectator and win the fairytale ending. This chapter shows that even though they approach it from different ends of the "value chain of meaning" (see chapter 2), Shakespeare's comedies and reality television deal with the same issue: the risks and rewards attendant upon the comportment of the self in competitive society.

Reality Shakespeare

Like Endemol's *Big Brother*, William Shakespeare's *The Taming of the Shrew* is a modern interactive commercial entertainment, produced by an entrepreneurial joint stock company and performed for profit to a secular, anonymous, popular audience of mixed class, age, and gender. Similarly, Endemol, co-founded by theatrical impresario Joop van den Ende and TV producer John de Mol, combined theater and live events with TV entertainment (Moran 1998: 33–7).[1] Like TV audiences, spectators in the Elizabethan playhouses were encouraged to reconsume formats, e.g. comedy, bear-baiting (Hawkes 2002: 83–7), but to watch a given production only once. Such shows, like *Big Brother* and *The Taming of the Shrew*, were full of "mirth and merriment," as one of them put it, but they also touched on important contemporary issues of identity-formation, including citizenship, domestic comportment, and self-management.

The Taming of the Shrew included various stock characters, as carefully chosen as the housemates on *Big Brother*, to portray familiar types within the target demographic of the popular audience: for instance a drunk (Christophero Sly), a braggart (Petruchio), a "shrew" or scold (Katharina), and the Elizabethan equivalent of a young cutie (Bianca). It was full of stagy artifice – disguises, inversions, cross-dressing – and was not above some bawdy humor. Like *Big Brother* it put these formulaic elements into an unfolding series of tests, observing how the characters dealt with situations and relationships about which the audience knew more than they did, and the game eventually produced a winner: Petruchio (V.ii.187–8).

All this theatrical artifice was in the service of a greater transparency. Like a contemporary television audience schooled in recombinant formats, re-versioning and re-mediation, Shakespeare's audience was "literate" as to the format and characters of comedies like *The Taming of the Shrew*. Spectators could see the "pleasing stuff" of the play and enjoy that; but they could also see *through* it to the conduct of human relationships within.

Readers will recall (from the previous chapter) that Scott Olson has claimed this kind of transparency for Hollywood narrative:

"Transparency is defined as any textual apparatus that allows audiences to project indigenous values, beliefs, rites, and rituals into imported media" (1999: 5–6). He suggested that an audience's *readings* of "transplanted" dramatic narratives, such as those from Hollywood that conformed to an identifiable typology, were "indigenous" to the culture where the audience was located. Here Olson was at one with Shakespearian scholar Terence Hawkes. For him, the whole point of Shakespeare, like Hollywood and television for later ages, was to draw disparate populations together, to address humanity in scale, to make national and other cultural boundaries "transparent" in order to facilitate cross-demographic communication. Hawkes argued that the Elizabethan theater was part of "communal experience":

> Its audience, and its plays, were genuinely "popular"; the result of an amalgam of the elements of the culture, and an artistically honest "projection" of it. When that amalgam disintegrated, the "universality" which can be felt in the plays vanished. . . . [Elizabethan] theatre can never be reproduced, but its true heir in our culture can only be television. Television constitutes the only really "national" theatre our society is likely to have. (Hawkes 1973: 231; and see Harbage 1941)

The "universality" for their own times that Hawkes felt in Shakespearean theater and in television was nothing other than the "transparency" Olson discovered in Hollywood narratives (but see Hawkes's own critique of decontextualized universalism, 2002: 117, 122). Olson's argument was couched in the language of national cultural competitiveness amid fears of media effects at the international as well as at the individual level. Hawkes's language was that of the humanist interpreter of drama, who saw television *as* Shakespearean theater, not least in its relationship with a popular audience that was by no means passive in either case:

> [Television] does encourage . . . participation, vocal and positive. . . . And this kind of participation . . . is of the same order as that which formed a distinctive part of the traditional theatrical experience in Shakespeare's theatre. The interjected comments of the audience on a play, and their "participation" in it became common enough practice for this to be included as part of plays themselves; e.g. . . . *The Taming of the Shrew.* (Hawkes 1973: 230–1)

For its part, *Big Brother* was taken as both indigenous (local housemates) and universal (human qualities, dilemmas, and ruses) in each of its territories: Africa, Argentina, Australia, Belgium, Brazil, Bulgaria, Canada, Columbia, Croatia, the Czech Republic, Denmark, Ecuador, Finland, France, Germany, Greece, Hungary, India, Italy, Mexico, Middle East, the Netherlands, Nigeria, Norway, the Pacific (South America), the Philippines, Poland, Portugal, Romania, Russia, Scandinavia, Second Life, Serbia, Slovenia, South Africa, Spain, Sweden, Switzerland, Thailand, the UK, and the USA.[2] It featured multinational transmission and interactive reception. It betrayed nothing of its Dutch origins in any version outside of the Netherlands. It was popular in the USA but did not originate there. *Big Brother* engaged audiences in much more activity than just narrative reception, using phone, modem and screen, extensive media coverage and tie-ins in the press, radio and live events, and the independent but linked efforts of advertisers, fans, and critics. It gathered international populations while recognizing national differences, and encouraged cross-demographic and multiplatform talk about human character, interaction, and plot.

For Shakespeare's own early-modern audience, caught imperfectly between cultures (e.g. medieval role and rank vs. modern job and identity), plays such as *The Taming of the Shrew* could be regarded as transparent narratives in Olson's terms, universal in Hawkes's, and interactive in *Big Brother*'s. Here was a textual apparatus about rich Italians (the Renaissance equivalent of Americans) for which hard-up English subjects were prepared to pay. Shakespeare's entertainments evidently spoke directly to the conditions in which the audience lived, drawing them in thousands to the unregulated south bank of the Thames, where they merrily projected their human "values, beliefs, rites, and rituals," both individual and socialized, into *The Taming of the Shrew*, even though it was set in Padua and performed by celebrity actors – one of whom was Shakespeare himself.

Like television, Shakespeare's theater was dedicated to cross-demographic communication. This was also its business plan, since the production costs of the plays and capital costs of the theaters required audience maximization. As in any modern commercial entertainment, the customers were in a pecuniary relationship with a capitalist corporation, but at the level of meaning the cash nexus did not prevent something worthwhile passing between producer and consumer. Posterity is clear on this point.

Because of the semiotic intensity of the English vernacular in the Elizabethan period, Shakespeare was part of a culture that transmitted through time as well as across demographic and national borders. His plays could be received by later audiences as applicable to, indeed part of, their own cultural and personal identity and therefore as "indigenous," "universal," and "participatory" all at once. Since the 1590s *The Taming of the Shrew* itself has been "re-versioned" into various new media formats, including the prose narrative of Charles Lamb's *Tales from Shakespeare*, Cole Porter's 1948 musical *Kiss Me Kate*, a 1957 Bolshoi opera, and a 1967 Zeffirelli blockbuster starring Richard Burton and Elizabeth Taylor. It was rescripted into the 1999 teen movie *Ten Things I Hate About You*, set at "Padua High School" and starring "Kat Stratford" (Julia Stiles), "Patrick Verona" (Heath Ledger), and Kat's cute sister Bianca (Larisa Oleynik).[3]

The Taming of the Shrew was indigenized in places culturally even more remote from Elizabethan London than a Tacoma high school. For instance, it was successfully produced in Moscow in 1937–8 by Alexei Popov, People's Artist of the Soviet Union, as a play for the Red Army: "Shakespeare's humanism is understandable and congenial to our men and to our officers" (Popov 1966: 165); and again by the Kazakh Theatre of Drama in Alma-Ata in 1943 – a testing year for the USSR. Its spirit lived on. Popov justified putting on a play that some thought "ideologically doubtful":

> Shakespeare the humanist makes it clear that the union of man and woman is only possible on a basis of mutual love and respect. And this makes Shakespeare a great ally in our struggle for a happy, self-respecting and strong humanity. . . . The popular eternal wisdom of Shakespeare leads him to resolve this question [how to achieve a happy marriage] *in the spirit in which it is resolved by all progressive minds.* (pp. 166–8)

This was narrative transparency incarnate, as was Hollywood and TV during the American Century; as is *Big Brother*. In each case – Shakespeare, Hollywood, television, reality – highly artificial and commercial forms worked because despite demographic differences audiences were able to "read" them as "we" rather than "they" for the purposes of exploring the vicissitudes of human relations as entertainment. Their transparency arose from their "universalizing" human interest within a popular dramatic tradition.

This required of audiences something that the critic S. L. Bethell called "multi-consciousness" (1944: 28–9). It was necessary for playgoers to attend to the unfolding immediacy of the diegetic world imagined in the play, while remaining delightedly aware of both its artifice and their own active presence within it. The show was put on in daylight, in the all-too-visible round of the "wooden O," and many plays featured direct address to individuals in the audience: for instance, Hawkes (2002: 97) analyzes a very challenging direct address in *The Winter's Tale*, spoken to "many a man" in the audience who "even at this present, / Now, while I speak this, holds his wife by th'arm, / That little thinks she has been sluiced in his absence" by "Sir Smile, his neighbour" (*Winter's Tale* I.ii. 189–96). *The Taming of the Shrew* capitalized on the fuzzy line between audience and show by opening with characters (Sly and his supposed wife), who settled down, in character, amid good-humored banter that was nevertheless scripted, to enjoy the show with (and *as*) the paying customers. In this multi-conscious context audiences attended, with the lively and interactive pleasure of "communal experience," to the narrative, action, and characters, and to the spoken dialogue that both contributed to and resolved the uncertainty of outcome over several hours of action.

How would the characters, especially various couples of marriageable age, deal with each other, with the trials and tribulations of the plot and with the artifice itself, using modern personal resources (e.g. native wit and mental stratagems) rather than medieval social position (e.g. paternal authority), as they strove – and this was the entertainment – to achieve personal goals and to manage interpersonal relations to maximum individual benefit within generic expectations and social norms? That was the question. How can men and women live, together, at home? It was a question posed directly, and often, by Shakespeare. *Big Brother* used the resources of multiplatform broadcast and interactive media to pose it again.

Like *The Taming of the Shrew*, *Big Brother* drew attention to its audience in a big way. In the Australian version (with which I am most familiar) the BB house was located in a theme park called Dreamworld in Queensland, where a live audience of up to 1,000 regularly gathered on set – about as drunk and randy as Shakespeare's Sly by the look of some of them – and the show constantly invoked, exhorted, and included them and the viewers at home, interactively through votes and polls, and in their dealings with commercial partners such as purveyors of pizza and soft drinks. Indeed, the triumph of the audience over the players was what made *Big Brother* an interesting phenomenon, but not by any means a one-off. It was the latest in a long line of developments that successively made each new medium seem both more transparent and more interactive in its dealings with audiences, at least to observers at the time. Like Shakespeare, *Big Brother*'s appeal was that it came over as unmediated (i.e. as reality) in relation to people's character, while remaining intransigently artificial in its form of presentation. Technique delivered transparency; artifice enabled human interaction – live, now.

Broadcast television itself was welcomed thus by its own pioneers. Writing at the end of the 1940s, Maurice Gorham, a top BBC executive, mused on what it was that made television into a distinctive medium in its own right:

> The ability to transmit images of things that are actually happening, whether or not they are enacted specially, is the hall-mark of television as compared with films. . . . The appeal is simplest and most unmistakable when it is a question of real events in which people are interested, and not events created by the effort of writers, actors, and producers. (Gorham 1951: 137)

Gorham thought "real events" meant public staged happenings that were independent of their transmission on television – sport and spectacle from horse racing to coronations. What really interested families at home was domestic life itself – their own relationships and self-formation within that context. Those "real events in which people are interested" turned out to be pitched at an anthropological as well as a social level, like meeting a potential romantic date (*Perfect Match, Blind Date*) or – and this was *Big Brother*'s appeal – getting along with people who might turn out, as in real life, to be both friend and competitor, neighbor and enemy/lover, a sleaze or a shrew. It took TV a while to perfect the techniques whereby such "real events" could be artificially produced, live and now, for prime-time entertainment. With *Big Brother*, audiences found a highly artificial but trustworthily transparent vehicle via which to observe and participate in human emotions, stratagems, characters, and relationships as they unfolded in a domestic setting, and as they were tested, sometimes to destruction. And *Big Brother* shared the authorial function with the audience, making the progress and outcome of the on-screen drama a collective "act."

Both *The Taming of the Shrew* and *Big Brother* began with a reflexive episode that drew attention to their status as shows. In the case of *Big Brother* in Australia, it was the scene-setting opening episode of the second series, April–June 2002. Would audiences "get in character" and follow the show, or would they heave a collective shrug of "been there, done that," and leave the new housemates to their fate? *Big Brother* rose to the challenge with a season opener that, according to one ratings expert at the time, "brained everything across the market" (Alan Robertson of Initiative Media, quoted in the *Age*, April 8, 2002). It was the number two show nationally that week. Ostensibly it was to "meet the house-mates," but the preview was also a revealing exposé of *Big Brother* itself: a show about the show. It tutored viewers in what happened on set and how it was done, including footage showing how potential housemates were auditioned and chosen on dramatic criteria, as characters in a cast. Simultaneously it relied on the audience's existing knowledge to increase their fun and involvement. It was about the "literacy" of viewers in the format; allusive, knowing, upgrading the skills and insights that viewers would need to get the most out of the series. It shared the gag with them while asking them to enjoy the show, displaying the artifice to expose the art.

The Taming of the Shrew also opens with an episode that is about the play to come. The "Induction" is a comic scene in which the low-life character Sly is sleeping it off after having been thrown out of the pub. He is found by a passing Lord, who decides to "practice on this drun-ken man" by concocting a "flattering dream or worthless fancy" that will make Sly "forget himself." His attendants will take the still sleeping drunkard to the Lord's own "fairest chamber." On awakening, Sly is to be treated like a lord, and convinced by everyone in the household, includ-ing the Lord's pageboy who will pose as the man's wife, that he is in fact a lord and not a beggar. One of them says: "we will play our part, as he shall think . . . he is no less than what we say he is" (Induction.i. 36–71).

The Lord has a lascivious fantasy about his page-boy as a woman:

> Such duty to the drunkard let him do
> With soft low tongue and lowly courtesy,
> And say "What is't your honour will command,
> Wherein your lady and your humble wife
> May show her duty and make known her love?"
> (Induction.i. 113–17)

The prospect of a compliant girl asking, with "kind embracements, tempt-ing kisses," how she might show her love, would certainly have attracted some participatory and lewd suggestions from the audience. The page duly meets the drunkard, who doesn't even know his supposed wife's name. Informed that lords call their wives "madam" he asks if she's "Alice madam, or Joan madam?" Without pausing for an answer, he invites her to "undress you and come now to bed." She entreats delay, at least until sunset, for the sake of his health. "I hope this reason stands for my excuse."

Sly's bawdy reply puns on the word "stands" – "Ay, it stands so, that I may hardly tarry so long" (Induction.ii.102–67). Sexual excitement is urgent and, it seems, all too physically manifest. Here the entertainment for spectators is to enjoy a scene where someone is so aroused by his proximity to a previously unknown but apparently up-for-it housemate that he gets a visible erection, with the added delight of knowing that the object of desire is not at all what "she" seems but (as all female parts were) a cross-dressed adolescent boy.

At this very moment the players arrive on stage to perform *The Taming of the Shrew*, being the entertainment Sly must watch while "tarrying" before bed. An ordinary bloke, who both *represents* the audience and *performs* it on stage, is put in an unfamiliar domestic setting, in a house belonging to an organization of vastly greater economic resource than his own, so that his behavior might be observed for the entertainment of the onlookers. He is surrounded by paid professionals whose scripted interactions come across to him as convincingly personal, while entertaining those in the know. Welcome to *Big Brother*, 1590s style.

Today's housemates don't need to be duped like Christophero Sly: they choose willingly to go into that unfamiliar house, to take on a lifestyle totally at odds with their own, in order to provide onlookers with an entertainment based upon inversions of status, experiments with identity, and the comedy of errors as people play with personalities they don't get to express in the outside world. But like Sly, some of them are all too immediately smitten with desire, and that pleases the audience as it did in Elizabethan London. The bottom line for both *The Taming of the Shrew* and *Big Brother* was marriageability, and the role or performance of the self in that context.

Kiss me Katrina

Why, there's a wench! Come on, and kiss me, Kate.
The Taming of the Shrew, *V.ii.181*

The second series of *Big Brother* in Australia (2002) introduced a new character to the world, by the name of Katrina. Unlike Shakespeare's Katharina, Katrina Miani was a real person. But her self-image appeared to be very different from what the other housemates, along with *Big Brother* editors, commentators, and audiences, made of her character. In one profile she likened herself to Audrey Hepburn, in another she thought she was "a bit of a mother figure." However, observers seemed to agree that here was a "Katharina" worthy of Shakespeare's shrew: "*Katrina* comes across as highly opinionated. . . . She seems to speak without thinking about the consequences of her comments. Some of these comments can be quite brutal and this appears to have rubbed some of the others in the group the wrong way" (BB Website).[4]

Kat was discussed in fan postings, which focused on her shrewishness: "*From Hot Chicky [27.Jun.02 − 5:02 PM]* Katrina – do you know that lots of people hate u, including me. I think u were a winger [*sic*] and a pain in the ass!!!"[5] Or this from a young blogger in Perth called Emma: "[Katrina] has narcissistic personality disorder. She uses people, has no regard for their feelings, thinks she always deserves praise, thinks she's above other people, refuses to accept that not everyone agrees with her, and does things solely so that she can feel more important than others and have them admire her for that."[6] Ouch!

Katrina received the most nominations for eviction from her housemates in the first week, and was all too visibly upset, angry, and incredulous. She didn't handle the situation well. But she wasn't evicted – in fact she received the lowest vote of the three nominees from the viewing public. They chose instead to evict a plausible but sly young man who'd been trying his luck with several of the girls (like a "Bianca" subplot). However, Katrina was nominated again in the second week. In the days before the vote was announced, Katrina was noticeably more in control, and performed several helpful tasks for the house. But this time she was evicted with 57 percent of the popular vote.

The contrast between her "hissy fits" on the show and her composure afterward led to further comment, and discussion of the extent to which editing was used to control viewers' reactions: "The people behind the scenes are responsible for making fools or stars out of the contestants. I bet tearful Katrina from Big Brother Two had little idea that she had become one of Australia's most annoying young women."[7] Big Brother himself (alias producer Peter Abbott) replied to this criticism:

Puppets On A String? As for the conspiracy theory that Big Brother chooses who's going to be a hero, and who's going to be a villain, BB finds the whole idea amusing. "We're neither clever enough to achieve it, nor stupid enough to try it," he said. . . . "Kat's crying, Damo's lines and Aaron's outbursts all happened – we all saw it. How the audience then choose to perceive those moments in their overall judgment of that housemate is up to them, not us," he said. So what does determine which footage makes it to air? Character development, and basic entertainment values, according to [supervising producer] Chris Blackburn. (May 25, 2002)[8]

Big Brother's live studio audience got in on the act, and into the national news. They commiserated with Kat about her pet goldfish Bubalah. His death had been reported to her by Big Brother while she was in the house, provoking one of her famous crying episodes. On her eviction, Katrina was greeted by fans sporting "RIP Bubalah" signs:

> *Katrina out in landslide.* When Katrina Miani emerged from the Big Brother house to see strangers mourning her dead pet goldfish, she gained a sudden appreciation for the reach of the reality phenomenon . . . "When I saw all these people with 'rest in peace' [signs] on their heads, I (thought) 'Oh my God – the nation knows that my goldfish died'," the 22-year-old . . . said. (Kathryn Torpy, *Courier Mail*, April 29, 2002)

The evening of Katrina's eviction on Channel 10 was also the night of the "Logies" – Australian TV's industry awards. Miani appeared in a live cross to that event, which was broadcast on rival Channel 9. *Big Brother* won Best Reality Program. "RIP Bubalah" went on sale as an icon for mobile phones.

Katrina unwittingly became an international political story.

> *Big Brother goes political.* Big Brother has become Australia's newest political battleground as Young Liberal and Young Labor supporters attempt to influence the reality TV show. The revelation that one of last week's eviction nominees, Katrina Miani, was a Victorian Young Liberal, sparked an email campaign by Young Liberals in her home state and New South Wales to keep her in the house. (Dale Paget, *Age*, April 24, 2002)

Not to be outdone, Young Labor supporters claimed her eviction as a political triumph:

> *No room for a party-girl, Big Brother's watching.* Katrina became the target of the campaign when news website crikey.com.au revealed that the perky Brighton dweller was – shock, horror – a Young Liberal. . . . NSW Young Labor president Chris Minns started the anti-Katrina campaign with an email to members. "It is time for a good old-fashioned 'Kick the Young lib off *Big Brother*' grassroots campaign," it read. (Olivia Hill-Douglas, *Age*, April 30, 2002)

Although she was later convinced that this, together with "certain photographs," explained her eviction, Katrina apparently took it in good spirit:

> *ALP claims Big Brother scalp.* "I am so not like anyone else in the Young Liberals," she laughed, adding that she was now contemplating canceling her membership. "I did have political aspirations but to make it in politics you have to be a particular type of person and I don't think I have the nastiness in me," Miani said. (*Age*, April 29, 2002)

But it was too late to abandon politics. This was already a global story, duly reported on news sites around the world; for instance, in Brazil: "*'Big Brother' australiano vira guerra política.*"[9]

Katrina's appearance in *Picture* magazine two years previously, where she had posed nude, was prominent in accounts of her career on *Big Brother*. Soon the pictures were made public again, both on the net,[10] and reprinted in *100% Home Girls* (17, 2002; see also *Picture* 564, 2000, and *100% Home Girls* 1, 2000). But when Katrina was evicted, it was the content of her character that was reckoned memorable, not (as one commentator put it)[11] her "wobbly bits": "*Catch Ya Later, Kat.* Love her, or hate her, there's no doubting Kat has been the most talked about housemate on Big Brother, thus far. Trials and tribulations, tantrums and talking to herself . . . Kat's antics on BB have made for must-see TV . . . One thing's for sure. For good or bad, she will be remembered" (BB website, April 28, 2002).

Once out of the house, Katrina could speak for herself:

> *How do you feel about yourself? Did you feel better after time went on?* There's been less crying episodes and I've been feeling a lot better about myself just this week. . . . I think having the task to throw myself into, and show that I am worthwhile and have a place in the group, was good. (BB website, April 28, 2002)

Asked "Who do you think will win?" she said: "I'm thinking Pete. He's just an all round good Aussie bloke." A latter-day Petruchio, although less of a braggart, Peter did indeed go on to win.

Katrina appeared in numerous media including *Rove Live* on Channel 10 (April 30, 2002) and on Radio National's *Media Report* (May 23, 2002), where presenter Mick O'Regan quizzed her about the reality of the show: "it's a very abbreviated version, but what was shown is definitely part of me." Finally he asked her:

O'Regan: Do you feel as though you've been sort of marketed as a media product?

Miani: No, actually. Like I came out, and you just get thrown in the deep end, and I thought, Boy, I wish I'd had some training. But now I've kind of realised that there are so many reality TV shows, and so many personalities have come out from that sort of stuff, that you basically get thrown in, and it's sink or swim, because there's just too many of us. So if you can handle it, you survive, and if you can't you go by the wayside. And it's just the battle of the fittest. The game is not in the house. The real game is out here.

O'Regan: Too right it is.[12]

Her media appearances tapered off after that, and Miani went back to work, although she continued to join post sessions on the web, and make appearances at clubs and events.

Like Katharina in *Taming of the Shrew*, Katrina was perceived as shrewish to begin with, and later redeemed herself, both on the show as she took on household tasks and saw them through, and afterward by her articulate and "tamed" comportment, not least during her eviction-interview with BB host Gretel Killeen; she was funny, insightful, and not in the least vengeful (see figure 9.1). But there remained a difference: Katrina was not tamed by a suitor and husband. In these Foucauldian times she had to learn to "govern" herself while playing a part. If she was tested by anything, it was by a television program rather than a suitor. Indeed she listed "self-exploration" as one of her motivations for going on the show:

> *Kat Talks Back.* BB: What did you personally get out of the BB experience?
> K: I think that BB helped my self-confidence. I know a lot of people have called me arrogant and stuck-up but I actually often feel intimidated more than anything else. Being in such a challenging environment made me see that if I put my mind to it I can achieve the things that I dream of if I just put in the effort. (July 10, 2002)[13]

Her second motivation was to take part in a "social experiment," having read George Orwell's *1984*. Such a thing, a *social* experiment of *self*-exploration, might be called "the taming of the self."

Figure 9.1 Katrina Miani – the taming of the self. *Big Brother*, series 2 (Australia, April 28, 2002). Photo: Steve Pohlner, Newspix

The Source of Meaning

What if Big Brother was already here, as the (imagined) Gaze for whom I was doing things, whom I tried to impress, to seduce, even when I was alone? What if the Big Brother *show only renders palpable this universal structure? In other words, what if, in our "real lives," we already play a certain role – we are not what we are, we play ourselves? The welcome achievement of "Big Brother" is to remind us of this uncanny fact.*

Slavoj Žižek (2002: 226)

Big Brother was a worthy successor to Shakespeare, as Katrina was to Katharina. But despite the interesting family resemblances between Renaissance theater and reality TV, the two are not the same. In the intervening period, something has happened to meaning. Its supposed source has shifted down the "value chain of meaning" (see chapter 2). In *contemporary* times, the source of meaning has drifted to the "consumer" end of the value chain. It has been taken to reside in the *audience* or *reader*. Given the anonymous popular sovereignty of mass democracy, this is an egalitarian approach to meaning. It requires large-scale sampling, aggregating, and ethnographic methods to get at what a given text might mean, because it means only what several million people say it does. The way to find that out is by poll, survey, and sample – by *plebiscite*. One of its imaginative or ritualized forms is *Big Brother*. Katrina Miani had no more control over her meaning than she did over her tear ducts. What she meant depended not on her own authorial intentions, or those of *Big Brother*'s producers, or even on its textual content. Katrina very clearly meant what her viewers – including journalists, political activists, bloggers, and the voting viewers – said she did.

While the fact that she was a real person experiencing real emotions guaranteed the transparency of *Big Brother*, her own sense of her reality had almost no bearing on how she was presented and received. Gossip media and bystanders concentrated on judging her character. Quality newspapers enjoyed all that too, but filed it under "political news." Some commentators used her image to discuss the artifice of the reality format itself. Others were interested in gazing at a desirable young woman or, conversely, in judging her adversely for the "pictures from the past." In each case Katrina meant what *they* said. But her dependence on the audience went further. As a contestant on *Big Brother* Katrina was also a character in an unfolding story in which the mass audience had an active part to play. They played it by making judgments about her character and actions in comparison with the other players, and voting accordingly. The meaning not only of Katrina but also of the entire show and format was determined by plebiscite, which was itself the high point of the entertainment, drawing much higher ratings to evictions than to the routine daily shows. Endemol itself claimed:

For the first time, ordinary people and the mass media have been given the opportunity to really interact. . . . If one thing has been proven, it's the eagerness of modern consumers to be involved in as many ways as possible. Spearheaded by massive TV coverage, the community has found its way to interactive media, with cross media links to all platforms. TV, website, email, SMS, WAP, and interactive TV refer to each other and keep the fans updated. More importantly, these media keep the community involved by means of voting, chatting, playing and other options.[14]

In such a context *Big Brother* represents one example, and reality TV one form, of an anthropological extension of "performance" to the whole population. Not only does everyone "perform the self," but everyone knows that they are doing it (and *how* to do it), so that the form taken by "self-exploration" is "playing a part." Some – like Katrina – are even driven to check the ratings and reviews to learn about themselves:

BB: Any low moments?
K: Well, there have been some. Probably the lowest was after reading the web forums about a week after I left the house. But even in my darkest moments when I thought "is it still worth it?" the answer is still a re-sounding yes! I think that the darker moments just make the good times feel even better. (July 10, 2002)[15]

This is a democratization of "playing"; the mass audience participating in their own Warholian "15 minutes of fame." That this is not always a comfortable quarter of an hour was itself a hard-learnt "part":

From Spearbear My question is: "What was your perception of fame before going into the House? And how has the experience changed your perception of fame?" Thanks.
   From miani69@yahoo.com . . . my answer for spearbear's question is yes, my perception of fame has changed. I grew up thinking that famous people were glamorous and rich and rich and didn't have any worries. I was very wrong. I feel just the same – except people now know who I am. That's the only difference fame makes. (July 13, 2002)[16]

The intimate "I" has become a public property to be judged by strangers.
   Because there is too much readily accessible meaning out there among the millions of people, media, sites, and sources, the *creation* of meaning is no longer an authorial act. It's an editorial one, resulting from

the textual practice of *redaction*; the creative editorial function of bringing existing materials together to make new texts and meanings. This is the art form of the age (and also the "method" of this book), a product and a promoter of the long-term drift of meaning to the consumer. Redaction adds value to the end of meaning's value chain. Once again, *Big Brother* makes the point, being itself a redactional text. Each episode of the show required heroic acts of creative editing to take the multi-camera, 24/7 footage of transparent, live, unmediated reality and to turn it into something like TV serial drama, or a very long frat movie, with three story lines per episode. At the macro level *Big Brother* also symbolized a redactional society – its overall meaning and its appeal were the amalgam of elements drawn from the house and housemates, the audience and commentators, surrounding media and business partners, adding up to a coherence that could only be achieved by editing those existing materials into something legible.

Such developments were accompanied by, and required, changes in literacy, of which they were also a symptom. The popular audience is achieving a *"read and write"* capacity in publicly distributed media, not least via their participation in shows like *Big Brother*. For Katrina to mean what consumers said she did, the viewing public has to be able to contribute in scale to the process of meaning creation. Those plebiscitary contributions need to be re-presented by redactional means, so that both actors and audience could learn how their very identity is an outcome of consumer choices beyond their control. That's how they can both perform the self and submit that performance to the judgment of the entire community, and how an "imagined community" uses TV's highest-rating entertainment show to explore questions of personality and relationship, and therefore also of marriageability and citizenship. That's how "shrewishness" is "tamed." That's what *Big Brother* has done, and it is an achievement of no less significance than Shakespeare's. As Katrina herself had said: "the game is not in the house. The real game is out here."

Notes

1   See www.endemol.com/corporate/history.jsp.
2   See www.bigbrotherworld.tv; and www.en.wikipedia.org/wiki/Big_Brother_(TV_series).
3   See www.movieweb.com/movie/10things/10things.txt.

4   See www.bigbrother.iprimus.com.au/news.
5   See www.geocities.com/sacchi_80/art_kat_forums.html; see also www.gusworld.com.au/tv/bigbro/bb2002.htm.
6   See tarnish.net/written/mundane/20020430.html.
7   See members.hn.ozemail.com.au/~voyager/letsgetreal/letsgetreal.html.
8   See www.bigbrother.iprimus.com.au/news.
9   See www.mundifm.com.br/news/index24042002.htm.
10 See watchersweb.com/30754.htm.
11 See www.ourbrisbane.com/entertainment/tv_guide/newsandgossip/2002_05_01.htm.
12 See www.abc.net.au/rn/talks/8.30/mediarpt/stories/s562394.htm.
13 See www.geocities.com/sacchi_80/katrina.html.
14 See www.endemol.com/interactive/formats_big_brother.jsp.
15 See www.geocities.com/sacchi_80/katrina.html.
16 See www.geocities.com/sacchi_80/art_kat_forums.html.

Sync or Swim? Plebiscitary Sport and Synchronized Voting

New things are happening at the interface of sport and media that may barely be visible from the perspective of regular sport, whether you're a player, a fan, or a spectator. If your sporting pleasures are mainstream, for instance if they involve any combination of men, a ball, and a team, then you might want to insist that an activity from which men are excluded, that requires smiling, a flamboyant costume, and trying as hard as possible to appear *exactly the same* as everyone else involved, can't be a real sport. But while that seems obvious today, the days of ball-assisted male combat as the ideal-type of sport may be numbered, or at least subject to competition from an unlikely alternative.

Growing up unnoticed in the thickets of popular entertainment and reality TV are new sporting attributes. They celebrate not individual heroics but spectator-oriented teamwork, where no matter how strenuous the performance, it must look effortless and stylish. Sporting values are feminizing. Instead of objective measurements – "faster, higher, stronger," as the Olympic motto *"citius, altius, fortius"* puts it – winners are picked by how they look to a panel of judges; by consumer choice, as it were.

Sport and media are converging and integrating. As they do so, what counts as sport, why it is valued, and what it symbolizes for contemporary culture are all changing. I take these changes to be emblematic of something emergent in the culture at large. The modernist paradigm, four hundred years in the making, is shifting toward a new consumerist paradigm (see chapter 2); and this is symbolized in new sports, of which the paradigm example is synchronized swimming.

Mars to Venus

I think I was the first scholar of cultural and media studies, possibly of any sort, to publish an analysis of synchronized swimming, in *The politics of pictures* (1992a). The cover picture of that book is a production still from a famous Hollywood film celebrating – perhaps even originating – this most unlikely sport. It shows Esther Williams, surrounded by mermettes (is that a word?), at the climax of *The Million Dollar Mermaid* (1952).[1] In other words, in my book, whose subtitle is "the creation of the public in the age of popular media," synchronized swimming is taken as nothing less than the *emblem* of the contemporary mediated *public*.

In this context, one aspect of a strange sport stands out as especially peculiar – compulsory smiling. I made it stand for other contemporary jobs in which smiling is compulsory, ranging from PR and TV presenters to retail assistants. Synchronized swimmers are an appropriate metaphor for the "smiling professions"; modern professionals in media, marketing, and the services who *represent the public to itself*. The smiling professions address and call into being, and also personify and embody, "the public" for large, diverse societies where the community can no longer experience itself as self-present. They do the work of holding together – by strenuous but invisible effort – the Andersonian "imagined community." They turn work into spectacle, competition into desirability, the imagined community into smiling faces. Synchronized swimming is their sport (Hartley 1992a: 137). In the *Historical Journal of Film and Television*, Tom Streeter noted my "description of the growth of the 'smiling professions' in the twentieth century . . . Hartley wittily uses synchronized swimming – a strenuous, highly skilled activity performed with a contrived smile – to illustrate the internal character, artfulness, and improbability of this new form of professionalism" (June 1996).[2] But like synchronized swimming, which suffers a "reputation deficit" compared with ball-sports, the smiling professions are among the most despised of all contemporary occupations. In both cases the put-downs bear no relation to the levels of training, skill, and dedication required to perform the job well. Socially, the reputation deficit also masks how important the smiling professions are to the daily functioning of hyper-democratized societies, just as the jocular dismissal of synchronized swimming masks the extent to which combat models of sport may be under threat from apparently weaker forces, as sporting values migrate from Mars to Venus.

Readers will recall from chapter 2 that it was Robert Kagan who coined the memorable line about Americans being from Mars and Europeans from Venus. Of course such a characterization oversimplifies, and Kagan refers to strategic rather than sporting power. But, nevertheless, as he writes, "the caricatures do capture an essential truth" (2003: 6). He draws attention to two divergent models of strategic policy: one based on unconstrained power (Mars), the other on the arts of *weakness*: "negotiation, diplomacy, and commercial ties, on international law over the use of force, on seduction over coercion, on multilateralism over unilateralism" (Venus) (p. 55). In Kagan's analysis, Europe has embraced Venus (miraculously, the "German lion has lain down with the French lamb" (p. 58), while, since World War II, the USA has taken over the Martial mantle from imperial ("Old") Europe.

Kagan's own interest is confined to strategic power – military supremacy and the willingness to use it on the world stage. He does not expand his analysis to include other spheres, including culture. But a parting of the ways has also occurred in that sphere. Some countries – notably France – want to protect their national culture, using the Venusian arts of negotiation and law (diplomacy, negotiation, "seduction not coercion"). Others – notably the USA – see culture in market terms, and market strength has become a metaphor for military might, following a "Hobbesian" model of power where competition throws up winners and winner takes all. From this perspective it's easy to see the values of Venus as illusory. But equally, many countries and individuals across the world reject the "power" model of competition in favor of the "law" model. It seems to me that the same forces are at work in sport. Here the distinction between Mars and Venus is not drawn along national borders but in the differences between different types of sporting endeavor. Put simply, there is hegemonic, modern, *power* sport, and there are "seductive," postmodern, *law* sports. It's the difference between football and synchronized swimming.

The turn from Mars to Venus in sport is indicative of more general changes, amounting to a paradigm shift. What interests me here is the "reputation deficit" that emergent forms suffer at the hands of those whose values they may be supplanting. I'm making synchronized swimming a metaphor for other forms that have suffered, and continue to suffer, a reputation deficit, namely the smiling professions and the popular media they serve. Compared to the world of official (political) power, popular media are Venusian synchronized swimmers. But, just as the Venusian value of "seduction not coercion" – despite its apparent weakness – is challenging Martial notions of power, so the popular media are a challenge to existing political and intellectual elites.

A Sprinkler System

Many of the components of what we recognize as modernity were assembled during the seventeenth century, including secular science based on reason and the theory of the modern state. A leading theorist in both of these endeavors was Thomas Hobbes, whose great work *Leviathan* was published in 1651. Hobbes thought the natural condition of humankind was "war of each against all," requiring a strong state – Leviathan – to maintain order. Hobbes was interested in power; like Kagan, he was on the side of Mars not Venus.

However, it was Hobbes himself who identified – by their very absence – the need for the smiling professions and popular media within his constitutional arrangements for the modern state. He imagined their political and cultural *functions*, the need for some sort of society-wide mediating system to teach the lay public the political and moral truths of the day, long before technology or a suitably trained profession were available to deliver them.

Hobbes was obsessed by the inadequacy of the only mechanism available in his own day to teach civil and moral doctrine to the population at large, namely the universities. He saw the universities as fountains not of truth but of error (papism and sophistry). He could only conclude *Leviathan* with this rather forlorn hope: "For seeing the Universities are the Fountains of Civill, and Morall Doctrine, from whence the Preachers, and the Gentry, drawing such water as they find, use to sprinkle the same (both from the Pulpit, and in their Conversation) upon the People, there ought certainly to be great care taken, to have it pure" (Hobbes 1968: 728, 378–86; Hartley 1992a: 122–30).

A fountainhead from which both *professionals and opinion leaders* (preachers and gentry) drew *ideological principles* (civil and moral doctrine) to use for *teaching* the lay population (sprinkled upon the people): this is a succinct description of the social-cultural function of mass media in modern nation-states. Hobbes just lacked the technology. He was very skeptical about universities. They weren't up to the job; they were more likely to define themselves *against* the authority Hobbes wanted people to "obey" in order to achieve "concord" in the body politic (Hobbes 1968: 380). Hobbes thought the universities were inclined to papism, to which he objected not on theological but political grounds because it fostered allegiance to a foreign prince. He also criticized "Aristotelity" (scholasticism or sophistry) in the universities, in contrast to what would now be recognized as modern empirical science based on mathematics and observation (pp. 708; 688). Thus, at the very outset of modernity, there was perceived to be a tension between the *need* for popular instruction in the service of a state of "concord," and the *means* to deliver it. Formal (university) education was divergent from necessary civic and moral education.

It was exactly this gap that popular media came to fill, starting during the same early modern period with popular entertainments like the theater and various forms of news – from juicy murders to constitutional debates – circulating via print and song. As industrialization kicked in, the media developed "mass" forms, from the radical "pauper press" to the commercial media empires that dominated the twentieth century. Such media were popular not because of the purity of their doctrine, but because they proved good at story-telling and spectacle; often finding a way to couch the great questions of turbulent times in a popular idiom, and by no means always to the advantage of the government of the day. Media professionals were not endowed with the authority of the state – quite the reverse in many cases – but this may have made them seem more trustworthy to lay people, even when their commercial might rivaled that of countries.

While Hobbes despaired of the official institutions for the mediation of ideas, the popular media were establishing a new "fountainhead" from which the population came to draw ideological water because they *liked* it. Media professionals had to strive above all to maintain people's goodwill toward the media themselves, their stories and sights, to keep them coming back for more not out of "obedience" but out of "concord." Because there was no compulsion, popular media had to seek approval from their users ahead of the political and ideological authorities. Perhaps this is why Hobbes missed them – he was a modernist, concerned with political theory, government, and the state – not with "smiling." Of "doctrine" he only thought that it should be "*pure.*" It did not occur to him to have it *palatable* too, even though he understood that Leviathan (i.e. the monarchical state) depended not on the mere *existence* or mere assertion of the rights or powers of the king, but on the people accepting those rights and obeying authority in "concord." (Hobbes 1968: 380). This failure to connect "concord" with consent, and consent with communicative media that people liked and trusted, left Hobbes's political theory incomplete at the end of *Leviathan*, and perhaps made his vision of the modern state much more authoritarian in the matter of popular instruction than it needed to be.

Leviathan was never put into practice as Hobbes imagined it. Instead, two independent systems for the creation and control of "the public" grew up across the span of modernity. One was the formal domain of politics and learning. The other was the informal arena of popular entertainment. The latter was essential to the constitution but intensely disliked by the denizens of the former, a situation that remains, as Stephen Coleman showed in his comparison of "PJs" ("political junkies") with BBs ("Big Brothers" – fans of reality TV), where PJs were irrationally hostile to BBs (but not vice versa) (Coleman 2003). Perhaps this explains why "civil and moral" teaching, using a popular idiom to "sprinkle" ideas on the people, remains despised by institutionally placed political, civic, and moral professionals. The popular media are disliked (by cause-and-effect rationalists especially) precisely because they are *media* – they come *between* political purpose and its object. They can be fun and they can't be directly controlled, and what's more they reach a part of the body politic that the authorities can't control either – the hearts and minds of lay people.

Reputation Deficit

Popular mediation as go-between, both connecting and disconnecting power and people, also offends the Protestant work ethic, another invention of the seventeenth century, because "consuming" media is taken to be part of the world of private pleasure not public affairs. Compared with sober public duty and the industrious creation of wealth, taking pleasure in stories and spectacle, using the dissembling arts of acting, the seductions of music and rhetoric, and the necessary lies of fiction seemed literally sinful, especially when such means were used to convey weighty public truths in the vehicle of entertainment. How, in short, could bear-baiting teach citizenship?

This vein of Puritan suspicion of the most popular media remains. It is manifest in the endless game of invidious comparisons where there's a reputation deficit on one side of any given pair of terms: quality versus trash, art versus entertainment, production versus consumption, serious versus sensational, etc. There's a hint of the same in the disciplinary suspicion expressed by some social science or political economy approaches (where media are *work*; a problem of control) toward the humanities (where media are *culture*; a source of pleasure). Since Hobbes's time, and especially since the nineteenth century when the press became fully industrialized, the media themselves have grown and prospered and some of them have become an accepted part of the governmental administration of life. The "deficit" model also operates here to distinguish the sheep from the goats – invidious comparisons that are designed to accord "official" status to serious outlets and approved modes of address, and to label *disapproved* versions (often the most popular) as aesthetically, educationally, politically, and/or morally deficient.

From within this modernist/workerist tradition that values power over rhetoric, decisions over drama, comes a strongly expressed disapproval for mediation of any sort. The same mental settings are evident in sport. Modern sport celebrates power, so it can't deal with a sport based on aesthetics – like synchronized swimming. The response is standard: many within the system refuse even to recognize it *as* sport, or they treat it with dismissive humor:

> Swimmer: I get really annoyed watching Roy and HG [a cult sports/comedy duo in Australia] and the Olympics. . . . I feel that they don't really appreciate what we do. They'd never do that to the swimmers or the track athletes, they'd never criticise them the way they criticise us; but I think it's just being a little bit naïve, I guess, because they don't really understand what goes on behind the scenes . . . here we are making it look easy when actually it is really, really hard and it takes years and years of training to get it to look easy. (Sarah Bombell & Eloise Amberger [Queensland champion duet in synchronized swimming] on ABC Radio, *The Sports Factor*, May 27, 2005)[3]

Leviathan to Mermaid

But times are changing again. Industrial society has evolved beyond the need for strong states and territorial loyalty (nations and their national games), while media have evolved beyond the broadcast era. The "business plan" of modernity, based on power and control, and on one-to-many, "read-only" ideological communication, is drawing toward the end of its useful life. The Hobbesian model of social life as "war of each against all" (for which sport is a ritual displacement) is shifting to a new model of Venusian, feminized competitiveness. New sports are emerging to symbolize the change.

Economic and symbolic emphasis has shifted down the value chain toward the consumer. This is part of a much more general process that can be observed across many cultural sites and communicative contexts, along the "value chain of meaning" (see chapter 2). The "behavioral" consumer of the long-dominant "media effects" model of communication – the despised or vulnerable feminized figure who for most of the twentieth century stood passive and manipulated at the supermarket shelf or in the polling booth, responding to commercial and political campaigning designed to make her behave as causal agents further up the value chain wanted her to – is giving way, even in marketing literature, to a new model of the consumer as "action." This much more interesting figure is the *user*, who is able to make as well as consume, write as well as read, who interacts with peers and organizations, and who drives innovation and co-creation in many dynamic sectors of the cultural and information economy, from the open source movement to games and online journalism.

It does seem to me that symbolic meanings can be associated with this historic shift down the value chain. For instance, the modern era differed strongly from the pre-modern or medieval period, when the source of meaning was thought to be divine and unarguable and truth was *revealed* as an article of faith. In contrast, *realism*, whether factual (journalism) or fictional (the novel, screen drama), suits the *modern* era's preoccupation with locating the source of meaning in objects; as for instance scientific observation of the properties of things in themselves, documentary evidence in law and history, the primacy of the text in literature and philosophy. But now it seems that an epochal change is under way again, in which the modern certainty that the source of meaning is to be found in objects, texts, and evidence is under attrition. In the *contemporary* ("globalized") era, realism is shifting to "*reality.*" Instead of one scarce truth there are plenty. Instead of one type of subjectivity there is difference and diversity (Hartley 2003: 3–5). There's a kind of hyper-democratization of meaning going on. Instead of investigating objects to determine what they mean, we ask consumers. The more who buy, vote or choose; the more something is worth. Instead of using criticism and aesthetic judgment of the internal qualities of an object, artwork, or text to determine its value, we use the plebiscite.

Symbolic values associated with sport are not immune to change. The long-term historical drift in the location of the source of meaning can be discerned in sports. They are drifting toward "reality," consumer plenitude, and the plebiscite. Some developments that seem pertinent are:

- *synchronized* sports – where choreographed collaboration within a team is prioritized, and where teams don't play each other as they do in many ball-sports (here the difference between synchronized swimming and water polo may be instructive). A good example is formation skydiving: the 2005 women's world record was won by "jumpforthecause.com" in aid of breast cancer research, where 151 women skydivers held a pinwheel formation for 4.8 seconds.[4]
- *feminized* sports – where there's a drift from male solo combat hero to female collaborative competitive being-looked-at; a shift from Mars to Venus.
- *plebiscitary* sports – where winning is an outcome of voting; not defeating an opposition directly but impressing spectators. An extension of such sports from the era of "realism" to the era of reality is the practice of throwing open voting from empanelled experts to spectators at large. Consumers determine the winner. Here ballroom dancing leads the way; it is already a world sport, but only with expert judges (as yet).
- *consumer-integrated* sports – where for example fashion (the costume) is *integral* – as in ballroom dancing and synchronized swimming of course, but also and increasingly in tennis, women's beach volleyball, surfing, etc. Consumer integration extends to sports where merchandising and mediation are pivotal, possibly primary, although this may apply to all sport now.

Consumer integration takes its most spectacular form when Olympic medalists turn their talents to entertainment: reigning Olympic and world champion rhythmic gymnast Ioulia Barsoukova was a hit as an ice-skater (go figure) for the Russian Ice Stars in *Nutcracker on Ice*; the same company toured *Sleeping Beauty on Ice* choreographed by legendary figure-skating coach Tatiana Tarasova; meanwhile the Cirque du Soleil extravaganza called *O* in Las Vegas features synchronized swimming Olympians coached by gold-medalist Sylvie Fréchette.[5]

Synchronized, feminized, plebiscitary, consumer-integrated sports include ice-skating (figure-skating/ice-dancing), rhythmic and artistic gymnastics, synchronized swimming and diving, trampoline, ballroom dancing, equestrian dressage, skydiving, surfing, and kite-surfing (where the 2005–6 world champion was an 11-year-old Catalan girl, Gisela Pulido).

Fascism to Fashion

Synchronized sports should not be confused with *regimented* fitness. People used to talk about *calisthenics*, and despite the fact that calisthenics had its origins in ladies' colleges in the mid-nineteenth century – the word comes from the Greek for "beauty" (kalos) plus "strength" (sthenos) – the dominant image is of mass physical exercises on parade grounds, with militaristic or fascistic overtones. Such displays were "synchronized" but on an industrial scale, regimented and standardized. The type of new possibilities that are being explored in synchronized sports is evident in the difference between those *1984*-style proletarian triumphs of the will and synchronized swimming itself, where make-up, hair gel, music, and nose-clips are specified equipment. Economic dynamism has shifted from production to consumption, from industry to services, work to entertainment. Media have begun to open up to interactive, DIY, user-led, or consumer co-created inputs. The political sphere and that of learning are both migrating away from traditional institutions and professions, toward private identity and the self. So perhaps there's less of a structural imperative now for adversarial combat sport, for masculine heroics and outdoor collective militaristic bonding.

Or perhaps this aspect of sporting combat is merely migrating to the clans and guilds in massively multiplayer online games (MMOs) like World of Warcraft. Here the "arrested development" (boyish make-believe) that Thorstein Veblen noticed in the modern "addiction to sports" is fused with the fantasies of escape, adventure, same-sex bonding, and romantic wish-fulfillment that characterize boarding school (real and fictional). In the safety of cyberspace, gamers can gang up to indulge sport's simplest underlying motives in ways that can rarely be experienced against living opponents (outside of real street gangs): the Martial "impulses of exploit and ferocity" (Veblen 1899: ch. 10). Gamers adopt an identity and join a clan as a means to navigate the vicissitudes of adolescent make-believe without inflicting physical damage or fascistic control. An innovation here is that even the gender of "boyish make-believe" is a matter of consumer choice, so women and men both play, using avatars of the other; ferocity, cunning, and sex appeal fused, Lara Croft style.

Just as Lara Croft evolved from tennis-playing English schoolgirl in *Tomb Raider I* to ruthless, determined, hyper-achieving knowledge-seeker with a body mass index to die for (*Tomb Raider: Legend*), a transformation assisted by Lara becoming the first animated cover-girl for style-bible the *Face* (June 1997), so real tennis players graduate from the "arrested development" phase of league sport to full-blown entrepreneurial careers in consumer culture. Often this step is achieved by fusing sporting and fashion values, preferably on the celebrity body of the sporting star herself. Thus, Serena Williams has launched her own fashion label Aneres. Anna Kournikova and Daniela Hantuchova achieved more success in fashion and beauty culture than on the tennis court. Maria Sharapova, enriched by "brand slam" endorsement deals with Canon, Nike, Palmolive, Motorola, Tag Heuer, Land Rover, and mobile game I-play among others, lent a more serious tone when she was appointed goodwill ambassador for the United Nations Development Program, joining Angelina Jolie (Lara Croft) in that role. Athletes too can compete in the fashion stakes. For instance, in a stunning transformation where all trace of "sport" seems to have been erased – except a glimpse of the powerful limbs that made it all possible – fashion photographer Daniela Federici took Olympian athlete Cathy Freeman, a world icon of power sport (Mars), and made her over *as* Venus, for Charlie Brown's winter 2004 collection (see figure 10.1).

Figure 10.1 Olympian Cathy Freeman in Charlie Brown (winter 2004 collection). Photo: Daniela Federici

Sporting values have entered fashion because even the haughtiest, most grown-up fashion houses now espouse sporting values. Indeed, we've become so used to seeing haute couture swimwear that it's hard to remember a time when such garments were not regarded as fashion apparel at all. Nevertheless, in the first half of the twentieth century, when Paris reigned supreme, swimwear rarely if ever featured on the catwalk or in *Vogue*, and modern women of style were not often seen in strenuous *action*. Fashion was seen in the *salon* not the stadium. Those days are long gone. Fashion and sport are now so integrated that you can't see the seam where they join. For instance, witness various typical sets featuring fashion icon Kate Moss, who has no sporting background. She starred on the cover of an issue of *Vogue* that was devoted to the proposition "Mode/Sport" by Mario Testino (*Vogue Paris*, November 2004, 852). The set showed her on the athletics track in starting blocks; throwing a javelin; being handled by a trainer; in anti-fashion running shorts and tracksuit. Soon afterward she appeared for *W* magazine in the USA as "Glamazon" by Mert Alas and Marcus Piggott (*W*, March 2005);[6] variously modeling sumptuous gowns and swimwear, sometimes indistinguishably, as in a shot of an Yves Saint Laurent jacket worn over an Eres bathing suit. Throughout the set her hair is coiled, synchronized-swimming style.

It is noteworthy that while sports and fashion are integrating, many of the sports in the "synchronized" category are at or beyond the edge of what is accepted as a "proper" sport. Synchronized swimming in particular seems to attract uncomprehending teasing from the locker-room jocks of competitive team contact sport. Like rhythmic gymnastics it is also one of the few women-only sports to have achieved Olympic status. There's more than a whiff of gender politics in the refusal to see a women-only event as a sport at all, especially one where compulsory smiling and fashion-linked costumes and make-up emphasize what some see as feminine traits rather than sporting prowess. In terms of reputation deficit, the feminized and spectator-oriented style of synchronized swimming is to masculine combat-contact sports as popular media entertainment is to serious politics.

Airbrushed, or History?

So where did such a strange fish come from? It transpires that the origins of synchronized, feminized, plebiscitary, consumer-integrated sport go

Figure 10.2 Annette Kellerman – portrait in *Physical beauty – how to keep it* (1918). New York: George H. Doran Company 1918

back to just one person, and an Australian at that. She was identified in her own day as *Venus*. Her name was Annette Kellerman (see figure 10.2):

> Kellerman was Australia's aquanaut, the beauty who – long before Elle Macpherson – was known as The Perfect Woman. The self-promoter who – long before Madonna – got herself arrested, knowing the commercial value of sensation. The thespian who – long before Nicole Kidman – was

a Queen of the Screen. The fitness guru who – long before Jane Fonda – showed middle-aged women how to stay sexy. (Meacham 2004)

This catalog of claims may seem hyperbolic, applied as it is to someone who is now largely forgotten even in the country of her birth. But in fact even this list falls well short of what Kellerman achieved. Not only was she the contemporary equal of Macpherson, Madonna, Kidman, and Fonda, but she was also a world champion sportswoman in both swimming and diving, and she was a sporting innovator, developing what was known at the time as "water ballet" – the precursor to synchronized swimming – and popularizing it worldwide via stage, screen, and stunt. As if all that wasn't enough, Kellerman is also credited with the invention and popularization of the one-piece swimsuit for women, making her an icon of fashion history too. And there's more.

It is likely, however, that more people today have heard of the film made about her life than have heard of her. For the film was Esther Williams's *Million Dollar Mermaid* (1952), which, as we've seen, is itself the very emblem of the contemporary mediated public. Esther Williams herself admired Kellerman as "a pioneer of women's rights." Williams told an interviewer in 2004:

> She knew there was more to being a woman than being kept in corsets. She wasn't content to float. She was determined to swim. . . . She was a woman who had a different opinion of what women could achieve. . . . Women have told me they learned to swim because they saw *Million Dollar Mermaid*. I loved that, and I know Annette would have loved it too. What she did was to persuade women to get in the water. I'm a continuum of that. (Quoted in Meacham 2004)

Williams met Kellerman, then in her sixties, while she was making *Million Dollar Mermaid*. She asked her:

> "Do you like the idea of me playing you in the movie?" because I was a champion swimmer and a dedicated athlete like she was. She told me: "I wish you could have been Australian." I replied: "Annette, I'm all you've got. I'm the only swimmer in the movies. There won't be another one. So let's see what we can do with an American girl playing an Australian." (Quoted in Meacham 2004)

Kellerman was born in Marrickville NSW in 1886, suffering rickets (some accounts say it was 1887, and polio), for which she had to wear leg braces until she was seven. She took up swimming to overcome this condition. She began to break records in her mid-teens. It was her swimming prowess that opened up the possibility of a career as a professional, an opportunity she took by sailing for England in 1904. She worked in Britain and Europe for the next few years, with three attempts to swim the English Channel, river races on the Thames, Seine, and Danube, and a coastal swim from Dover to Ramsgate. She emerged as a world champion in both distance swimming and high-diving. While still in her teens, according to the citation in the International Swimming Hall of Fame, she attracted the "largest live audience ever to see a swim race." Half a million Parisians watched her race 17 men down the Seine.[7] Then she went to the USA, where she became the "million dollar mermaid" . . . and the rest is history. Some of that history was recovered in a 2004 biopic: *The Original Mermaid*, directed by Michael Cordell and screened in Australia on SBS-TV (the multicultural channel!).[8]

To the Macpherson–Madonna–Kidman–Fonda list must therefore be added one more name to signify her *sporting* renown and influence, which far exceeded that of Australia's current greatest swimming hero, Ian Thorpe. But where Ian Thorpe is famous for swimming (and big feet), it remains the case that Kellerman was *also* famous as a beauty (Macpherson), self-promoter (Madonna), film star (Kidman), and fitness guru (Fonda).

Her reputation for beauty is based partly on her contribution to *fashion* – the invention of the one-piece swimsuit. This innovation also explains the reference to Madonna-like self-promotion. It was this garment – or lack of very much of it at all – that attracted the attention of both the Prince of Wales and Lord Northcliffe (owner of the *Daily Mirror*, which sponsored her appearances) while Kellerman was in the UK. The Powerhouse Museum marks the moment:

> At a time when female swimmers wore restrictive, cumbersome bathing costumes, Kellerman came up with the idea of a more practical one-piece swimsuit. When invited to give an exhibition of swimming and diving before members of the Royal Family at London's Bath Club, she was forbidden to show any bare leg. Her solution was to buy a long pair of black stockings and sew them onto a boy's short racing swimsuit. The women's one-piece swimsuit had arrived.

After she went to the USA in about 1910, it was this garment that got her newsworthily arrested on a Boston beach. In turn that incident attracted academic attention, leading to her reputation as "The Perfect Woman." Biographer Emily Gibson tells the story:

> [Harvard professor Dr Dudley Sargent] actually heard about her because she was doing a swim from Revere beach in Boston, and she went down in her Australian boy's bathing suit, and was arrested for indecent exposure because nobody liked seeing legs in those days. So it was in the papers and Dr Sargent heard about her and asked her to come along to Harvard where he measured her. Before her he'd measured thousands of women, which I don't think would have been such a bad job for a Harvard professor. What his standard was, was the Venus de Milo, and none of them had even come close to those measurements; and Annette Kellerman did. He even measured Annette's wrists. There are wrist measurements in Dr Dudley Sargent's little jottings, and the Venus de Milo, as we know, didn't have any wrists, but anyway. (Interviewed on *The Sports Factor* with Mick O'Regan, ABC Radio National, May 27, 2005)[9]

Annette Kellerman had one more claim to fame up her sleeve: she prefigured the exercise video (Fonda). In 1918 she published a book called *Physical beauty – how to keep it*, and later in life ran a business called Physical Instruction by Mail (Meacham 2004).

The International Swimming Hall of Fame makes it clear that her place in history was secured because of the all-too corporeal nature of her swimming achievements:

> Annette Kellerman starred in motion pictures such as the *Diving Venus, Queen of the Mermaids, A Daughter of the Gods*, and *Neptune's Daughter* [see figure 10.3, p. 216, for one of her mermaid costumes]. She crisscrossed the US and circled the world in the famed "Annette Kellerman black one-piece suit" which *made swimming attractive to men and liberated for women*. She performed stunts and dives which made her first among the fore-runners to synchronized swimming and women's high diving. (International Swimming Hall of Fame, Fort Lauderdale Florida)[10]

She commented on her own fame later in life: "I come from a nation of swimmers but no one remembers me now, yet I was once one of the most famous women in all the world. They called me the 'diving Venus', the perfect woman, a daughter of the gods" (quoted in *The Sports Factor* with Mick O'Regan, ABC Radio National, May 27, 2005).

"Officially" modeled on the goddess Venus, attractive to men, liberated for women, world champion, star of stage and screen (and river),

Figure 10.3 Costume worn by Annette Kellerman. Collection: Powerhouse Museum. Sydney, *Object number 2000/66* (Gift of the Denis Wolanski Library, Sydney Opera House, 2000). Photo: Marinco Kojkanovski, PHM

inventor of a film genre, progenitor of *two* sports (synchronized swimming and women's high-diving), inventor of the one-piece swimsuit, inventor of home-fitness instruction – and forgotten. The modernist era of sport didn't know how to deal with an attractive celebrity entertainer who contributed to fashion, films, and female fitness. Kellerman was ahead of her time.

Synchronized Voting

The combination of publicity, showbiz, skimpy costumes, and a perfect body, masking but also popularizing world-class athleticism and female achievement, was too much for traditional sporting culture to handle. But now we are witness to the integration of all such values into sport. The shift from sports based on Mars (power, victory) to those based on Venus ("seduction not coercion," law) is nearly complete. The "law" component comes into play in the mechanism used to decide winners. Instead of literally beating the opposition, sports like ice-skating, diving, and synchronized swimming require a choice to be made in a rule-governed environment – the contemporary equivalent of the mythical "judgment of Paris" (see the Wikipedia for this), where Venus won the prize as "the fairest of all" goddesses by promising Paris the hand of Helen, the most beautiful woman on earth. Judges today are understood to be just as open to persuasion as Paris was, so they too are "synchronized" as it were, by being multiplied up to seven from different competing countries, whose scores are combined and sometimes discounted, to ensure that national interest or hegemonic power does not prevail. The mode of scoring brings such sports into the realm of media, where the arts of Venus, performance, look, style – and smiling – can carry the day.

Somewhere beyond what we currently recognize as sport lies reality TV, some of which is strongly based on sports values. *Plebiscitary sports* are beginning to draw from reality TV the image of consumer choice as the ultimate arbiter of sporting achievement. These not-quite sports represent a dispersal of competitiveness itself from the individual combative hero to the feminized image of the consumer. For a taste of things to come, behold *synchronized dancing*.

The progenitor of this emergent form is one of the oldest and longest-running shows on international television: the BBC's *Come Dancing*, which debuted in 1949 and lasted until 1995. Its demise was short-lived, however, for the BBC replaced it in 2004 with *Strictly Come Dancing*. The title borrows a bit of glam from Baz Luhrmann's 1992 movie comedy *Strictly Ballroom* to enliven the rather naff image of *Come Dancing*. It worked wonders. The show immediately became a major hit in the UK and internationally. It has been spun off and re-versioned ruthlessly by the BBC, making it one of the Corporation's biggest export earners (Sherwin 2005). In Australia it topped the ratings as *Dancing with the Stars*. In Italy it burnt the floor as *Ballando con le Stelle*. It has also been bought by Austria, Belgium, Denmark, Israel, the

Netherlands, New Zealand, Poland, Russia, South Africa, Sweden, and the USA. There's a children's version called *Dance Factory*, and an amateur-only version called *Strictly Dance Fever*. There are one-off specials like *Strictly Ice Dancing* (a Christmas show) and *Strictly African Dancing*. The latter was screened in July 2005 to coincide with Live8 and the G8, as part of the BBC's "year of Africa." It featured sporting and showbiz celebrities of Afro-Caribbean background, paired with traditional African dance troupes. After training, and visiting Africa to see where the dances came from, each one performed their dance live in front of a studio audience, with a panel of experts judging their skills while viewers could vote for their favorites.

Finally, the ultimate citadel was stormed – *Dancing with the Stars* conquered the USA. The Disney-owned ABC bought it to rival *American Idol* on Fox. It became the surprise summer hit of 2005; a surprise because no one in the USA thought it could succeed. The ABC even had to bring over the original BBC team to make the local version:

> "I am fully aware that this may sound like the craziest show anyone in the US has ever heard of," Andrea Wong, ABC's vice-president, said. . . .
> Ms Wong said: "In a world where it's easier for reality series to imitate than innovate, I just love how fresh this format is. And the show's global success demonstrates how audiences around the world find it surprising and, undeniably, fun." (Quoted in Sherwin 2005)

Eventually the format got what it deserved: an award for Best International TV Sales at the 2006 Broadcast Awards. The BBC Press Office crowed: "Judges praised the transferability of the format to a global audience, saying: 'This is the holy grail: a primetime format that can travel around the world and work in every market you can think of.'"[11] In every version the basic proposition is the same: viewers get to see someone who can't necessarily dance being put through their paces, in synchronized competition with other pairs who are eliminated by a combination of expert judges and viewer plebiscite until a winner emerges at the end of the series. The format is usually a celebrity paired with a dance professional (*Strictly Dance Fever* used all-amateur couples). Often the viewers' vote is at odds with the judges' score. It seems that viewers enjoy watching people who dance as badly as they do, so frequently an incompetent but plucky celeb will survive long after rivals who can dance.

Voting is a matter of public interest. In Australia a major national scandal broke out when teen celebrity Nikki Webster was eliminated from the 2005 series of *Dancing with the Stars*. Webster shot to international fame in 2000 as the 13-year-old in a sundress who aerially guided four billion TV viewers through the Sydney Olympics opening ceremony (see chapter 5). But she was booted out of *Dancing with the Stars* when a judge on the show awarded her tango a score of one out of ten – too low to be offset by the other judges' scores or viewers' vote. A tabloid feeding frenzy ensued.[12] Ratings soared.

Competitive dancing is not new. It was central in *They Shoot Horses, Don't They?* – a Horace McCoy novel made into an iconic film starring Jane Fonda. That was a vision of dancing as Mars, not Venus. What is new about the *Strictly/Stars* format is that it pioneers *plebiscitary sport*. Whatever the version, the key to commercial (if not competitive) success is consumer choice. Elimination is achieved not by brute endurance but by the extent to which skill, attractiveness, fashion, and the human appeal of flawed celebrity or plucky amateur combine into something that can be voted on via a mobile text-message. Given the controversy surrounding judging panels in both accredited sports and reality TV, can we be very far away from the *plebiscitary Olympics*, where the winners will be made in the image of the feminized viewing-voting consumer-citizen? Conversely, when can we expect politics to abandon Martial Leviathan and embrace Venusian synchronicity? When will we see "*Strictly Come Voting* (politicians waltz in an election special)"? At the moment that's only a spoof imagined by some wag at *The Times* (Sherwin 2005). It can't be long before it becomes politico-sporting "reality."

Notes

1 See www.imdb.com/title/tt0044903/; and see wwwmcc.murdoch.edu.au/ReadingRoom/6.2/Lucy.html.
2 See www.findarticles.com/p/articles/mi_m2584/is_n2_v16/ai_18897276.
3 See www.abc.net.au/rn/talks/8.30/sportsf/stories/s1376333.htm; and see www.royandhg.com/thedream/29Aug/thedream.html.
4 See jumpforthecause.com/2005_wwr.html.
5 See observer.guardian.co.uk/osm/story/0,,849759,00.html and www.cirquedusoleil.com/CirqueDuSoleil/en/showstickets/o/O-acts2.htm.
6 See www.style.com/w/feat_story/020205.

7   International Swimming Hall of Fame: www.ishof.org/74akellerman.html.
8   See: www.abc.net.au/abccontentsales/s1132527.htm; www.roninfilms.
     com.au/video/1886377/30/2387690942; www.roninfilms.com.au/related/
     2387690942-0.pdf.
9   www.abc.net.au/rn/talks/8.30/sportsf/stories/s1376333.htm
10   www.ishof.org/74akellerman.html
11   See "Strictly Come Dancing quicksteps to victory at Broadcast Awards":
     www.bbc.co.uk/pressoffice/bbcworldwide/worldwidestories/pressreleases/
     2006/01_january/broadcast_award_strictly.shtml
12   "Dancing Controversy", *Age*, March 17, 2005. www.theage.com.au/
     news/TV—Radio/Dancing-controversy/2005/03/16/1110913657005.html;
     and see Channel Seven: seven.com.au/seven/dancing_webster

Part IV

What Can TV Be?

Metaphysics of TV

What is the "is" of television? Luckily for those who don't like metaphysical questions, the answer is that it doesn't have one. Television is a product of history and is therefore subject to change. Because it doesn't have an essence it is defined by its context. However, that does not mean that it can be – or become – whatever anyone wants. So to understand television's conditions of being, one must look at history; and also at *historiography*, the way history is undertaken. That's the task set in chapter 11. It seeks to hammer out a general template for advancing the currently patchy and informal historiography of television, and to do this while focusing on one particular national example. Australian TV history is peculiar to Australia, of course, but the way that television has been memorialized and turned into a history of nation-building in that country across various discursive sites (namely publishing, cultural institutions, television, ProAms) is far from unique.

The final chapter focuses on TV studies (rather than on TV itself), in order to show that the conditions of knowledge that influence how we think about television are embedded in existing institutional forms and practices, especially those associated with university education. The purpose of the chapter is to show how universities themselves are caught in the same paradigm shift that affects popular knowledge more generally, as has been argued throughout the book. It follows that changes in the way knowledge is produced and circulated in the wider environment will – or should – impact on the way things are done in universities. At this point the chapter moves beyond description toward "intervention analysis" by proposing the kind of educational renewal that is needed to bring into the domain of formal education the dynamism and change that have repurposed popular knowledge. The chapter argues that the long-standing purposes of modern education – political emancipation and economic opportunity – are still what universities are *for* in the global era, but that achieving them in the fields of study connected with TV and new media requires a shift from a "sit-back" to a "sit-up" mode of attention.

A model is offered of the kind of educational initiatives that are needed for active engagement with both political and economic aspects of the growth of knowledge. It takes the form of the "creative industries" initiatives with which I've been associated in Queensland (see Hartley 2005). The chapter lists the principles and strategies necessary to cant the creaky old windmill of higher education around to face the winds of change blowing from the "new economy." At the very least, graduates of tomorrow will need to navigate the tensions between closed expert systems and open innovation networks, between market forces and DIY citizenship. They also need to integrate theory, practice, and critique (into *innovation*) so as to acquire the individual knowledge and skills, the independence of thought and passion, to do for themselves what for so long television was said to do for them – using the available means of communication to represent the life of the imagination and to pursue the truth.

11

"Laughs and Legends" or the Furniture that Glows? Television as History

With Joshua Green and Jean Burgess

Television as History

The year 2006 marked the seventieth anniversary of television broadcasting in the UK and the fiftieth anniversary in Australia. TV was launched in London on November 2, 1936. In Sydney and Melbourne it was launched in 1956, just in time for the Melbourne Olympic Games. So it seems timely to look at the ways in which television itself has become a historical object; to consider some of the ways in which television is memorialized. This chapter is concerned not so much with the events of this history as with the way in which it is written; with television *historiography* rather than the history of television.

Television *as* history can be distinguished from histories of things *on or about* television, such as programs, broadcasters, genres, technology, policy, audience, and the like. Particular historical studies are not uncommon, but if you wanted to explain to someone what constitutes our discipline's major object of study, you would be hard put to identify a work that tackled that job *as history*. Commenting on an earlier version of this chapter on the online TV Studies journal *Flow*, Garth Jowett wrote: "I have through my survey of the current literature been made aware how few serious works there are dealing with this subject in a manner which would satisfy scholars in other fields seeking some sort of guide to the role and impact of television in modern life."[1] Media, cultural, and television studies routinely construct television within the endless present tense of science, policy, journalism, and critique. The attempt to render it historically has barely begun. Both Anne Curthoys (1991) and

Albert Moran (1991) made a similar point in an issue of *Continuum*, but little has changed in the interim, either in Australia or globally. This is despite regular returns to the problem, such as an edition of *Media International Australia* focused on Australian media history edited by Graeme Turner (No. 99, May 2001), and Liz Jacka's ruminations on the problem (Jacka 2004).

Much writing about television tends to use the scientific present-continuous tense, but that doesn't mean that what we do is science. Scientists tell us that for any new endeavor there is a pre-scientific period, the type of whose knowledge can be characterized by what Robert Provine has rather disparagingly dubbed "logic and anecdote" as opposed to "empirical data" (2000: 11; see also Billig 2005: 3), although that does seem a pretty accurate description of humanities-based approaches to media. This precedes a properly scientific phase based on the testing of hypotheses using large-scale empirical data.

But television *as history* hasn't even reached the "logic and anecdote" stage yet. It is just anecdote. Generically, historical *anecdotes* about TV are apt to head off in one (or both) of two directions: *folklore* or *ideology*. Either way – popular memory or corporate self-interest – legends are spun that serve the interests of the teller. Such stories tell us more about the source of the narrative, whether a national, academic, commercial, producer, or consumerist speaking position, than they do about television as such. They are "data" not "discipline."

Data and anecdotes cannot turn into history by themselves. In a context where the history of TV still seems to be mostly "folklore" or "ideology" rather than "discipline" or "science," it seems premature to attempt the history of "television as history," but it may be timely to apply some logic to the anecdotes. Two purposes may be served: First, a period of what Marx used to call "primitive accumulation" of know-ledge is needed about the pastness of TV's past in order to produce sufficient "surplus value" to enable a properly scientific historical inquiry to ensue. Jacka opens her article with a quotation from Paddy Scannell about the impossibility of conducting meta-commentary when the basest data is elusive – in Scannell's case, chronological accounts of the formation of broadcasting activities at the BBC (Jacka 2004: 27). In this regard, it transpires that a latter-day knowledge-equivalent of Inca gold, i.e. an *accelerant* to the process of "primitive accumulation" that may precipitate epochal change, has recently been discovered and is ripe for exploitation in order to kick-start that scientific phase. It is called the internet. It is toward that "future of history" that we point at the end.

Second, analysis of the various extant versions of television history may reveal both generic patterns and ideological tendencies: we'll be able to tell you what television as history has been *for*, hitherto. That is the purpose of the present chapter.

No Origin; No "It"

Television *as* history (as opposed to the history of things on television) is confronted by a problem at the outset. There is no coherent object of study. Television is too complex, contingent, and context-dependent to have an essence, either technically or as a broadcast system. "It" was improvised, emerging as the work of many hands, individual, corporate, and governmental, over a lengthy period, in many countries, and so its history is one of multiple starts.

The point that is picked to stand for the beginning of TV depends on whether its origin is ascribed to technology, to nation, to broadcast system, or to context of viewing; and also on who is the narrator – for instance, the point of origin is different for an academic historian from what it would be for a TV network. Technologically, television was invented at least twice; electromechanically and electronically. Nationally it was invented anew in many countries; "firsts" of various kinds are claimed by the British, Germans, Americans, and others. Each country set up its own national system of technology, standards, legislation, broadcasting organizations, programs, and of course audiences. Subsequent histories are nation-centric. The British "forget" the part played by Germany; Americans "forget" the part played by the British (e.g. in the Wikipedia entry on Television).

Such national differences mean that any anniversary is arbitrary, even if you concentrate on the launch of broadcast systems as opposed to technical inventions. Thus, 2006 was the fiftieth anniversary of regular broadcasting in Australia, but the seventieth in Britain; sixty-ninth in Germany, sixty-fifth in the USA; fifty-fourth in Canada . . . and so on up to Bhutan, where television was but six years old that year. Then there is the question of what is celebrated as the anniversary. Each of the pioneer countries developed different standards, including internally competing ones. Like other "early adopters," the Soviet Union invented television twice – first as an electromechanical and then as an electronic system. The context of viewing was not uniform either. The BBC targeted a domestic audience in order to boost receiver sales, which meant in effect that the *very* first broadcast TV audience was confined by and large to electrical retailers, and in terms of both programming and people's experience of the new medium the first broadcast was the test transmission. In 1936, the BBC scheduled programming specifically for the electrical retailers during the afternoons, so that they might demonstrate the sets. In contrast, television was launched in Nazi Germany as a public rather than domestic medium, projected in television viewing halls, and in the USA its use during this early period was largely confined to department stores.

The origins of broadcast systems themselves are misremembered or cheerfully faked, especially to make them coincide with the present purposes of corporate players. TV was invented in Australia on multiple occasions before the "official arrival" in 1956. Australian experiments with mechanical television and early electrical systems took place before World War II, including a visit in 1938 and rumored demonstration by John Logie Baird himself. After the war, there are multiple claimants to the origins of television, as Albert Moran (1991) has usefully outlined. One of them was at the Powerhouse Museum, which itself played a role in the lead-up to the "Australian invention" of TV, for instance via public demonstrations of an imported Pye 625-line television set from 1954.[2]

The quest for a single point of origin is not only fruitless, it is also metaphysical, a version of Derrida's "origin of society" problem – the idea of a fixed point always implies a "before" that therefore unfixes both the point and with it the notion of a singular origin (Derrida 1976: 7). So television as history has no origin; there is no "it." The Derridean moment for Australian TV (the "point" of origin) is generally held to be Bruce Gyngell's opening line, "Good evening and welcome to television," uttered on-screen when TCN9 opened in Sydney on September 16, 1956. The frequently repeated clip of this moment, however, is not the originating moment of television at all. It is something rather different; one of the first, if not the very first, of the *memorializations* of television in Australia. The famous Gyngell clip was in fact made a year later to celebrate the first anniversary of Sydney TV station TCN9 (Stone 2000: 47–8).

In any case the anniversary applies to Sydney alone. Television didn't "begin" across Australia; it rolled, as it did in most countries. Regular broadcasts began in urban Sydney and Melbourne in 1956. It didn't reach the other mainland states till 1959. Tasmania and Canberra waited till the early 1960s, and the Northern Territory did without TV till 1971. Notwithstanding the success of Imparja, established in 1988, it may be argued that Indigenous Australia *still* awaits a television service to match national systems like the ABC and SBS, with a bid for a NIBS (National Indigenous Broadcasting Service) languishing permanently "under review."[3]

Television has no singular point of origin because it is not a singular object. Although memorializations are plentiful, it is difficult to claim that television "as such" has a history, because it doesn't have a "such." It is too various a phenomenon to be reduced to an invention with properties that can be defined and tested. In other words its history is not that of a technology but of many different socio-cultural, politico-legal, and commercial activities, relationships, and structures.

Working with Joshua Green and Jean Burgess, I undertook a project designed to begin the "primitive accumulation" of knowledge about television as history by investigating the way it has been memorialized across various different institutional and discursive sites. We wanted to answer the question, "what is claimed or assumed to *count* as the history of television?" We looked at four sources:

1 *published* histories (trade and academic),
2 exhibitions and shows in *cultural institutions*,
3 memorializations of television *on television*, and
4 memorializations by "*ProAms*" (Leadbeater & Miller 2004) both in physical sites and on the internet.

What follows represents a preliminary survey of these four fields. We have drawn on national, private, and university archives, watched many hours of Australian television specials, and searched library catalogs, newspaper indexes, and the worldwide web. While in some cases this process of primitive accumulation has produced little more than lists of available resources, we have begun to create taxonomies and conceptual categories. Through synthesis and comparison within and across these sites and categories, we have been able to identify some of the implications of the diverse ways in which television in Australia has been memorialized, and along the way to take early steps toward the future of television history.

1 Published Histories

Most of the published history of television is incidental to other purposes, and this is true all the way from large-scale, magisterial academic works (histories of nation-building by historians such as Manning Clark or Geoffrey Blainey) through to special newspaper sections published to celebrate successive anniversaries, such as one in the *Australian* commemorating TV's fortieth (September 1996), which included no fewer than 31 articles. Exhibition catalogs might contain interesting perspectives on television history while thinking about something else, for instance architect Derham Groves's publications arising from an exhibition to commemorate the 1956 Olympics (Groves 1996, 2004). Groves traces changes in architecture and domestic life associated with the arrival of television in Melbourne, examining advertising, editorial cartoons, newspaper and magazine articles, knitting patterns, *Australian Home Beautiful*, and furniture catalogs.

Portions of the history of Australian television appear in histories or treatments of other things – for example, "the nation." Philip and Roger Bell's books on Americanization (1993, 1998) consider American content on TV and the acknowledgement and discussion of this by the Australian press. The Australian Heritage Commission website, "Australia: Our National Stories – Linking a Nation," locates radio and TV within a narrative about "transport and communications," beginning with ports and horses and ending with car ownership.[4] Jenny Black (1995, 2005) celebrates television within the context of rural Australia. Beyond such incidental histories, we have allocated published histories of TV to two categories, "trade" books (i.e. the book trade – publications for the general market, rather than for academic or government specializations) and academic books.

Trade

"Trade" books include the full spectrum of "anecdotal," "folklore," and "ideological" treatments of television. An early example of a history that sets the tone for later studies is Sandra Hall's *Supertoy: 20 years of Australian television* (1976; and see Sandra Hall 1981). It treads what has become a familiar path in describing the history of Australian television, covering pre-history, policy, industry players and individual stations (both commercial and public), audiences (children and ratings), and various programming genres (variety and drama). Sandra Hall is not a media academic or historian but a feature-writer, literary editor, and film and TV critic. She has written a novel and short stories and edited an anthology of erotic writing. It is not likely that she invented the taxonomy of TV that she uses; it may be nearer the mark to say that this is a commonsensical array of topics, likely an import from similar treatments in Europe and America. Whatever the case, it is still commonly used in both general and academic accounts of television. Gerald Stone's *Compulsive viewing: The inside story of Packer's Nine Network* (2000), which Ketupa.net calls "a *60 Minutes* flavoured account" of the leading commercial network: "colour, action, a fascination with the big fella and legal stoushes,"[5] is a typical example of anecdotal history. However, the institutional inside stories are valuable given the guarded nature of broadcasters. Biographies, autobiographies, and memoirs of television personalities, journalists, and aging stars also provide data toward an evidence-based history: for instance Tabberer (1998) or Littlemore (1996), which Graeme Turner uses to contextualize his analysis of *This Day Tonight* (Turner 2005). "Folkloric" accounts include Peter Beilby's (1981) *Australian TV: The first 25 years*, a large-format "scrap book" including short, journalistic pieces and a multitude of pictures and memorabilia. The anniversary format was also used by MacCallum (1968) and Beck (1984).

It would be unsafe to draw a hard and fast line between trade and academic histories. An example of a hybrid form is Cate Rayson's *Glued to the telly: A history of Australia television* (1998), a book associated with a "comedic" documentary of the same title made by Vixen Films in 1995 and shown on ABC TV and at the Melbourne International Film Festival. Both the book and the documentary combined wry observation with plentiful comments, including some from media academics such as McKenzie Wark, Meaghan Morris, and myself. Made by a commercial production house that otherwise specialized in advertisements, the documentary won a "Gold Apple" educational media award in the USA,[6] and the book belied its coffee-table look with thought-provoking content.

Academic histories, including government agency reports and publications

Academic histories of television are less common than you might think, especially those concerned with programming as opposed to broadcasting systems (but see McKee 2001). The academic study of television remains largely in the present tense as it engages with scientific or policy discourse, pondering questions of media effects, audience behavior, technology, power, and profit. Works that do trace historical events tend to use history to illustrate contemporary concerns, not to account for the pastness of the past (see for example O'Regan 1993; Moran 1992). Policy agencies occasionally cast their own concerns as history; for instance, Aisbett (2000) follows the fortunes of regulated "C" (children's) time, while Jones and Bednall (1980) provided a regulator's view of TV history via the ratings. General historians have tended to include broadcasting in histories of national infrastructure, referring to "transport" when talking about "communication" (Osborne & Mandle 1982: 153–63; and see n. 3 in this chapter). The academic neglect of television history is especially pronounced in Australia; we await both our Asa Briggs (1985), a magisterial institutional history by an historian, and our Horace Newcomb (2004), a comprehensive encyclopedia of television including historical entries. No attempt has been made to integrate television into nation-building narratives such as that associated with Manning Clark.

2 Cultural Institutions and Exhibitions

Academia is not alone in its neglect of television. Television as *cultural* history is strangely elusive. The major institutions of cultural memory – museums, galleries, and archives that claim national status – have almost completely ignored it. On the whole, where they have noticed it at all, cultural institutions have not been kind to television. They have perhaps been too prone to what Roland Barthes once called "either/or-ism": *either* Cultural institutions, *or* the dreaded Tube (see table 11.1).

Table 11.1 Either/or-ism: cultural institutions versus the tube

Cultural institutions	TV
Extraordinary	Ordinary
Institutions of collection	Medium of diffusion
Public	Commercial
City and civic experience	Suburban and domestic experience
♂ tendencies	♀ tendencies
Education/art	Consumption/entertainment
Contemplation	Behavior
Historicize art and culture	*Memorialize schlock, dreck, kitsch*
. . . and so on	

This familiar set of oppositions drives a persistent tendency, most notable among those who value cultural institutions, to associate value with one side of the ledger and – therefore – disrepute with the other. So if you're interested in popular media, the great national institutions have been something of a cultural wasteland, at least until 2006. Before then, it was very difficult to find an exhibition that took the medium and its practitioners seriously in the way that artists, photographers, and filmmakers are handled in art galleries. What would television history look like if it were curated for the Tate Modern or MOMA? The closest thing we have found to an answer to that question in Australia was the inaugural exhibition at Sydney's Museum of Contemporary Art (MCA) in 1991, to celebrate 35 years of Australian TV. "TV Times" was curated by David Watson and Denise Corrigan, and featured a publication of the same title to which I contributed a photo-ethnography of the way people sited TV sets in their homes (Hartley 1992a: 99–116). One of the main exhibits was a room-sized black box with peepholes through which visitors could spy, as if from the back of an open fridge, into a domestic set where a suburban couple (played by actors) sat watching television, leafing through magazines, etc. Very Foucauldian, and an artwork in its own right. But the MCA collapsed financially soon afterward and had to be re-launched with a different business plan. Memorializing the popular arts in a serious way seems not to be part of it.[7] Co-curator David Watson later complained: "The contemporary art line is that television is the anathema, television is the enemy. A lot of art has been made about the meaninglessness of telly, rotting your brain, couch potatoes. If I hear that one more time . . . it's such a cliché. Television is an easy target" (quoted in Rayson 1998: 80).

As a cultural exhibit, television stands for our collective fears, desires, and follies; part criminal, part fool, a technological "melancholy clown." In serious mood it is the history of technology (read: determinism); of social and cultural impact (read: negative); of corporate players (read: capitalist power); or of cultural imperialism (read: Americanization). But meanwhile, we are called upon to wallow in nostalgia and see the ads, comedy shows, kids' TV, and sport from, well, yesteryear. We are invited to laugh at the mullets, cringe at the flares, and wince at how our favorite celebrities used to look. Such topics may also correspond to various target demographics and their accompanying modes of consumption: nostalgia and "the history of me" for the oldies; arch critique and knowing kitsch for the urban sophisticates; the enjoyment of celebrities and games for the kids.

There is no Australian cultural institution devoted solely to the history of broadcasting, like the Museum of Television and Radio in New York and Los Angeles, or the Museum of Broadcast Communications in Chicago. TV has been collected as the supplement to cinema and radio. Inheriting the legacy of the National Historical Film and Speaking Record Library (going back to 1935), the National Film and Sound Archive (NFSA) was created in 1984, changed its name to ScreenSound in 1999, but reverted to the NFSA when it was subsumed into the Australian Film Commission (AFC) in 2003.[8] The archive maintains an official collection of television footage in a permanent collection of news and "representative" programming. It relies on TV networks or production companies donating self-selected examples of interesting, innovative, significant, or landmark content. Archives like the NFSA are challenged by the sheer volume of the content they are trying to collect. Another challenge is that because of the differing and rapidly changing technical requirements of film, tape, and digital content, they are also required to become hybrid institutions, combining the principles of museums (preservation of artifacts), libraries (providing for users), and archives (preservation of "documents") (Edmondson 2004: 33–4). Despite the size and complexity of its task, the NFSA is the only organization in its category in Australia that has not been awarded statutory status along the lines of the National Archives, the National Museum, the National Maritime Museum, or the National Gallery. Instead it is part of the Australian Film Commission, whose own history is that of an industry promotion body and audience-builder. "Preservation and availability" have been added to the AFC's industry and policy remit.

The NFSA has contributed its own take on Australian TV history. A permanent exhibition at the NFSA HQ in Canberra, "Sights and Sounds of a Nation," uses the archive's holdings to trace an integrated history of Australia's film, photography, television, radio, and recording industries. Organized by decade, the exhibition navigates phases of development of the Australian audio-visual industries using various unifying themes. Another exhibition, "Take '84" (2004), celebrated the year that the NFSA first opened. It included items compiled from ScreenSound's collection, including television news and that year's "Logies" TV awards.

The role played by audio-visual archives is further complicated by commercial imperatives that overshadow their collections. As much as they aid in the preservation of national culture, most audio-visual archives also serve as stock inventories, centralizing content for re-use in future productions, subject to the negotiation of copyright royalties. For these purposes, television also boasts its own industrial archives, from those held by regional TV stations right up to the Olympic Television Archive Bureau (OTAB). The maintenance of large archives by the commercial and public networks enables the broadcasters to exert control not only over the re-use of content (achievable through copyright provisions) but also over access to their recorded histories. Commercial donors may retain rights in material donated to archives and university holdings. Copyright regulations restrict access to members of the educational institution that holds the recording, although inter-institutional borrowing may also be permitted.

We have found examples of television's memorialization in exhibitions mounted at *state and regional museums*. These tend to fall into three categories – those that celebrate specific programs, those that seek to portray an era or industry; and those that seek to memorialize television itself.

Program-specific exhibitions

Frequently, landmarks and milestones trigger the memorialization of television, especially in relation to children's shows; for instance, the National Museum of Australia's touring exhibition "Hickory Dickory Dock," which celebrated 39 years on-air of the ABC's *Play School* in 2004. "Mr Squiggle: Who's Pulling the Strings?" (2005) was subtitled "The Life and Art of Norman Hetherington." It celebrated the puppet-making and artwork of Squiggle's creator/alter ego. "Li'l Elvis and the Truck Stoppers" was a touring exhibition by the Australian Children's Television Foundation, based on a 13-part TV series of the same name. Part of the ACTF's education program, it sought to inform visitors about animation processes. Designed to be hands-on, it included original cells and a "motion simulator" to enable children to manipulate optical illusions and place themselves in the animation.

A permanent exhibit (not driven by an event or anniversary) is the Grundy-donated "*Neighbours* Kitchen" belonging to the Robinson family in the show, replete with Scott and Charlene's plaster wedding cake in the fridge, which is now an installation at the Australia Gallery of the Melbourne Museum. The *Herald Sun*, describing "exhibits you must not miss" when the museum opened in 2000, declared that the set and *Neighbours* itself present "suburban Melbourne to the world." And the world presents itself to Melbourne, for busloads of backpacker fans make the pilgrimage out to "Ramsay Street" – turning Pin Oak Court in Vermont South and other *Neighbours*-related places into a global sacred site of soap-opera memorialization.[9]

Portraits of an era or industry

The promise of a broader memorialization of Australian television appeared in the catalog for "Back of Beyond: Discovering Australian Film and Television," an exhibition mounted in Sydney and exported to the US in 1988. A collaboration between the Australian Film Commission (under the aegis of Phillip Adams) and the UCLA Film and Television Archive, it set out to showcase Australian film and television directors and their work, as part of the 1988 bicentennial celebrations. The television content on show is the kind that looks most like director's cinema – the mini-series, in particular those produced in the 1980s by George Miller's production company Kennedy Miller: *Bodyline*, *The Dismissal*, *The Dirtwater Dynasty*, *Vietnam*, *Bangkok Hilton*, and *The Cowra Breakout*. Television is celebrated to the extent that it aspires to a legitimate Australian national cultural form – film.

Television has featured in exhibitions as a link to the domesticity of "yesteryear." In 1997 the Heide Museum of Modern Art in Heidelberg, Victoria, offered "1956: Melbourne, Modernity and the XVI Olympiad." Here television was seen as the cause of architectural trans-formations in the family home to accommodate "the box in the corner" (Groves 1996, 2004). Again, it featured as a component of a bygone domestic lifestyle in "Living in the Seventies," mounted by Adelaide's National Automotive Museum. This exhibition accompanied the launch of the new Holden Monaro, by looking at the "cars, clothes, politics, film and television" of the 1970s. TV is included among a familiar line-up of "iconic" representations of the era when the original Monaro was famous (*Advertiser*, December 17, 2001).

Exhibiting TV

It seems rare that television "as such" has been the subject of an exhibition. In addition to "TV Times" at the MCA, we have managed to uncover only one other example. In 1994 the Victorian Arts Centre's Performing Arts Museum featured an exhibition of photographs and publicity shots entitled "Welcome to Television," showing personalities from the 1950s through to the mid-1970s. It drew on a collection of

100,000 negatives, many unpublished, donated by entertainment photographer Laurie Richards. The *Age*'s Entertainment Guide described this exhibition as "dethroning" Australian television icons (*Age*, June 10, 1994). The surprise expressed in the article about, for instance, the fact that Channel 9 newsreader Brian Naylor had a previous history on children's program *Swallow's Juniors*, or that Bert Newton spent his early days "as a TV stud," hints at the gaps in the public memory of television. Journalist Barbara Hooks used the exhibition to explore the status of women in early Australian television. She interviewed Susie Boisjoux, featured in some of the stills, who was a "pointer" on *The Astor Show* and *The Tarax Show*, as well as a hostess on daytime and children's TV, appearing on *In Melbourne Tonight*, making commercials, and hosting *Sincerely Yours*, her own Friday night show (*Age*, June 23, 1994). Thus the exhibition was made to say as much about gender as it did about television.

TV exhibitions remain quite rare events in Australia, and indexed information about them perhaps even rarer. Like Sandra Hall's instant taxonomy of TV history, they tend to conform to what Raymond Williams once called "the culture of the selective tradition." Some aspects of a cultural form are selected over others, such that "the history of television" is standardized. We learn what to expect.

However, things picked up for the fiftieth anniversary. The year 2006 featured two new exhibitions by major national cultural institutions: "On the Box: Great Moments in Australian Television 1956–2006" at the Powerhouse Museum in Sydney, and "TV50" at the Australian Centre for the Moving Image (ACMI) in Melbourne. Curated by Peter Cox, "On the Box" attracted considerable public interest around its April 6 opening (e.g. *Australian*, March 30 and April 8, 2006). The museum promised "the largest collection of television costumes, props and memorabilia ever displayed in Australia," and Cox described the exhibition as dense and full of detail, but not "encyclopaedic" (*Illawarra Mercury*, May 20, 2006).

As befitted ACMI, an institution devoted to disseminating screen culture rather than collecting artifacts, "TV50" featured rich content on many screens. It resulted from a unique collaboration between ACMI and my research center. It was curated by ACMI's Mike Stubbs and Alessio Cavallaro from a "creative concept" developed by me (Hartley 2006), with creative and research input by a team from Queensland University of Technology (QUT) (Joshua Green, Ellie Rennie, and Jerry Watkins) and design by ACMI's Felicity Hayward. It was fascinating to be involved in the very practical problems associated with trying to produce well-researched history and a good show at the same time. Not the least of the issues was a familiar conundrum for any curator or artistic director interested in popular culture: what would persuade potential visitors to switch off the TV set at home and come in to the city . . . to watch TV? It all seems counter-intuitive. But 85,000 people came nonetheless.

3 Television on Television

Television's memorialization of itself, principally in the form of anniversary specials and station idents or promos that celebrate TV's role in "our" lives (especially those of baby-boomers everywhere), has over time become the closest thing there is to an "official" history of television. However, the selective tradition is at work here too; produced by winners, appealing to nostalgia, and consisting almost entirely of anecdote. More than one observer has presented Australian television as a series of "great moments" (e.g. *Who Weekly*, McKee 2001, and the Powerhouse Museum). How such moments come to be "great" seems to be via repetition at each milestone, eventually establishing an unauthored but apparently authoritative narrative out of an oft-repeated cast and plot. Television becomes what the tale says it is: local (Australian) content, technological innovation, personalities, and live rather than scripted shows, especially early variety programming. Things that may be almost unique to Australian television – the multicultural/multilingual channel SBS, for instance – are routinely ignored, as is the fact that most programming on most channels is made overseas.

Early shows *about* television celebrated the medium either as a booming post-war *industry* or as a technological *marvel*. On the industry side, Astor sponsored *This is Television* (1956). It promoted TV as a nation-building industry, focusing on the manufacture of TV sets, domestic content, and transmissions of the latest overseas programs, education, Australia variety and quiz shows, and films. On the marvel side was the General Motors Hour, also called *This is Television* (GTV9, 1956). Interspersed with ads for Holden cars and an overview of the functioning of a studio, the show featured Eric Pearce explaining the science behind the wonder of electronic image transmission.

TV – or at least Channel 9 – marked its twentieth and twenty-first anniversaries with back-slapping gala events in ballrooms packed with personalities. Hosted by Bert Newton and regularly featuring "special guests" from television's past and musical acts extolling the virtues of television's future, these events resembled the Logies. Tracing a familiar path from September 1956 through classic TV shows like *Pick-a-Box* or *In Melbourne Tonight*, key news events, memorable sporting broadcasts, children's television, imported drama events, and the successes of local programming, they prefigured what was to become a stable format for television's memorialization of itself: the "anniversary special."

As television matured, anniversary specials moved out of the ballroom and into the studio. The thirtieth and fortieth anniversaries were less focused on the live experience of *making* television and more on formats and favorites – the magical moments that television has provided for the delighted viewer. The emphasis was on genre divisions and viewer nostalgia, leavened by celebrity presenters making scripted jokes. More recently the anniversary special seems to have made a further shift into film-can-filled "vaults" and using "archive" sets to present the shows, adding an additional layer of historicity. This has proven especially the case for "legends" like Graham Kennedy and Bert Newton, who are in a league of their own *as* television history. The moment chosen to reveal Kennedy's supposedly vitriolic response to being booted off the air in the 1970s is accompanied by a trip to the Channel 9 archive. Here, surrounded by the recorded history of the network, Ray Martin (himself a TV legend) shows the audience a canister containing a reel of film on which the incident is recorded. Popular memory, celebrity, and channel ID are conflated – without embarrassment, even though it was Channel 9 that earned Kennedy's rebuke in the first place.

In 1991 Channel 9's *35 Years of Television* made history of its own, claiming to be the first anniversary show that covered commercial TV as a whole, rather than only one channel (although it did complain that "the other networks" were reluctant to share their material). It was presented by stars and personalities from all three commercial networks and ran for a full two hours in place of Channel 9's Sunday night movie. Personalities or (in the case of Mary-Anne Fahey's Kylie Mole) characters presented relevant genre segments. Needless to say there was no cross-referencing to "TV Times" over at the MCA. Channel 7 followed up with *40 Years of Television* (1996, ATN7), a large-scale, studio-based affair hosted by comic Garry McDonald. In addition to clips, McDonald presented song-and-dance numbers and vignettes celebrating "the box." This was in turn matched by Channel 9's *40 Years of Television: Then and Now* and *40 Years of Television: The Real History.*

Celebrations for television's fiftieth anniversary were under way long before the relevant date. Channel 9 aired a special called *Five Decades of Laughs and Legends*, almost a year early, on the curious grounds that we were within the "anni" of the anniversary. As Graeme Blundell commented in the *Australian* (October 16, 2005), "*Five Decades* smacks of a grab for ratings desperately – and cheaply – fashioned from the junk pile and the banal hysteria of TV's supermarket." He conceded, however, that despite the less than lofty motives of the networks, the history of TV can't help being compelling viewing: "It does illustrate just how far we've come" since 1956. Given that the "we" Blundell invokes is "the Australian nation," these more recent shows hint at a kind of television history that, while both partial and partisan, at least transcends the level of individual institutions. In these moments, the idea of television as shared cultural history is foreshadowed, but not yet delivered.

4 ProAm TV History Online

Legions of amateurs, fans, retired technicians, and announcers from the heyday of broadcasting have stepped in to fill the void left by both cultural institutions and television itself. They maintain museums in barns and sheds. They have migrated enthusiastically to the net. They are the "ProAm" consumer co-curators of television history. The ProAms tend to fall into two broad groups, organized around *technologies* on the one hand and *programming* on the other. Between them they collect everything from old TV sets and parts to images, screen captures, video clips, theme music, surrounding ephemera (TV magazines and memorabilia), idents, intros, and test patterns. There is program-specific fandom, cult, camp, retro, nostalgia, and the fetishization of obsolescence.[10]

The technologists divide (very roughly) between "pros" and "ams." The pros (professionals) are those who have worked in the industry and can discuss details down to the question of whether the electron beam in early cathode ray tubes swept right to left or left to right. The ams (amateurs) are those who love, collect, and learn about the furniture that glows. They are also apt to invest in physical sites, to show the collected wares.[11] Those interested in programming tend to be the fans, cult-show followers, or ordinary people giving voice to their personal enthusiasms and nostalgic desires. A Google search for any title will land you at the personal webpage of an amateur enthusiast who has posted images, anecdote, press clippings, and trivia about the show.[12] More popular shows might attract a well-organized and systematic fan website. An example of the latter is "Perfect Blend," an extensive fansite for *Neighbours*. It "aims to create the most accurate and comprehensive information source ever assembled . . . and we have been proud to act as factual consultants to the recently relaunched official BBCi *Neighbours* site."[13] As an article in the *Age* put it:

> It babysat generations, distracted countless teenagers from homework and, as Homer Simpson sagely observed about television, became our "teacher, mother, secret lover." Sure, the shows may have been ludicrous – think *Webster*, *The A-Team*, *Charles In Charge* – but they became part of our lives nonetheless. So what do you do when they end? Immortalise them online. ("Retro Vision," *Age*)[14]

In this context it is worth considering that the extreme diversity of aesthetics and logic of selection in such immortalizations, while making it difficult to find ways to harness the collective knowledge of fans and amateurs, also provides a richer picture of the diverse meanings and everyday uses of TV content than do the rigor and homogeneity of professional curation.

In museology, the practice of popular collecting is usually distinguished from the professional practice of curating. The latter is seen as reasoned custodianship, selection, arrangement and/or exhibition of objects for public consumption, and the ability to reflect critically on and explain the reasoning behind the choices made. Mere collecting is often viewed pejoratively, but Paul Martin (1999) has argued for the benefits of collaboration between the amateur, everyday cultures of collecting and the cultural institutions for which curation and exhibition are core business. He makes the point that individual collections of apparently trivial objects provide more depth of knowledge on their specialized subjects than institutional collections and curatorial practice can possibly provide. He argues that museums need to transform their own practices in relation to popular collecting, if only to let some of it in. In the case of online television memorialization, a good example of this would be the European early television project "Birth of TV," which plans to build in the ability for members to contribute information.[15] In short, new media have begun to transform the hidden history of popular collecting into a shared resource.

In fact, ProAm memorialists may be doing a better job of working toward a systematic shared history for television than the cultural historians and institutions. In the field of TV history, James Paterson and Tom Bosic's "Australian Television Archive" is probably the best example of Leadbeater and Miller's (2004) model of ProAm creative innovation.[16] It is organized, purposeful, serious, collaborative, and regulated. It has a mission statement and detailed terms and conditions of membership and use. It is a non-profit venture that harnesses the power of collaborative knowledge production, offering archival footage/trading and historical and technical information contributed by members. Download access is only available to those who contribute footage, vintage equipment, information, or money to the archive. Its taxonomy of television history is logical. In addition to archiving footage and information, since 2005 the website has featured an "Archivist's Reference Manual," an ongoing collaborative project that invites members to write quality articles on issues relating to the archiving of audio-visual material. The aim is "to provide a comprehensive and ultimately authoritative text on the subject." The ProAms are proving to be more interesting and useful to the cause of television *as* history than are the great cultural institutions of memory. Like eBay, their websites make accessible curios that would have been impossible to find before. And unlike "official" curators they're interested in TV history, in which many of them have played an active role, on both sides of the screen. Some of them even seem to be working for broadcasters now. The BBC especially seems drawn to the possibilities.[17]

Conclusion: The Future of History

It's clear that television history is not the work of one agency or even one "discursive regime." The work of producing it is shared among academics, cultural institutions, and ProAms (including fans and TV professionals), and the history that emerges is different in each case, and in each country. Each of these cultural sites of memorialization constructs a different (and necessarily partial) mythological object and "story" for television. In particular, the popular memorialization of television constructs a very different picture of what matters in TV history than do official, institutional, or published histories. For instance, the popular fetishization of obsolescent technology is in tension with an industry discourse of technological progress; the underplaying of soap operas by the industry is in tension with the high level of fan activity around them. If there is to be such a thing as a thorough, shared memorialization of television as history, it would need to draw on and integrate these perspectives, a task which seems complex to say the least.

The future of television history promises to be more interesting than its past. As we've investigated the cultural memorialization of television it has also become clear that something new is afoot. The internet offers entirely new possibilities for TV as history, and the number of potential participants in the work of piecing it together has dramatically increased with the inclusion of the ProAms. At the moment the various parties to this work have little in common and less mutual contact. The next question is how the dispersed and idiosyncratically organized resources and spaces of ProAm memorialization might be more productively networked, both with each other and with the cultural institutions whose remit is to remember television for the public. Existing platforms for filtering and aggregating ProAm knowledge and online resources include webrings (e.g. Australian Television Webrings) and the peer knowledge portal About.com.[18] The About.com pages are guides to very specific subjects, particularly web resources related to those subjects. Each one is maintained by an expert (frequently, an amateur expert) in the field. It has proven to be a reasonably effective way of filtering and annotating specialist content; however, collaborative information collection and filtering is far more efficient (as in Wikipedia). Following that, we may be able get beyond the era of "primitive accumulation" and attempt a more systematic academic history of television that will more adequately represent our discipline's object of study.

Notes

1 See jot.communication.utexas.edu/flow/?jot=view&id=1214.
2 See www.ben.com.au/articles/47/0C028547.asp.
3 See www.aba.gov.au/tv/overview/FAQs/AusTVhistory.shtml#1; www.imparja.com.au/company.htm; www.dcita.gov.au/__data/assets/pdf_file/12663/IndigenousTVReview.pdf.
4 See www.ahc.gov.au/publications/national-stories/transport/chapter9.html.
5 See www.ketupa.net/packer.htm, also www.caslon.com.au.
6 See www.jolane.com/vixen.htm.
7 See www.mca.com.au/default.asp?page_id=4.
8 See www.nfsa.afc.gov.au/screensound/screenso.nsf.
9 See backpackerking.com.au/theage_with_the_king.html.
10 See for instance: Classic Australian TV, www.classicaustraliantv.com/index.html; aus.tv.history, www.austvhistory.com; television.au The History

of Australian Television, televisionau.siv.net.au/index.htm; Australian Television Information Archive, www.australiantelevision.net/list.html; and MILESAGO – Television – The Logies, www.milesago.com/TV/logies.htm.

11 Victor Barker's Television History, my.integritynet.com.au/barkertv/; Australian Museum of Modern Media, www.tvworld.com.au/; Television History – The First 75 Years, www.tvhistory.tv.

12 See Countdown Memories, www.countdownmemories.com.

13 See perfectblend.net/about.htm.

14 See www.smh.com.au/articles/2004/03/12/1078594553600.html.

15 See www.birth-of-tv.org/birth.

16 See austv.hostforweb.com.

17 See www.bbc.co.uk/bbcfour/tvontrial.

18 See l.webring.com/hub?ring=austv; classictv.about.com.

12

Television in Knowledge Paradigms

A modern society's goal should be to maximise the production and distribution of knowledge, to combine in a single ideal democratic and economic imperatives . . . Political empowerment and economic opportunity stem from the same root: the spread of knowledge.

Charles Leadbeater (1999: 222)

This chapter takes up the theme of the "spread of knowledge," finding that both TV itself and the formal study of media are shaped by historical forces and processes. Here is where the paradigm shift in what TV studies is *for* can be most clearly discerned, as the chapter shifts the focus of the book from past to future, from popular culture to creative industries, and from structure to agency.

"Your Starter for Ten"

I first thought of "television" as a discipline back in the 1970s. The idea came from TV itself. Do you remember *University Challenge*? It's a veteran quiz show, modeled on the even more venerable US *College Bowl* (1959).[1] For 25 years from 1962 *University Challenge* was hosted by Bamber Gascoigne, before being dropped and then revived with Jeremy Paxman from 1994 by the BBC, where it's still running.[2] Bamber Gascoigne exuded posh, urbane scholarliness, during a time when universities were unchallenged as finishing schools for top people and professional experts. Gascoigne "came up" to Magdalene College Cambridge in 1955 to "read" English,[3] and he always introduced contestants on the show by saying what they "read" at university. From mid-1978 onward I always hoped to hear him introduce some scion of learning as: "So-and-so, University of Somewhere, *Reading Television*." This was because I had just co-authored a book with that very title (Fiske & Hartley 1978). Of course it never happened. It never could – the disciplinary paradigm and prestige participants in the show ensured that such a dream remained merely a bad pun coined by two obscure polytechnic lecturers. As far as I know there still is no degree in "television" anywhere in the world, although of course students study TV for degrees with broader titles.

Early in *University Challenge*'s run, British universities themselves were challenged to adapt to the changing social and economic circumstances of the affluent welfare society. After the Robbins Report (1963) they succumbed to an irreversible trend to open up to the hoi polloi and the oiks. Some of the latter – I was one – learnt a little about what universities might be like by watching the show: "For many of the viewers, it was their first contact with that alien beast, the student, and did much to make university more accessible to people who hadn't been to Eton."[4]

Perversely, popular audiences persistently liked know-alls, whether highbrow from *University Challenge* to *Mastermind*, or the other sort of brow from *Double Your Money* to *Who Wants to be a Millionaire?* It may even be said that this light-hearted entertainment softened up the general public for the "knowledge economy" by showing knowledge and the ability to deploy it confidently and quickly to be a *competitive advantage*.

But the influx of plebeian students could not "read" television in the way that their predecessors may have "read" Greats (classics) or PPE (philosophy, politics, and economics). The times were not propitious for so demotic a pursuit, not only because TV was widely dismissed as unworthy, but also because everyone was already an expert. Knowledge of TV was neither scarce nor valuable. Watching TV was in the domain of consumption not production; tacit not explicit knowledge; domestic privacy not public life. There was no special disciplinary method or professional expertise to be learnt. As for "doing" TV, the business side involved generic marketing and business skills for which an MBA would do nicely (certainly not the now-derided "media studies"), while practical production crews were unionized proletarians not artistic graduates. What's to study?

Given such barren ground, "television studies" grew only indirectly. It wasn't a discipline but a "problem" in other disciplines like sociology and psychology, where studies were devoted to showing how TV affected *other* people's behavior (the masses, women, children, etc.). *Liking* TV was akin to liking junk food – your problem, not a proper topic for Higher Education. In the "old" humanities like history, English, art, or politics, TV was largely ignored, or it was a "bad object." The point of including it on the curriculum was to teach students how to resist it, in the name of national values, "critical reading," public culture, or a polity unsullied by mediated commercial entertainment. As a result, TV studies was developed first and most influentially by those who pathologized, feared, or opposed TV.

Theory

Sometime during the 1970s and 1980s, TV theory as a stand-alone endeavor and corpus of work did begin to grow out of an amalgam of "critical" humanities and "behavioral" or "generalizable" social sciences. It was devoted to understanding on the one hand *values* (human, aesthetic, cultural) – the domain of the *critic* – and on the other hand *behaviors* (psychological, social) – the terrain of the *clinic*. Mix in the influence of politicized "*high theory*" (structuralism, psychoanalysis, Marxism, postmodernism) and countercultural "new social movements" associated with *identity* (class, gender, race, ethnicity, sexual orientation, age, first peoples, subcultures based on consumption), and you have the makings of "theory" for television. Notice how little of this amalgam requires familiarity with what's on TV or the contextual experience of watching it.

TV studies was elaborated on the ground of these values, behaviors, theories, and identities. Unfortunately, that perspective didn't posit TV as a "we" sort of system. When English (the academic discipline, not the language) forced its way into the academy in the latter nineteenth century, literary studies – like film studies, later on – was founded on a *positive*: that literature was a "good thing" and it was OK both to like it as a consumer and to harbor ambitions toward professional practice; there was honor in both. But TV studies was founded on a *negative*, like the study of deviance and criminality, which it closely resembled. TV was theorized as a "they" sort of problem: a symptom of whatever needs to be resisted or opposed in the formation of selves in modernity.

Do you recall the terms "U" and "non-U"? They were popularized by Nancy Mitford in the 1950s to identify class difference in language (Mitford 1956). "U" people said "napkin" while "non-U" people said "serviette." This was code for class hatred on all sides; a deep well of mutual loathing that watered British TV comedy for decades, with snobbish social climbers like Margot Leadbetter (*The Good Life*), Sybil Fawlty (*Fawlty Towers*), and Hyacinth Bouquet (*Keeping Up Appearances*). The distinction extended to the academic world, where it remains a force. For instance, it is "U" to be a film "theorist" or "critic" but "non-U" to be a film "buff." The "buff" reeks of unsystematic thought and amateur enthusiasm, signifying nothing but personal consumption of dubious taste. Weirdly, TV studies – especially the versions of it derived from screen studies – is "U" if it is about *values, behavior, theory, and identity* (see "theory," above); "non-U" if it's about *television* as such.

Practice

Television practice was interested in neither value nor behavior. How might a bright person make a career in television? Don't study it. If you wanted to be a producer, writer, or director, then you might study accounting, English, or art, respectively. Or take a "Nike diploma" – "just do it." Plenty of the best did.

Production did become part of university courses, but rarely as an industry training scheme (other than in journalism schools). If taught as "film" it was art. If taught as "media," it was an extension of "critical reading"; not done as an apprenticeship to industrial discipline, but as an attempt to "demystify" the workings of an "ideological apparatus" by getting students to "encode" as well as "decode."

Critique

"Critique" arose from a combination of Frankfurt School critical philosophical and literary theory (critique of ideology). The original idea was to make a systematic study of the conditions and consequences of knowledge, an endeavor of major consequence and impressive achievement. But in the hands of some latter-day commentators, the term became a euphemism for the practice of applying negative evaluations to contemporary life. Since it is quite easy to "critique" television and popular culture, the more important term that we need to inherit from the Frankfurt school is "systematic." Did "critique" explain television "in itself" by making a *systematic* study of its conditions and consequences? Perhaps the nearest serious attempt was the Birmingham Centre for

Contemporary Cultural Studies' *Policing the crisis* (Stuart Hall et al. 1978). It wasn't about television directly but in every other respect was the "critical" full Monty, and still serves as a model of what is needed to locate the sources of ideological knowledge both historically and conceptually. The work of Herbert Schiller may also be mentioned in this context, from the American perspective. More frequent by far, however, have been "critical readings" that analyzed something on or about television with the purpose of finding it wanting; a practice that Toby Miller dubs "narcissism" (Miller et al. 2005: 44–5). Such critics could get jobs as academics, but they were unlikely to work in TV, or want to.

Teaching

TV studies was not propagated through the great "sandstone" universities where professional, business, and government elites were educated. It took them 25 years – a generation – to let it in. It was taught by "critics" (see above); those for whom TV was a problem at best and anathema at worst.

But it was *studied* by students – especially at polytechnics, technical institutes, and colleges of higher education (eventually bundled together as "new universities") – for whom TV was the principal form of leisure entertainment and a pretty good career option. TV studies spread like a prairie fire through the "junior branch" of higher education. This was where the beneficiaries of mass consumerism and rapidly rising post-World War II affluence were gathered; the children of white-collar suburbia and blue-collar full employment. They represented the penetration of tertiary education to places where it had never in human history aspired to go before – deep into the working class and among girls, even reaching significant numbers among the welfare-dependent poor, ethnic minorities, and immigrants. Such folk were not critics, not professionals, not revolutionaries. But they were consumers. They liked television and some wanted to work in the media. Without cultural capital from family or class or professional expertise, they needed a general education and some certification to get there.

These same people were also citizens, and their civic education attracted the passionate interest of those who wanted to extend among all citizens various educational ideologies of the day – critical literacy (Hoggart 1957; Williams 1961), countercultural critique (Stuart Hall), identity politics (e.g. feminism), or emancipation – however construed – via universalizing tertiary education. This weird combination of citizen (*resist!*) and consumer (*desire!*) sustained TV studies right through from Hoggart to the end of the broadcast era, to which we shall now fast-forward.

From Margot Leadbetter to Charlie Leadbeater

Television remained a dubious object of study, but the purpose of *universities* had not been questioned since the expansionism of the 1960s, despite which they retained more than a whiff of "U." With the realignment of British politics in 1997 under New Labour, when social democratic centrism was wrenched decisively from the grasp of the Tories, the modernizers (e.g. Demos[5] and the *New Statesman* under Ian Hargreaves and John Lloyd) came out in force. Among the challenging questions that they asked (in light of the knowledge economy) was: what are universities *for*?

This was a good question, despite the unsettling implication that the "wrong" answer might reduce public funding. It drew attention to what university had become since the 1960s – a finishing school for the "lumpen-manageriat" and the comfortably complacent sons and daughters of Margot Leadbetter, Sybil Fawlty, and Hyacinth Bouquet. Academics were demoralized about their own loss of status and reward, but too many of them connived in teaching self-regarding theory, practice, and critique that actively discriminated against anything with "new" in the title – the "new economy," New Labour, new ideas. The problem for any rhetoric that sought to modernize universities for the era of knowledge networks was that there was plenty for the existing academic workforce to be demoralized about. The extension of knowledge-based and IT-enabled industries across the whole economy entailed a concomitant proletarianization of intellectuals themselves. A certain "critical" stance *did not want* to prepare students for this new world, because it was seen as a move toward casualization of intellectual labor and submission to the yoke of global capital, rather than a chance for people trained in critical, humanistic, and arts subjects to contribute to the creation of economic as well as symbolic value. Despite energetic local efforts the university *system* was still not responsive enough to the educational needs of the majority of the population, who had no option but to work in a context where knowledge was the major component of capital investment, and where an ability to operate as a freelance, doing more than one type of work in more than one industry, often in teams that dissolved after each project, was no more than the generic capability of a creative, knowledge-based workforce. If universities weren't part of an urgent modernization of business, government, and society by training young people to cope with its opportunities and challenges, then what indeed were they for?

In 2000 I went to QUT in Australia to try something "new." I wanted to combine *symbolic* with *economic* values in a project of *educational renewal* that was designed both to grow jobs and GDP and to *repurpose the arts and humanities.* At QUT we looked at the economic, social, and educational forces that might influence the direction and capacity for survival of the university. Something new was afoot in various domains:

- *technical*: convergence, integration, and interactivity;
- *policy*: the new economy, information society, and creative industries;
- *employment*: the drift of employment from large-scale industries to project teams and service provision; and
- *consumer*: "do-it-yourself" consumer co-creation, user-led innovation, open source, and network.

Even though existing corporate players remained strong, the writing was on the wall for the one-to-many, expert-vs.-behavioral model of media and consumption. Naturally there had been false starts to the interactive era, like the "dot.com" boom and bust. But just as railways had survived the stock market crash of 1856 and automobiles the slump of 1929, so mobilized content would survive the "tech wreck" and begin to change what might be meant by "television." And equally, these new possibilities grew up on ground that was thoroughly occupied by existing players, business models, and organizations. This meant both that good old-fashioned broadcast TV would persist, and that the most powerful and prescient players would adopt (or strangle) new-paradigm ventures, just as a big tree will crowd out and starve saplings of even its own species in the competition for light. Nevertheless, despite the shaky start to the "interactive" era, and despite the monopolistic tendencies of big old media, a change of more profound and causal importance was discernible in the tangle of productive and defensive stratagems. It was this: the progressive disintegration of the rigid division of labor between producers and consumers in industrial economies, and the role of creative ideas and knowledge-based innovation as the dynamic "wrecker" of the industrial-era expert paradigm.

Convergence and integration

The creative cat had been let out of the technological bag. People at large were no longer confined to passive consumption. They could and did perform acts of creative innovation. Technologically enabled media of communication had shifted decisively from a "read-only" to a "read-and-write" mode. And user-led co-creation – in open source, games, blogs, web applications, "viral" marketing – was itself at the sharp end of business innovation.

This wasn't an inevitable process, nor was its extension among all countries or demographics inevitable. Like other epoch-making changes of the modern period (e.g. democracy), it could be hedged about, begrudged, delayed, and denied, not least by academic "critique," and also, perhaps more effectively still, by monopolistic vested interests. But it could also be encouraged, taught, promoted, and extended as a capacity that might be developed to the advantage of the general public. That seemed a worthwhile project for an educational initiative. It was at this point that I concluded that the external environment required decisive change within contemporary universities. I closed QUT's Faculty of Arts, of which I was the last dean, to launch the world's first Creative Industries Faculty in July 2001. It was a response to these general trends. The arts, computers, entertainment media, and telecommunications were no longer separate industries but aspects of the *same* emergent phenomenon in a post-broadcast era. It was no longer viable to think of infrastructure (IT), connectivity (telecoms), and content (media) as separate disciplines, and to keep all of these away from "culture" and the creative and performing arts. Furthermore, if the new economy was to be based on consumer *action* not *behavior*, and on innovation in the services sector, there was a need to get beyond behaviorist models of the consumer and marketing models of society. Graduates needed capabilities that would enable them to act with confidence both as consumers and as citizens, and to create affluence both economic and symbolic out of their own talents and actions.

Innovation = integration of theory and practice

It was – in short – necessary to *integrate* theory, practice, and critique. A borrowed word from business describes the result: *innovation*. Borrowing it from business did not require anyone to abandon their theoretical sophistication ("theory"), political commitments ("practice"), or social beliefs ("critique"), although it did sometimes necessitate putting on a business suit. The resultant amalgam – "innovation" – is a dynamic and forceful concept that unites theory and practice and requires constant and detailed critique, but makes all of these *useful* by "falling forward," as it were, rather than remaining as a "stance" or "position" that disabled action. "Falling forward" is of course a description of "walking." Innovation is theory, practice, and critique in action, purposed toward future destinations.

Innovation is R&D for the knowledge-based economy, and it is what creativity needs if it is to find a *use* and therefore *value*. Charles Landry distinguishes "creativity" from "innovation": creativity is the process through which new ideas are *produced*; innovation is the process through which they are *implemented* (Landry & Bianchini 1994; see also Hartley 2002: 117). Therefore, creativity is a precondition for innovation, but innovation – the evaluation and assessment of the creative idea and its implementation as a practical process – is what will make the difference in the development of products and services.

For innovation to occur, it may be necessary to step outside of familiar routines or structures. It may therefore be the result of critique, which doesn't have to be abandoned; rather it needs to be directed and made useful. Innovation may be a product of experimentation, or the ability to use old ideas as the raw materials for something new. As Thomas Edison is supposed to have said, it requires the ability to "*fail* forward towards success" (Hargreaves 2003: 35). Success is like learning to walk: maintaining impetus and controlling the fall.

Emancipation = integration of knowledge and powers

Modernity was characterized by the ascendancy of the *useful* over the *fine* arts; new technology over old master. C. P. Snow's idea that society had fractured into "two cultures" – science and the arts – was widely accepted (even though it may have had no basis in historical fact: Egerton 2006: 197–210). But modern communications and design media combine science and technology with artistic and aesthetic content. All of them require engineering as well as aesthetics. Such true art–science hybrids cannot exist without scientific inventions, but would find no public without their artistic content. They have grown up over the past 200 years in forms that competed directly with traditional arts. They are now at the heart of one of the most dynamic sectors of the global economy.

Popular aesthetics, as opposed to artistic *taste*, was always an art–science interface. The idea that truth could be revealed by technological means, rather than by a shaping artistic vision that too often turned out to be manipulative, was inherent in the popularity of the aestheticization of science itself, via photos from outer space, wildlife documentaries on TV, or the entire dinosaur industry. The human condition, previously the domain of literature, painting, and the pursuit of "beauty," became a province of science. Beauty was found in truth, not imagination.

People trusted truth more than they did art. They were right. And universities need to pursue this destiny, not pine for traditional "critical" (i.e. gentlemanly) values. Creativity and innovation, arts and sciences, knowledge and business, truth and imagination: they all need to get together, to modify each other's genes, and multiply.

In the new economy, knowledge has to be distinctive. It has to be "easy to replicate but hard to imitate" (Leadbeater & Oakley 2001: 19). Further, it has to be put into an entrepreneurial context, to mobilize capital resources and find a market. Such knowledge differs from the kind of "public-good" (i.e. publicly funded) knowledge exemplified by traditional arts and disciplines. But knowledge generated in a commercial context may still sustain public, critical, even utopian ambitions. Charles Leadbeater has argued that the new economy is about creating human and social value as well as financial. Here again is the quotation from him at the head of this chapter:

> A modern society's goal should be to maximise the production and distribution of knowledge, to combine in a single ideal democratic and economic imperatives. Societies become more democratic as people become more literate, numerate, and knowledgeable, capable of making informed choices and challenging authority, so allowing them to take charge of their lives. . . . Political empowerment and economic opportunity stem from the same root: the spread of knowledge. (1999: 222)

That's what innovation is or ought to be about: new-economy R&D for political and economic emancipation via the useful application of creative ideas.

University Challenge – Twenty-First-Century Style

There is a need to reform education to take up this new "university challenge." Graduates are said to lack "industry readiness." Universities find it hard to model and teach adaptability, flexibility, teamwork, and just-in-time project work. The split between higher *education* and "vocational" skills *training*, and pejorative distinctions between public art and commercial entertainment, don't help. Inherited disciplinary and bureaucratic silos make innovation difficult. And it is a big ask for students, for whom the risks and insecurities of employment are combined with the privatized costs of education. They must develop their creative and critical talents, but simply training in a specialist area is not nearly good enough. They must learn how to manage a portfolio career, not staying long with a single employer or even industry, self-employed or working as casual labor.

Work itself may be project-based, in teams with multiple partners who change over time, in an international environment. Project management and entrepreneurship are core skills, "life design" an increasing priority. Continuing education is necessary. Entry-level workforce jobs are very different from wealth-creating destinations. Young people now are not pre-programmed to regard commercial enterprise with suspicion or to revere public culture. On the contrary, they don't trust people in the public sector any more than they trust global corporations, but many of them do want to start a business of their own.

A short history of the university

Universities have proven themselves adaptable over the long term. Classical and Arabic in origin, they're among the oldest surviving organizations, along with the Catholic church and the Tynwald (the Isle of Man parliament). Emerging from the medieval cloister from around 1600, modern universities showed themselves useful as boot camps for professional cadres: clergy, lawyers, doctors, soldiers; and more recently for the administrators of modernity: bureaucrats and the business "manageriat." Since the nineteenth century some of them, especially in the state-directed tradition, have also been active in scientific invention. In the mass age of the twentieth century, universities became the chosen mechanism for the mass communication of mechanized expertise. This enabled the elite ones at least to be in at the birth of the inventions and innovations that produced the information revolution. Now, we're facing "new times"; and universities must adapt again. How will barely post-medieval institutions cope with the accelerating tempo of technologically driven change in the twenty-first century? What are universities *for*?

Continuing survival is based on fulfilling some fundamental human needs, like the *puberty rite*, which we now call "teaching"; and the *need to establish pecking orders without violence*, which we now call "research." Such functions still underpin tertiary education at an anthropological level, but more elaborate justifications are needed in a competitive funding environment. As alternative sources, networks, and technologies of knowledge proliferate, what stories will universities need to tell in order to win acceptance from the general public and the public purse for what they do? They are suppliers of expertise (certificated credentials) and professional labor – is this still enough?

Closed innovation process . . .

In the past, universities were built around stored knowledge (the library; the lab). Modernization meant abandoning the medieval library and switching from the preservation to the expansion of knowledge. The model of innovation – the implementation of creative ideas – was borrowed from manufacturing industry. Industrial-era knowledge was best produced by a closed, linear process of innovation, as discussed in chapter 1. This model of innovation as a closed production line is shared by research labs, elite universities, the creative departments of companies, city planners, etc.

. . . vs. open innovation networks

But it is breaking down. Expertise is migrating out of organizations along with technologies, and organizations are open to external sources of innovation, not least through globalization, travel, and increasing participation in tertiary education. Innovation is myriad-sourced. Consumption is increasingly co-production; it is active not passive, making not just taking, using not behaving. And while learning is a fundamental requirement of innovation, it cannot be confined to the elite organization or research center. Learning becomes a porous, distributed system, and innovation becomes an open network. In the ProAm economy consumers are sources of ideas, redefining products. Inventions are not complete until explored, extended, or even reinvented by users. In open models, innovation is democratic not technocratic; it needs the widest possible base of participation, not isolated expert elites, patented applications, and controlled value chains. Innovation is also a true science–arts hybrid – it has a science or engineering component but a

culture of *use*. Innovation requires the promotion of diversity and interaction, as well as research.

Exclusion of consumers

To date, lay people have been more or less excluded from formal production of knowledge – it is their job to learn how to be wise consumers
of various commodified representations of knowledge. The division of
labor between producer and consumer is one of the most extreme in
modernity. Production is the sphere of government, business, organization, control, and in this context innovation is a closed system of applied
expertise. Consumers are reduced to passive, feminized *behavior* (not
action), manipulated by marketing, which is controlled by psychological expertise, so that the innovations prepared for them will be taken
up and accepted; the more docilely the better. The interests of business,
government, and expert elites on the one hand and consumers on the
other were never fully aligned in the industrial era. (In the gap between
them grew up the entertainment industry.)

Mediation of knowledge

Professional scientists often fail to connect with the public at all. Looked
at from the outside they seem to be organized as a pre-modern
priesthood. Science requires extreme length of apprenticeship, arcane
knowledge, bizarre and not very appealing dress codes, living in
institutions, a kind of celibacy. Meanwhile popular interest in science has
never been higher. The demand for truthful knowledge is evidenced by
the success of National Geographic; the Discovery and History channels
on pay-TV; the popularity of science-based drama from forensic and
medical shows to science fiction; and not least by the passionate uptake
of science-based causes, from conservation to HIV/AIDS activism,
genetics to global warming.

The imperative therefore is to bring elite science together with
public understanding, via media formats that people are known to like
and understand. The entertainment industry really does know how to
teach uncommitted citizens about truths they don't necessarily want to
face. We call that miracle "the news." Since the first realistic novel was
published it has been the entertainment industry's job to translate
observation, truth, science, creativity, and innovation into a popular idiom;
to recruit the lay public to the story of modernity.

But there's a growing disconnect between the lay population and elite knowledge institutions. Very little attention has been given to consumer demand, because the market for it to date has been restricted to companies and governments, not the general population. But at the same time, with every improvement in digital interactive technology, the possibilities for lay people to engage directly but informally in creative innovation grow as fast as Moore's law; that is, exponentially.[6] For example, check out consumer co-creation of games content; the open source movement; Digital Storytelling; the "ProAm" economy; music sharing; podcasting; blogging; online journalism; the Wikipedia. Learning and research organizations like universities must venture much further into that intermediate space between expert elites and the citizen-consumer, because this intermediate space of popular realism is the "medium" for growing user-led, consumer co-created innovation.

Businesses of the twenty-first century will themselves be more like design workshops (ateliers). It will no longer be enough to manage industrial scale and efficient processes. Instead of organizing firms around permanent staff and ongoing tasks, where success flows from controlling big budgets and many employees, firms are increasingly organized around projects, with teams that may dissolve and re-form, and maximum interaction and creative feedback from clients and customers. Success here is codified in the form of an individual's or firm's "credits," an effective shorthand for projects that have successfully brought together an *idea, a team, resources, clients,* and a *process,* hopefully to critical and popular acclaim.

Education + Innovation = Emancipation

Education needs to be integrated into this environment, not completed beforehand. In fact most students are already working; perhaps that's why project management and entrepreneurship are becoming core skills, and "life design" (work–life balance) an increasing priority. But why aren't most workers also studying?

In this context, academic work itself needs to evolve beyond the "industrial" form of organization, with a large permanent workforce who see management responsibilities as a spectator sport, to which the appropriate response is abuse and catcalls from the sidelines. Academics should not be organized as workers, trained (never to be retrained) for ongoing tasks like timetabled teaching that remain the same throughout a career. Instead, academics need to become more like "producers" of the film and TV variety – managing short-term projects that successfully bring together:

- *an idea* – flexible curriculum based not on "disciplinary truths" but on "learning services";
- *a team* – (where seven is the magic number) that may include adjuncts and outsourced professionals; a pool of freelance talent working and teaching as part of their own portfolio, as is common in creative arts;
- *resources* – including fundraising and competitive project funding;
- *clients* – students, but not only neophytes enrolled in time-based programs; they may be senior industry players extending their skills while working; and
- *a process* – appropriate pedagogy, not taking a semester, or three years, to do what can be done intensively, or doing on campus what may better be delivered in the workplace.

Success here results not from seniority of place within a hierarchy but from academic entrepreneurship. The risk in any one project is that the idea or team may not attract enough clients or resources; and in any case not everything proposed will be funded. Actually academics are well used to this regime. It already governs competitive research funding and the research process. It's an intriguing model for teaching, because although it is fraught with insecurity it does model what is done in the economic sector that we face, and it encourages innovation rather than repetition in the classroom, including the possibility of "failing forward towards success."

The organizational unit that houses creative education for the creative industries (including TV) won't look anything like a department. On the model of a creative production house it might be called a "creative educational incubator." It might be privately owned; perhaps its own staff would expect equity in it to be among their incentives and rewards. If universities are to become "creative education incubators" they must be integrated into consumer services, career development, and the "experience" economy. Any such organization would need to embrace at least the following values:

1 *Research led*: scoping the external environment not disciplinary legacy –
   a end-user focus not supply-side expertise;
   b institutional renewal driven by research as the model for teaching.
2 *Interdisciplinary* –
   a among creative disciplines, to bring together creative and performing arts, media and communication, and digital technologies, oriented to the "new economy" and commercial applications of artistic talent;
   b among many disciplines, e.g. law, business, IT, education; because innovation requires regulation, entrepreneurship, technology, and human capital (workforce and consumer).
3 *International* –
   a "whatever the question, the answer is China" – or India;
   b with trade in educational qualifications in this era of global creative services, and development programs to extend capabilities to less favored regions.
4 *Distributed*: involving partners in –
   a industry;
   b different levels of educational provision (schools/higher education/vocational and educational training);
   c agencies to promote transition from education to economic productivity.
5 *Bicameral*: increasingly –
   a undergraduate education for general education toward "creative consumer-citizenship";
   b postgraduate training for "craft" (this is already the case in US higher education).
6 *Integrated values* –
   a theory, practice, and critique folded into innovation;
   b symbolic and economic values folded into educational outcomes.

Since they're the drivers of innovation and economic growth in a service economy, the question must be asked: what do *consumers* want from education, science, innovation, and new technologies? Despite their dependence on student demand, universities have not fully engaged with this community, seeing it as the destination rather than the source of knowledge. However, the successful university will be one that joins an open innovation network to learn from active, co-creative consumers. Television is integrated into consumer services and what's known as the "experience" economy, touching many sectors including education, government, journalism, and sport. It is as reliant on law and regulation as it is upon technology. It needs enterprise skills as much as creative talent. It thrives on consumers – but they're changing into very different animals in front of its very eyes.

Good work in TV studies may be in a position to *shape* some of the changes that are beginning to spurt from the fissures that have opened between the broadcast era and the interactive age. It may also be able to influence educational renewal more generally. If so, we should stop doing what we've been doing so well, because the intra-mural "invention" of television thus far has produced a field of study which is better at lambasting its object of study than improving it. That's our *university challenge*. If we get the answer right, we may even help to answer the question of what *universities* can be for in the interactive era of consumer co-creation. A research-led, interdisciplinary, international, distributed, bicameral education with integrated values seems worth a try.

What about the students?

Karl Popper ("world's tenth greatest philosopher" – see pp. 155–6) had views on that subject.

> "Do no harm" and "give the young what they most urgently need in order to become independent of us, and to be able to choose for themselves" would be a very worthy aim for our educational system, and one whose realization is somewhat remote although it sounds modest. Instead, "higher" aims are the fashion, aims which are typically romantic and indeed nonsensical, such as "the full development of the personality." (Popper 1945: vol. 2, 275–8)[7]

To the latter, Popper prefers personal modesty (not fame-seeking individualism), critical dissatisfaction, and eagerness for improvement. If that is what education is for, the question is how to combine the quest for innovation in the object of study with the best prospects for achieving independence and choice among those who study it.

A species of TV studies that seeks to explain the medium by discoursing about nothing but television, even if it uses multidisciplinary languages to do so, does seem unlikely to produce more than self-expression writ large (this has been the fate of some film theory); but equally a TV form of studies that knows in advance what needs to be criticized is unlikely to promote independent thought and eagerness for improvement among the students, who may learn to get good grades by agreeing with their teachers – not a sound way to promote innovation, leadership, and dynamic change. How then should we think about television? As control and choice shifts from the expert "publisher/provider" model to the self-regulating "navigator/aggregator" (see chapter 2), we need to ask: is formal, expertise-based knowledge doomed?

Popper's own method for arguing the case for an open society, one in which "do no harm" and "encourage independence and choice" were the watchwords and a complex open system the means, was to interrogate intellectual history in order to elaborate the principles of an open society and to disentangle them from the line of totalitarian thinking that he traced back directly to Plato. Given the importance of education both formal (universities and schools) and informal (popular culture and media) to the present endeavor, it seems right to follow Popper's lead.

Notes

1 See www.collegebowl.com/arch/history.asp.
2 See www.ukgameshows.com/index.php/University_Challenge.
3 See www.magd.cam.ac.uk/alumni/gascoign.html.
4 See www.bbc.co.uk/pressoffice/pressreleases/stories/2002/08_august/15/ univ_ chal_40years.shtml.
5 See demos.co.uk/; see also demos.org/(USA).
6 A good account of Moore's law is at en.wikipedia.org/wiki/Moore's_law.
7 Also cited in www.the-rathouse.com/RC_PopperEdu.html.

References

Nicholas Abercrombie and Brian Longhurst (1998) *Audiences: A sociological theory of performance and imagination.* London: Sage.

Kate Aisbett (2000) *20 years of C: Children's television programs and regulations 1979–1999.* Sydney: Australian Broadcasting Authority.

Richard D. Altick (1957) *The English common reader: A social history of the mass reading public 1800–1900.* Chicago: University of Chicago Press.

Perry Anderson (1991) *Imagined communities.* 2nd edn. London: Verso.

Aristotle (350 BCE) *Politics.* Internet Classics Archive, Web Atomics. classics.mit.edu/Aristotle/politics.7.seven.html.

Bain Attwood (1996) "Mabo, Australia and the end of history." In Bain Attwood (ed.) *In the age of Mabo: History, Aborigines and Australia.* Sydney: Allen and Unwin, 117–35.

Marjorie Mandelstam Balzer (1999) *The tenacity of ethnicity: A Siberian saga in global perspective.* Princeton, NJ: Princeton University Press.

David Barboza (2005) "Hunan TV cancels the bland to bring the offbeat to China." *International Herald Tribune* (November 27).

Chris Barker (1999) *Television, globalization and cultural identities.* Buckingham and Philadelphia: Open University Press.

John Barrell (1986) *The political theory of painting from Reynolds to Hazlitt: "The body of the public."* New Haven, CT: Yale University Press.

Christopher Beck (ed.) (1984) *On air: 25 years of TV in Queensland.* Brisbane: One Tree Hill.

Peter Beilby (ed.) (1981) *Australian TV: The first 25 years.* Melbourne: Nelson/Cinema Papers.

Philip Bell and Roger Bell (1993) *Implicated: The United States in Australia.* Melbourne: Oxford University Press.

Philip Bell and Roger Bell (eds.) (1998) *Americanization and Australia.* Sydney: UNSW Press.

Quentin Beresford and Paul Omaji (1996) *Rites of passage: Aboriginal youth, crime and justice.* Fremantle: Fremantle Arts Centre Press.

S. L. Bethell (1944) *Shakespeare and the popular dramatic tradition.* London: Staples.

Michael Billig (2005) *Laughter and ridicule: Towards a social critique of humour.* London: Sage.

Jenny Black (1995) *The country's finest hour: Fifty years of rural broadcasting in Australia.* Sydney: ABC Books.

Jenny Black (2005) *The country's finest hour: Sixty years of rural broadcasting in Australia.* Sydney: ABC Books.

Graeme Blundell (2003) *King: The life and comedy of Graham Kennedy.* Sydney: Pan Macmillan.

Pierre Bourdieu (1998) *On television*, trans. Priscilla Parkhurst Ferguson. New York: New Press.

Todd Boyd (2003) *Young black rich and famous: The rise of the NBA, the hip hop invasion and the transformation of American culture.* New York: Doubleday.

Kees Brants, Joke Hermes, and Liesbet van Zoonen (eds.) (1998) *The media in question: Popular cultures and public interests.* London: Sage.

Asa Briggs (1985) *The BBC: The first fifty years.* Oxford: Oxford University Press.

Richard Butsch (2000) *The making of American audiences: From stage to television, 1750–1990.* Cambridge: Cambridge University Press.

California Voter Foundation (2005) *California Voter Participation Survey.* Davis, CA: California Voter Foundation. www.calvoter.org/issues/votereng/votpart/voter_participation_web.pdf.

John Carey (1992) *The intellectuals and the masses.* London: Faber and Faber.

Guglielmo Cavallo and Roger Chartier (eds.) (1999) *A history of reading in the West*, trans. Lydia Cochrane. Cambridge: Polity; Amherst: University of Massachusetts Press.

Richard Caves (2000) *Creative industries: Contracts between art and commerce.* Cambridge, MA: Harvard University Press.

Chua, Beng Huat (2000) "Multiculturalism compared: Singapore, Australia and Canada." Talk given to the Centre for Media Policy and Practice Seminar Series: Queensland University of Technology.

Michael Clarke (1952) "Television prospect: Some reflexions of a documentary film-maker." In Roger Manvell and R. K. Neilson Baxter (eds.) *The cinema 1952.* Harmondsworth: Penguin, 174–87.

Stephen Coleman (2003) *A tale of two houses: The House of Commons, the Big Brother house and the people at home.* London: Hansard Society.

Stephen Coleman (2005) *Direct representation: Towards a conversational democracy.* London: Institute for Public Policy Research (ippr exchange). www.ippr.org.uk/ecomm/files/Stephen_Coleman_Pamphlet.pdf.

Stephen Coleman (2006) "How the other half votes: *Big Brother* viewers and the 2005 UK general election." *International Journal of Cultural Studies*, 9:4, 457–79.

Samuel Taylor Coleridge (1972 [1830]) *On the constitution of church and state according to the idea of each.* London: J. M. Dent.

Robert Cooper (2002) *The new liberal imperialism.* Full-text version of "Why we still need empires." *Observer* (April 7). Both accessible on *Guardian Unlimited.* observer.guardian.co.uk/print/0,3858,4388912-110490,00.html. observer.guardian.co.uk/comment/story/0,6903,680096,00.html.

Cornell University (2006) "Early childhood TV viewing may trigger autism, data analysis suggests: Authors urge further study by autism experts into a possible connection." Cornell University Press Relations Office (October 16). www.news.cornell.edu/pressoffice1/oct06/tv_autism.shtml.

Stuart Cunningham (2001) "Popular media as public 'sphericules' for diasporic communities." *International Journal of Cultural Studies*, 4:2, 131–47.

Ann Curthoys (1991) "Television before television." *Continuum*, 4:2, 152–70.

Michael Curtin (1995) *Redeeming the wasteland: Television documentary and cold war politics.* New York: Rutgers University Press.

Peter Dahlgren (1995) *Television and the public sphere.* London: Sage.

Peter Dahlgren (1998) "Enhancing the civic ideal in television journalism." In Brants et al. (1998: 89–100).

Jacques Derrida (1976) *Of grammatology.* Baltimore. MD: Johns Hopkins University Press.

Umberto Eco (1972) "Towards a semiotic enquiry into the television message," trans. Paola Splendore. *Working Papers in Cultural Studies*, 3, 103–21 (first published in Italian 1966).

Economist (2005) "Democracy idol." *Economist* (October 9), 376(8443), 42.

Ray Edmondson (2004) *Audiovisual archiving: Philosophy and principles.* Rev. edn. Paris: UNESCO. portal.unesco.org/ci/en/ev.php-URL_ID=15592& URL_DO=DO_TOPIC&URL_SECTION=201.html.

David Egerton (2006) *Warfare state: Britain, 1920–1970.* Cambridge: Cambridge University Press.

Hans Magnus Enzensberger (1992) "A modest proposal for the protection of young people from the products of poetry." In *Mediocrity and delusion: Collected diversions*, trans. Martin Chalmers. London: Verso, 3–18.

Rita Felski (1989) *Beyond feminist aesthetics.* Cambridge, MA: Harvard University Press.

Jane Feuer (1983) "The concept of live television: Ontology as ideology." In E. Ann Kaplan (ed.) *Regarding television: Critical approaches – an anthology.* Frederick, MD: University Publications of America/American Film Institute, 12–22.

John Fiske (1989) "Moments of television: Neither the text nor the audience." In Ellen Seiter, H. Borchers, G. Kreutzner, and E. Warth (eds.)

Remote control: Television audiences and cultural power. London: Routledge, 56–78.

John Fiske and John Hartley (2003 [1978]) *Reading television: 25th anniversary edition.* London: Routledge.

Michel Foucault (1984) *The Foucault reader,* ed. Paul Rabinow. New York: Pantheon; London: Penguin.

Nancy Franklin (2004) "See how they run; on television." *New Yorker* (August 30), 80(24), 100.

Edward Gibbon (1995 [1776–88]) *The history of the decline and fall of the Roman empire.* New edn. London: Penguin.

Mark Gibson (2001) "Monday morning and the millennium." PhD thesis. Perth, Australia: Edith Cowan University.

Gregor T. Goethals (1981) *The TV ritual: Worship at the video altar.* Boston, MA: Beacon Press.

Maurice Gorham (1951) "Television: A medium in its own right?" In Roger Manvell and R. K. Neilson Baxter (eds.) *The cinema 1951.* Harmondsworth, Penguin, 131–46.

Chad Graham (2004) "The other presidential race." *Advocate,* 921, 49–50.

Herman Gray (1995) *Watching race: Television and the struggle for "blackness."* Minneapolis: University of Minnesota Press.

Jonathan Gray (2005) "Why A. C. Nielsens aren't invited to my birthday party." *Flow,* 3(8). jot.communication.utexas.edu/flow/?jot=view&id=1354.

Green Left Weekly (1992) "Money for crud." *Green Left Weekly* (July), 1:61. www.greenleft.org.au/1992/61/2980.

Tom Griffiths (1996) *Hunters and collectors: The antiquarian imagination in Australia.* Cambridge: Cambridge University Press.

Derham Groves (1996) "There's more to 'televiewing' than meets the eye." In Max Delaney et al. (eds.) *1956: Melbourne, Modernity and the XVI Olympiad.* Bulleen: Museum of Modern Art at Heide.

Derham Groves (2004) *TV houses: Television's influence on the Australian home.* Melbourne: Black Jack Press.

Sara Gwenllian-Jones and Roberta E. Pearson (eds.) (2004) *Cult television.* Minneapolis: University of Minnesota Press.

Jürgen Habermas (1989) *The structural transformation of the public sphere: An inquiry into a category of bourgeois society,* trans. Thomas Burger. Cambridge: Polity.

Sandra Hall (1976) *Supertoy: 20 years of Australian television.* Melbourne: Sun Books.

Sandra Hall (1981) *Turning on, turning off: Australian television in the eighties.* Sydney: Cassell.

Stuart Hall, Chas Critcher, Tony Jefferson, John Clarke, and Brian Roberts (1978) *Policing the crisis: Mugging, the state and law and order.* London: Macmillan.

Alfred Harbage (1941) *Shakespeare's audience.* Chicago: University of Chicago Press.

David Hargreaves (2003) *Education epidemic*. London: Demos. www.demos. co.uk/files/educationepidemic.pdf.

John Hartley (1992a) *The politics of pictures: The creation of the public in the age of popular media*. London and New York: Routledge.

John Hartley (1992b) *Tele-ology: Studies in television*. London: Routledge.

John Hartley (1996) *Popular reality: Journalism, modernity, popular culture*. London: Arnold.

John Hartley (1999) *Uses of television*. London and New York: Routledge.

John Hartley (2000) "Communicative democracy in a redactional society: The future of journalism studies." *Journalism: Theory, Practice and Criticism*, 1:1, 39–47.

John Hartley (2002) *Communication, cultural and media studies: The key concepts*. London and New York: Routledge.

John Hartley (2003) *A short history of cultural studies*. London: Sage.

John Hartley (ed.) (2005) *Creative industries*. Oxford: Blackwell.

John Hartley (2006) *TV50: Fifty years of Australian television*. Melbourne: ACMI.

John Hartley and Alan McKee (2000) *The Indigenous public sphere: The reporting and reception of Aboriginal issues in the Australian media*. Oxford: Oxford University Press.

Terence Hawkes (1973) *Shakespeare's talking animals*. London: Arnold.

Terence Hawkes (2002) *Shakespeare in the present*. London: Routledge.

Stephen Heath and Gillian Skirrow (1977) "Television, a world in action." *Screen*, 18:2, 7–59.

Joke Hermes (1998) "Cultural citizenship and popular fiction." In Brants et al. (1998: [Q: Pages?]157–67).

Joke Hermes (2005) *Re-reading popular culture: Rethinking gender, television and popular media audiences*. Oxford: Blackwell.

John M. Higgins and Deborah Starr Seibel (2004) "*American Idol* vs. speed dialers." *Broadcasting and Cable* (May 24), 134, 21.

Matt Hills (2002) *Fan cultures*. London: Routledge.

Thomas Hobbes (1968 [1651]) *Leviathan*, ed. C. B. Macpherson. Harmondsworth: Penguin.

Richard Hoggart (1957) *The uses of literacy*. London: Chatto and Windus.

James Holston and Arjun Appadurai (1996) "Cities and citizenship." *Public Culture*, 8:2, 187–204.

Homilies (1850 [1574 []) *The book of homilies: Certain sermons appointed by the Queen's Majesty to be declared and read by all parsons, vicars and curates, every Sunday and holiday in their churches; and by Her Grace's advice perused and overseen for the better understanding of the simple people*. Cambridge: Cambridge University Press.

Liz Jacka (2004) "Doing the history of television in Australia: Problems and challenges." *Continuum*, 18:1, 27–41.

Susan Jakes (2005) "Li Yuchun: Loved for being herself." *Time Asia* (October 2).

Henry Jenkins (2006) *Fans, bloggers and gamers: Media consumers in a digital age.* New York: New York University Press.

Colin Jones and David Bednall (1980) *Television in Australia: Its history through the ratings.* Sydney: Australian Broadcasting Tribunal.

Peter Jull (1994) "Mabo politics in a 'first world' context." In Murray Goot and Tim Rowse (eds.) *Make a better offer: The politics of Mabo.* Sydney: Pluto Press, 203–16.

Robert Kagan (2003) *Paradise and power: America and Europe in the new world order.* London: Atlantic Books; New York: Knopf.

Declan Kiberd (1999) "Wilde and the Belfast Agreement." *Textual Practice*, 13:3, 441–5.

Jon P. Klancher (1987) *The making of English reading audiences 1790–1832.* Madison: University of Wisconsin Press.

Nigel Kneale (1959) "Not quite so intimate." *Sight and Sound* (Spring), 86–8.

Arthur Koestler (1967) *The ghost in the machine. The urge to self-destruction: A psychological and evolutionary study of modern man's predicament.* London: Hutchinson.

Charles Landry and Franco Bianchini (1994) *The creative city. Working paper 1: Key themes and issues.* London, Comedia.

Marcia Langton (1993) *"Well I heard it on the radio and I saw it on the television."* Sydney: Australian Film Commission.

Richard Lanham (2006) *The economics of attention: Style and substance in the age of information.* Chicago: University of Chicago Press.

Charles Leadbeater (1999) *Living on thin air: The new economy.* London: Viking.

Charles Leadbeater and Paul Miller (2004) *The ProAm revolution.* London: Demos.

Charles Leadbeater and Kate Oakley (2001) *Surfing the long wave: Knowledge entrepreneurship in Britain.* London: Demos.

Chin-Chuan Lee (ed.) (2003) *Chinese media, global contexts.* London and New York: RoutledgeCurzon.

Li, Yu (2005) "What is 'Supergirl?'" *Legal Mirror* (China) (August 8). bj.ynet.com/view.jsp?oid=6200618. Translated at www.danwei.org/archives/002157.html.

Tamar Liebes (1990) *The export of meaning: Cross-cultural readings of "Dallas."* New York: Oxford University Press.

Stuart Littlemore (1996) *The media and me.* Sydney: ABC Books.

Yuri M. Lotman (1990) *Universe of the mind: A semiotic theory of culture.* Bloomington, IN: Indiana University Press.

Catharine Lumby (1999) *Gotcha! Living in a tabloid world.* Sydney: Allen and Unwin.

Catharine Lumby and Duncan Fine (2006) *Why TV is good for kids: Raising 21st century children.* Sydney: Pan Macmillan.

Martyn Lyons (1999) "New readers in the nineteenth century: Women, children, workers." In Cavallo and Chartier (1999: 313–45).

Jane Macartney (2005) "TV talent contest 'too democratic' for China's censors." *The Times* (August 29), 25.

Mungo MacCallum (ed.) (1968) *Ten years of television.* Melbourne: Sun Books.

D. E. MacDonnel (1822) *A dictionary of quotations, in most frequent use, taken chiefly from the Latin and French, but comprising many from the Greek, Spanish and Italian languages, translated into English; with illustrations historical and idiomatic.* London: G. and W. B. Whittaker.

Maria Cristina Marconi (1999) *Marconi my beloved.* Boston: Dante University of America Press.

Robert Marquand (2005) "In China, it's Mongolian Cow Yogurt Super Girl." *Christian Science Monitor* (August 29), 1.

T. H. Marshall (1963) "Citizenship and social class." In *Sociology at the crossroads and other essays.* London: Heinemann, 67–127.

Paul Martin (1999) *Popular collecting and the everyday self: The reinvention of museums?* London: Leicester University Press.

Robert McChesney (1999) *Rich media, poor democracy.* Champaign, IL: University of Illinois Press.

Hamish McDonald (2005a) "Pop culture grabs limelight." *Age* (August 29), 9.

Hamish McDonald (2005b) "Pop singers give new range to cultural democracy." *Sydney Morning Herald/AFP* (August 29), 8.

Alan McKee (1997) "'The Aboriginal version of Ken Done . . .': Banal Aboriginal identities in Australia." *Cultural Studies,* 11:2, 191–206.

Alan McKee (2001) *Australian television: A genealogy of great moments.* Melbourne: Oxford University Press.

Marshall McLuhan (1964) *Understanding media.* New York: Mentor.

Marshall McLuhan and Quentin Fiore (1967) *The medium is the massage.* New York: Bantam.

Steve Meacham (2004) "Beauty who swam in the big pool." *Sydney Morning Herald* (April 14). www.smh.com.au/articles/2004/04/13/1081838727299.html.

Steve Mickler (1998) *The myth of privilege.* Fremantle: Fremantle Arts Centre Press.

Toby Miller (1995) "Exporting truth from Aboriginal Australia: 'Portions of our past become present again, where only the melancholy light of origin shines.'" *Media Information Australia,* 76, 7–17.

Toby Miller (1998) *Technologies of truth: Cultural citizenship and the popular media.* Minneapolis: University of Minnesota Press.

Toby Miller, Nitin Govil, John McMurria, and Richard Maxwell (2001) *Global Hollywood.* London: BFI Publications.

Toby Miller, Nitin Govil, John McMurria, Richard Maxwell, and Ting Wang (2005) *Global Hollywood 2.* London: BFI Publications.

Nancy Mitford (ed.) (1956) *Noblesse oblige.* London: Hamish Hamilton.

Jason Mittell (2005) "An arresting development." *Flow*, 3:8. www.flowtv.org.

Albert Moran (1991) "Some beginnings for Australian television: The first governor-general." *Continuum*, 4:2, 171–83.

Albert Moran (ed.) (1992) *Stay tuned: The Australian broadcasting reader.* Sydney: Allen and Unwin.

Albert Moran (1998) *Copycat TV: Globalisation, program formats and cultural identity.* Luton: University of Luton Press.

David Morley (1992) *Television audiences and cultural studies.* London: Routledge.

Meaghan Morris (1993) "Panorama: The live, the dead and the living." In Graeme Turner (ed.) *Nation, culture, text: Australian cultural and media studies.* London: Routledge, 19–58.

John Morton (1996) "Aboriginality, Mabo and the republic: Indigenising Australia." In Bain Attwood (ed.) *In the age of Mabo: History, Aborigines and Australia.* Sydney: Allen and Unwin, 117–35.

William Mougayar (2002) "Small screen, smaller world." *Yale Center for the Study of Globalization* (October 11). claudius.its.yale.edu/globalization/display.article?id=204.

Fred R. Myers (1991) *Pintupi country, Pintupi self: Sentiment, place and politics among western desert Aborigines.* Berkeley, CA: University of California Press.

Tom Nairn (1997) *Faces of nationalism.* London: Verso.

Tom Nairn (2000) *After Britain.* London: Granta.

National Inquiry (1997) *Bringing them home: The report of the National Inquiry into the Separation of Aboriginal and Torres Strait Islander Children from their Families.* Sydney: Human Rights and Equal Opportunity Commission.

Horace Newcomb (ed.) (2004) *Encyclopedia of television.* 2nd edn. New York: Routledge.

Horace Newcomb and Paul M. Hirsch (2000) "Television as a cultural forum." In John Hartley and Roberta E. Pearson (eds.) *American cultural studies: A reader.* Oxford: Oxford University Press, 162–73.

Scott Robert Olson (1999) *Hollywood planet: Global media and the competitive advantage of narrative transparency.* Mahwah, NJ: Lawrence Erlbaum.

Walter J. Ong (1958) *Ramus. Method, and the decay of dialogue: From the art of discourse to the art of reason.* Cambridge, MA: Harvard University Press.

Tom O'Regan (1993) *Australian television culture.* Sydney: Allen and Unwin.

Tom O'Regan (1996) *Australian national cinema.* London and New York: Routledge.

Graeme Osborne and William F. Mandle (eds.) (1982) *New history: Studying Australia today.* Sydney: Allen and Unwin.

Thomas Paine (1937 [1792]) *Rights of man: Being an answer to Mr. Burke's attack on the French Revolution*, ed. Hypatia Bradlaugh Bonner. London: Watts.

People (2004) *"American Candidate." People* 62 (August), 40.

Mark Pesce (2005) "Piracy is good?" 2 parts; online. *Mindjack* (May 13). www.mindjack.com/feature/piracy051305.html. www.mindjack.com/feature/newlaws052105.html

Armando Petrucci (1995) *Writers and readers in medieval Italy: Studies in the history of written culture,* trans. and ed. Charles M. Radding. Cambridge, MA: Yale University Press.

Armando Petrucci (1999) "Reading to read: A future for reading." In Cavallo and Chartier (1999: 345–67).

Alexei Popov (1966 [1940]) "Shakespeare and the theatre". Extract from *"The Taming of the Shrew" in the Central Theatre of the Red Army.* In Roman Samarin and Alexander Nikolyukin (eds.) *Shakespeare in the Soviet Union.* Moscow: Progress, 165–76.

Karl Popper (1945) *The open society and its enemies.* London: Routledge and Kegan Paul.

Michael Porter (1985) *Competitive advantage: Creating and sustaining superior performance.* New York: Free Press.

Robert Provine (2000) *Laughter: A scientific investigation.* London: Faber and Faber.

Cate Rayson (1998) *Glued to the telly: A history of Australia television.* Melbourne: Elgua Media.

Henry Reynolds (1996) *Aboriginal sovereignty: Three nations, one Australia?* Sydney: Allen and Unwin.

I. A. Richards (1929) *Practical criticism.* London: Kegan Paul.

Thomas Richards (1993) *The imperial archive: Knowledge and the fantasy of empire.* London: Verso.

George Ritzer (2004) *The McDonaldization of society.* Rev. edn. Thousand Oaks, CA: Pine Forge Press/Sage.

Lionel Lord Robbins (1963) *Higher education. Report of the committee appointed by the prime minister under the chairmanship of Lord Robbins, 1961–1963: "The Robbins report."* London: HMSO.

Dan Roberts (2005) "Is the world falling out of love with US brands?" *Yale Global Online* (January 5). yaleglobal.yale.edu/display.article?id=5109.

Bernard Rosenberg and David Manning White (eds.) (1957) *Mass culture: The popular arts in America.* Glencoe, IL: Free Press.

Howard Rosenberg (1999) "Man commits suicide – live!" *Media Studies Journal,* 13:2, 70–1.

Tim Rowse (1992) *Remote possibilities: The Aboriginal domain and the administrative imagination.* Darwin: North Australia Research Unit, Australian National University.

Tim Rowse (1993) *After Mabo: Interpreting Indigenous traditions.* Melbourne: Melbourne University Press.

Royal Commission on the Press (1948) *Minutes of evidence, 26th day.* London: HMSO.

Michael Schudson (1998) "Changing concepts of democracy." In *Democracy and digital media conference*. MIT. web.mit.edu/m-i-t/articles/schudson.html.

Michael Schudson (1999) *The good citizen: A history of American civic life*. Cambridge, MA: Harvard University Press.

Jeffrey Sconce (2000) *Haunted media: Electronic presence from telegraphy to television*. Durham, NC, and London: Duke University Press.

James Secord (2000) "Progress in print." In Marina Frasca-Spada and Nick Jardine (eds.) *Books and the sciences in history*. Cambridge: Cambridge University Press, 369–89.

Deborah Starr Seibel (2004) "*American Idol* outrage: Your vote doesn't count." *Broadcasting and Cable* (May 17), 134, 20.

Adam Sherwin (2005) "*Come Dancing* set to have a twirl on American television." *Times Online* (March 24). www.timesonline.co.uk/article/0,,2-1538643,00.html.

Lynn Spigel and Michael Curtin (eds.) (1997) *The revolution wasn't televised: Sixties television and social conflict*. New York: Routledge.

Robert Stam (1995) "Eurocentrism, polycentrism, and multicultural pedagogy: Film and the quincentennial." In Román de la Campa, E. Ann Kaplan, and Michael Sprinker (eds.) *Late imperial culture*. London and New York: Verso, 97–121.

Gerald Stone (2000) *Compulsive viewing: The inside story of Packer's Nine Network*. Ringwood: Viking/Penguin Australia.

Maggie Tabberer (1998) *Maggie*. Sydney: Allen and Unwin.

John Tomlinson (1999) *Globalization and culture*. Cambridge: Polity.

Sasha Torres (2003) *Black, white, and in color: Television and black civil rights*. Princeton, NJ: Princeton University Press.

Graeme Turner (1997) "First contact: Coming to terms with the cable guy." *UTS Review*, 3:2, 109–121.

Graeme Turner (2004) *Understanding celebrity*. London: Sage.

Graeme Turner (2005) *Ending the affair: The decline of current affairs in Australia*. Sydney: UNSW Press.

Graeme Turner (2006) "The mass production of celebrity: 'Celetoids,' reality TV and the 'demotic turn.'" *International Journal of Cultural Studies*, 9:2.

Rahul Tyagi, Infosys Technologies Ltd. (2003) "Apparel globalization: The big picture." *Apparel Magazine*. www.apparelmag.com/bobbin/reports_analysis/article_display.jsp?vnu_content_id=1786051.

Thorstein Veblen (1899) *The theory of the leisure class*. Project Gutenberg. www.gutenberg.org/dirs/etext97/totlc11.txt.

Hendrik D. L. Vervliet (1972) *The book through 5000 years*. London: Phaidon; Brussels, Editions Arcade.

Victor S. (2005) "Democracy comes to China! (Well, actually just for Mongolian Cow Yogurt Super Girl)." *Apostate Windbag* (October 12).

http://apostatewindbag.blogspot.com/2005/10/democracy-comes-to-china-well-actually.html.

McKenzie Wark (1994) *Virtual geography: Living with global media events.* Bloomington, IN: Indiana University Press.

McKenzie Wark (1997) *The virtual republic: Australia's culture wars of the 1990s.* Sydney: Allen and Unwin.

McKenzie Wark (1999) *Celebrities, culture and cyberspace: The light on the hill in a postmodern world.* Sydney: Pluto Press.

Raymond Williams (1961) *Culture and society.* Harmondsworth: Penguin.

Bob Woodruff (2006) "Go-karts, paintball appeal to young Iranians: Country's youth stand in contradiction to hardline government." *ABC* [USA] *World News Tonight* (January 3). http://abcnews.go.com/WNT/story?id=1467301&CMP=OTC-RSSFeeds0312.

Virginia Woolf (1945 [1929]) *A room of one's own.* Harmondsworth: Penguin.

Jim Yardley (2005) "The Chinese get the vote, if only for 'Super Girl.' " *New York Times* (September 4), 4, 3.

Slavoj Žižek (2002) "Big Brother, or, the triumph of the gaze over the eye." In Thomas Y. Levin, Ursula Frohne, and Peter Weibel (eds.) *Ctrl [space]: Rhetorics of surveillance from Bentham to Big Brother.* Karlsruhe: ZKM; Cambridge, MA: MIT Press, 224–7.

Index